50 HIKES
IN THE CAROLINA
MOUNTAINS

OTHER BOOKS IN THE 50 HIKES SERIES

50 Hikes in Pennsylvania

50 Hikes in New Jersey

50 Hikes in Eastern Massachusetts

50 Hikes around Anchorage

50 Hikes in the Lower Hudson Valley

50 Hikes in Michigan

50 Hikes in the Adirondack Mountains

50 Hikes in the Sierra Nevada

50 Hikes in Connecticut

50 Hikes in Central Florida

50 Hikes in the Upper Hudson Valley

50 Hikes in Wisconsin

50 Hikes in the Catskills

50 HIKES
IN THE CAROLINA
MOUNTAINS

FIRST EDITION

Johnny Molloy

THE COUNTRYMAN PRESS

A Division of W. W. Norton & Company

Independent Publishers Since 1923

AN INVITATION TO THE READER

Over time trails can be rerouted and signs and landmarks altered. If you find that changes have occurred on the routes described in this book, please let us know so that corrections may be made in future editions. The author and publisher also welcome other comments and suggestions.

Address all correspondence to:
Editor, 50 Hikes Series
The Countryman Press
500 Fifth Avenue
New York, NY 10110

For information about permission to reproduce selections from this book, write to Permissions, The Countryman Press, 500 Fifth Avenue, New York, NY 10110

For information about special discounts for bulk purchases, please contact W. W. Norton Special Sales at specialsales@wwnorton.com or 800-233-4830

Manufacturing by Versa Press
Book design by Chris Welch
Maps by Michael Borop (sitesatlas.com)

The Countryman Press
www.countrymanpress.com

A division of W. W. Norton & Company, Inc.
500 Fifth Avenue, New York, NY 10110

www.wwnorton.com

978-1-68268-586-0 (pbk.)

10 9 8 7 6 5 4 3 2 1

This book is for all the past, present, and future hikers of the Carolina mountains, ranging from the Virginia state line down to Georgia.

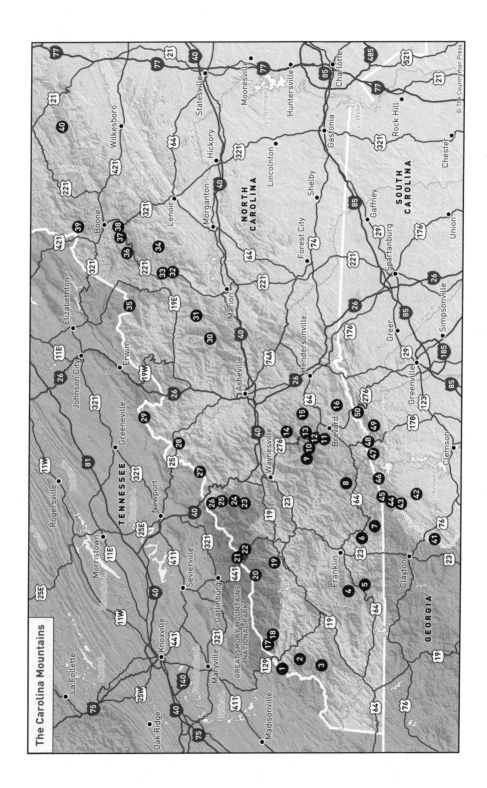

The Carolina Mountains

Contents

Hikes at a Glance

	Hike	City	Distance (miles)	Views
Southwest North Carolina Mountains	1. Joyce Kilmer-Slickrock Wilderness Loop	Robbinsville	10.7	
	2. Joyce Kilmer Memorial Forest	Robbinsville	2.0	
	3. Three Waterfalls of Snowbird Creek	Robbinsville	12.6	
	4. Siler Bald Loop	Franklin	3.4	✓
	5. Upper Nantahala River Route	Franklin	8.9	
	6. Bartram Trail Vistas	Franklin	9.6	✓
	7. Chinquapin Mountain and Glen Falls	Highlands	5.0	✓
	8. Panthertown Valley Highlight Hike	Lake Toxaway	12.3	✓
	9. Black Balsam Knob	Brevard	4.9	✓
	10. Waterfalls of the Graveyard Fields	Brevard	3.4	✓
	11. Cat Gap Loop	Brevard	5.6	✓
	12. Looking Glass Rock	Brevard	5.6	✓
	13. Twin Falls	Brevard	5.8	
	14. Mount Pisgah	Asheville	3.2	✓
	15. South Fork Mills River Loop	Mills River	8.4	
	16. DuPont State Forest Waterfall Hike	Pisgah Forest	6.2	✓
North Carolina Smokies	17. Gregory Bald Circuit	Fontana Village	15.6	✓
	18. Shuckstack Fire Tower	Fontana Village	6.6	✓
	19. Waterfalls of Deep Creek	Bryson City	2.4	
	20. Andrews Bald	Cherokee	3.4	✓
	21. Charlies Bunion	Cherokee	8.4	✓
	22. Sweat Heifer Creek Cascades	Cherokee	7.2	
	23. Big Fork Ridge Loop	Maggie Valley	9.2	✓
	24. Little Cataloochee Hike	Maggie Valley	8.2	
	25. Mount Sterling	Maggie Valley	5.4	✓
	26. Mouse Creek Falls and the Midnight Hole	Maggie Valley	4.0	

Waterfall	Campground Nearby	Trail Camp	Kid Friendly	Comments
✓		✓		Waterfalls, big wilderness, swimming
			✓	Incredible old-growth forest, ancient trees
✓		✓		Multiple waterfalls, stream scenes
		✓	✓	Open meadow atop mountain, views galore
	✓	✓		Aquatic splendor in mountain setting
		✓		Views from open granite slabs, solitude
✓			✓	Extensive views; huge, long waterfalls
✓		✓		This loop has it all, can be shortened
		✓	✓	Panoramas amid spruce-fir highlands
✓			✓	Cataracts in highland valley
✓		✓	✓	Granite slab vistas, waterfalls
		✓		Climb to panorama, classic Carolina mountain trek
✓		✓		View two falls at once
	✓		✓	Panoramas from iconic Carolina mountain
		✓	✓	Streamside extravaganza, wildflowers
✓				View some of the biggest waterfalls in the Carolina mountains
✓		✓		Classic Smokies loop, backpacking, superlative scenery
				Hike AT to historic fire tower with 360-degree panorama
✓	✓		✓	Perfect family day hike to view cataracts
			✓	Family day hike to highest bald in the Smokies
		✓		Top notch vistas on AT in Smokies high country
✓		✓		Smokies hike to unsung waterfall
		✓		Big trees, pioneer history
				Historic hike to restored cabin and church
		✓	✓	Hike through spruce-fir forest to tower with 360-degree vista
✓	✓		✓	Swimming hole, waterfall on gorgeous Smokies stream

	Hike	City	Distance (miles)	Views
Northeast North Carolina Mountains	27. Max Patch	Hot Springs	1.5	✓
	28. Lovers Leap	Hot Springs	4.1	✓
	29. Big Firescald Knob	Hot Springs	10.8	✓
	30. Mount Mitchell Hike	Black Mountain	5.6	✓
	31. Crabtree Falls	Little Switzerland	2.8	✓
	32. Tower of Babel Loop	Linville Falls	5.7	✓
	33. Linville Falls	Linville Falls	4.2	✓
	34. Raider Camp Creek Circuit	Lenoir	9.5	✓
	35. Balds of Roan Mountain	Bakersville	4.8	✓
	36. Calloway Peak via the Profile Trail	Linville	8.2	✓
	37. Boone Fork Circuit	Blowing Rock	5.4	
	38. Flat Top Tower	Blowing Rock	5.8	✓
	39. Elk Knob	Boone	3.8	✓
	40. Caudill Cabin	Elkin	9.8	
South Carolina Mountains	41. Opossum Creek Falls	Long Creek	4.6	
	42. Station Cove Falls via Historic Oconee Station	Mountain Rest	3.1	
	43. Pigpen Falls and Lick Log Falls	Mountain Rest	2.0	
	44. King Creek Falls and Big Bend Falls	Mountain Rest	7.6	✓
	45. Ellicott Rock Wilderness Hike	Salem	8.4	
	46. Lower Whitewater Falls	Salem	4.4	✓
	47. Laurel Fork Falls at Lake Jocassee	Rocky Bottom	10.6	✓
	48. Beech Bottom Falls	Rocky Bottom	1.8	
	49. Table Rock State Park Hike	Cleveland	8.0	✓
	50. Raven Cliff Falls	Cleveland	3.8	✓

Waterfall	Campground Nearby	Trail Camp	Kid Friendly	Comments
		✓	✓	Start high and enjoy continuous vistas, family hike
		✓	✓	Views on AT above French Broad River
✓		✓		Big loop with big features, backpacking and solitude
	✓	✓		Hike to the highest point in the East
✓	✓		✓	Classic Blue Ridge Parkway hike
✓		✓		Challenging but rewarding wilderness hike
✓	✓		✓	Superlative scenery in network of interconnected trails
✓		✓		Excellent aquatic loop with huge falls
		✓	✓	Open meadows, high country, wildflowers along AT
				Stellar hike at Grandfather Mountain State Park
✓	✓			Excellent Blue Ridge Parkway loop with waterfalls
			✓	Easy walk on carriage roads to fire tower with views
			✓	Grand vistas from newer state park
✓		✓		Blue Ridge hike up gorgeous stream to historic cabin
✓		✓		Solitude to Chattooga River and wild waterfall
✓			✓	Visit historic site en route to falls
✓		✓	✓	Easy hike to two falls, plus Chattooga River
✓	✓	✓		Two different falls, trailside beauty
✓		✓		Hike past waterfalls and river in untamed land
✓		✓		Grand view of waterfall and gorge
✓		✓		Stunning valley hike along stream to falls and lake
✓			✓	Newer family hike to rugged cataract
✓				Classic highlight-filled hike at South Carolina icon
✓			✓	Walk rim of gorge to view 320-foot waterfall

Acknowledgments

Thanks to the builders and maintainers of the trails upon which we enjoy the Carolina mountains, and to my wife Keri Anne for treading the trails with me.

VIEW FROM THE BLUE RIDGE PARKWAY IN NORTH CAROLINA AHEFLIN/ISTOCKPHOTO.COM

Preface

My first encounters with the mountains of North Carolina and South Carolina were outgrowths of my explorations of the Southern Appalachians beyond the place where I first "discovered" the mountains—Great Smoky Mountains National Park, near where I attended college at the University of Tennessee. Having gotten the hiking bug and running around in hiking circles, it wasn't long before I heard whispers of superlative Carolina mountain hiking destinations—Linville Gorge, Chattooga Wild & Scenic River, Shining Rock Wilderness, Mount Mitchell, the Foothills Trail, the Appalachian Trail and assorted pathways along the Blue Ridge Parkway, and on and on. The possibilities seemed endless with the wealth of trails in North Carolina's Pisgah and Nantahala National Forests, along with Tar Heel state parks and forests. And in South Carolina, the Sumter National Forest and South Carolina's state parks protected thousands of more acres to discover via still more trails.

Hiking adventures in Great Smoky Mountains National Park were followed by forays to Carolina mountains including backpacking trips at Joyce Kilmer-Slickrock Wilderness, car camping trips at campgrounds on the Blue Ridge Parkway, and paddling adventures on Carolina highland lakes and rivers, as well as day hikes at special destinations like Roan Mountain and Station Cove State Historic Site. Later exploits lay ahead as I branched out—backpacking Panthertown Backcountry, long trips on the Appalachian Trail, the Bartram Trail and the Foothills Trail. I saw high waterfalls, distant panoramas, and historic places that displayed just how many exciting trails there are to hike in the Carolina mountains.

Later, I turned my passion for the outdoors into a vocation as a writer. I kept the Carolina mountains on the front burner, going on more adventures and writing about them, searching for more opportunities to document what the Carolina mountains offered. I was given the opportunity to write this guidebook, then began systematically re-exploring the mountains of North Carolina and South Carolina for the best hikes. I found more wildlands and more trails to hike then share with you. It was a real pleasure (most of the time) to hike the Carolina mountains from the waterfalls along the Chattooga River gorge to the overlooks of the Fishhawk Mountains to the historic sites of Smokies to the crags of Grandfather Mountain. Along the way, I found some unexpected hikes that pleasantly surprised this grizzled veteran. And with the joy of completing a book and the sadness of an adventure ended, I finished my research. But I will continue putting my lessons to work, enjoying more of the Carolina mountains in future outdoor adventures.

What It's Like: Hiking in the Carolina Mountains

It's seeing colorful wildflowers on the South Mills River Trail.
It's photographing Beech Bottom Falls after a heavy rain.
It's slithering between boulders at Table Rock State Park.
It's seeing the Steve Woody Place in Cataloochee Valley.
It's walking amid the splendor of Ellicott Rock Wilderness.
It's pounding your feet on the granite slabs of the Bartram Trail.
It's seeing Looking Glass Rock for the first time.
It's finding Sweat Heifer Creek Cascades.
It's viewing two waterfalls at once on the Twin Falls hike.
It's climbing 3,570 feet to Gregory Bald.
It's navigating the rock gardens along Boone Fork.
It's seeing a deer along the Nantahala River .
It's wondering how Lick Log Falls got its name.
It's traversing Laurel Fork on a cool suspension bridge.
It's hearing the roar of the High Falls .
It's appreciating the simplicity of the Caudill Cabin.
It's feeling the breeze atop Black Balsam Knob.
It's being amazed by the continual views at Max Patch.
It's standing atop Calloway Peak.
It's imagining Civil War soldiers on Caldwell Fork.
It's being disheartened at trash left by thoughtless hikers.
It's not believing the depth and clarity of Big Creek .
It's walking atop Chinquapin Knob.
It's all the stream fords on the Raider Camp Creek Circuit.
It's hiking at Panthertown Valley on a crystal blue fall day.
It's feeling the fury of Lower Whitewater Falls.
It's seeing the very ruggedness of the Tower of Babel.
It's photographing the historic church at Little Cataloochee.
It's being amazed by the views from atop Mount Sterling.
It's the sheer numbers of hikers at Deep Creek.
It's the solitude of the Big Firescald Knob.
It's watching turkeys scatter on a wooded hill near Station Cove.
It's just being in the Carolina mountains.

Introduction

This book details 50 hikes that take place in the mountains of North Carolina and South Carolina, in South Carolina from the Chattooga River on the Georgia state line to Jones Gap State Park astride North Carolina; and in North Carolina from the Nantahala National Forest near Robbinsville in the southwest to the wildlands along the Blue Ridge Parkway in the northeast near Virginia. This guide also includes hikes on the North Carolina side of Great Smoky Mountains National Park. Specific emphasis was placed on the most scenic destinations and unique places that make the Carolina mountains so special, places like the Linville Falls with its rock formations and charging cataracts or the ancient trees of Joyce Kilmer Memorial Forest. Some hikes in this book take place on the Appalachian Trail, the master path of the Appalachians. Other long trails are represented, including the Bartram Trail, the Palmetto Trail and the Foothills Trail.

Still other hikes take place within federal and state lands scattered throughout the Carolina mountains. Hikes of varied lengths and difficulties are included. Sometimes we feel like going on a rugged hike; other times an easy stroll will do. Time constraints, companions, and time of year are major considerations when choosing a Carolina mountain hike. Grandma is not going to feel like fording remote rivers, and a weekend backpack with your old Scout buddy will likely entail challenging terrain. An introductory stroll with your little nephew will call for friendly pathways.

Many hikes take place on federal lands—the Nantahala, Pisgah, and Sumter National Forests as well as Great Smoky Mountains National Park and the Blue Ridge Parkway. These federal lands cover nearly a million acres in the Carolinas and not only have hiking trails but also campgrounds, waterways to float and fish, special scenic areas, hunting, and more, allowing you to combine hiking with other outdoor activities. Still other hikes are on state property, whether it be a state park, state forest or state natural area. As the Carolina mountains become more populated and appreciated, the land and its resources become more valuable. No matter what entity manages the land, there is plenty to see—remarkable waterfalls framed in rich forests, rock outcrops where panoramic views extend to the horizon, geological formations, rare spruce-fir forests, waterways big and small.

The best way to reach these places is on foot. The rewards increase with every step beneath the towering forests of these majestic highlands or in deep defiles where translucent streams run wild and free. A respite into the Carolina mountains will revitalize both mind and spirit. To smell the autumn leaves on a crisp afternoon, to climb to a lookout, or to contemplate pioneer lives at an old homesite will put our lives into perspective.

That is where this book will come into play. It will help you make every step count, whether you are leading the family on a short day hike or under-taking a challenging backpack into the back of beyond. With your precious time and the knowledge imparted to you, your outdoor experience will be realized to its fullest.

This book presents 50 hikes to choose from. Included are some of the Carolina mountain classics such as Charlies Bunion, Crabtree Falls, and Table Rock State Park. However, the many of the hikes are off the beaten path, offering more solitude to lesser-known yet equally scenic sights, such as Opossum Creek Falls, Snowbird Creek, and Elk Knob. This will give you the opportunity to get back to nature on your own terms.

Two types of day hikes are offered: there-and-back and loop hikes. One-way hikes lead to a particular rewarding destination, returning via the same trail. The return trip allows you to see every-thing from the opposite vantage point.

You may notice more minute trailside features on the second go-round, and returning at a different time of day may give the same trail a surprisingly differ-ent character.

To some, returning on the same trail just isn't as enjoyable. Certain hikers just can't stand the thought of covering the same ground twice with miles of Caro-lina mountain trails awaiting them. Loop hikes avoid this. Many of these hikes offer solitude to maximize your experience—though, by necessity, portions of some hikes traverse potentially popular areas.

Day hiking is the most popular way to explore the Carolina mountains, but for those with the inclination, this book offers overnight hikes. Some of the best locales for overnight stays are detailed for those who want to see the cycle of the highlands evolve from day to night and back again. The length of these hikes was chosen primarily for the weekend

MAP LEGEND

———	Described trail	═══	Interstate highway
- - - -	Important trail	═══	Secondary highway
◄———	Hike direction arrow	———	Minor highway, road, street
———	Perennial stream	- - - -	Unpaved road, trail
- - - -	Intermittent stream	+—+—+	Railroad
———	Major contour line	— ·· —	International border
———	Minor contour line	- · — · -	State border
	National/state park, wilderness	🅿	Parking area
	National/state forest, wildlife refuge	🚹	Trailhead
	Perennial body of water	•	City, town
	Intermittent body of water	⤳	Overlook, scenic view
	Swamp, marsh	⋀	Campground, campsite
	Wooded area	⼧	Shelter
		✕	Mountain peak
		▪	Place of interest

backpacker. Backpackers should follow park regulations where applicable and practice "Leave No Trace" wilderness use etiquette.

The wilderness experience can unleash your mind and body, allowing you to relax and find peace and quiet. It also enables you to grasp beauty and splendor: a stone outcrop with a window to distant lowlands, a black bear disappearing into a brushy thicket, or a pine-bordered clearing marking an old homestead. In these lands you can let your mind roam free, to go where it pleases. So get out and enjoy the treasures of the Carolina mountains.

How to Use This Book

The 50 hikes in this book are geographically arranged. Each hike is contained in its own chapter. An information box is included with each hike. Following the hike name are total distance, hiking time, vertical rise, and maps. Below is an example of a box with a hike:

TOTAL DISTANCE: 4.6 mile there-and-back

HIKING TIME: 2:15

VERTICAL RISE: 770 feet

RATING: Easy–moderate

MAPS: Sumter National Forest—Andrew Pickens Ranger District; USGS 7.5' Rainy Mountain GA-SC

TRAILHEAD GPS COORDINATES: N34°46'23.8", W83°18'14.8"

CONTACT INFORMATION: Sumter National Forest, Andrew Pickens Ranger District Office, 112 Andrew Pickens Circle, Mountain Rest, SC 29664, (864) 638-9568, www.fs.usda.gov/scnfs

---

From the box, we can discern that the hike is 4.6 miles long. In determining distance I walked (and in most cases rewalked or walked numerous times in my life) every hike in this guidebook using a Global Positioning System (GPS). You may notice discrepancies between the distances given in this book and those given on trailhead signs, or other guides, or trail literature distributed by the governing bodies that administer the trails. Sometimes trail distance is passed down from one government body to the next without knowing where it even originally came from. Same goes with trail signs. I have full confidence in the mileages given in this book, because I obtained them myself from my own hiking, field experience if you will, with GPS in hand. Distances are given from the trailhead to the destination and not from the parking area.

This is a there-and-back hike, meaning you walk to your destination, returning to the trailhead the way you came. Other hikes could be a loop, in which case you would walk a new trail from the hike's beginning then return to the trailhead without backtracking.

The hiking time is 2:15 hours. Hiking time is based on the actual time spent on the trail, plus a little time for orienting and stopping. Hiking times are averages and will be different for each hiker and hiking group. Before endeavoring a trip, adventurers need to factor in the physical fitness of the group, rest times desired, and eating and drinking breaks, as well as relaxing and contemplation of nature times, into their own projected hiking times.

The vertical rise is 770 feet. In this case, the vertical rise is the climb from Chattooga River back up to the trailhead. Vertical rise is calculated as the largest uphill vertical change. It may be anywhere along the hike, and not necessarily on the first climb from the trailhead. It is not the sum of all climbs during the hike. The vertical rise was obtained from elevation profiles derived from plotting the GPS tracks onto a mapping program.

This hike is rated easy-moderate. On this hike, the rating is based on the descent and return from the trailhead, along with being a well-marked and maintained trail with few rocks to navigate. Hikes can be anywhere from easy to moderate to difficult. The difficulty rating arises from the following factors: trail length, overall trail condition, including trail maintenance and ability to follow with added emphasis on elevation changes. Longer, rougher hikes with large elevation changes will be rated difficult. In contrast, short, level and well-marked trails, such as the Beech Bottom Falls, will be rated easy.

The Maps section first includes the United States Geographical Survey 7.5' Quadrangle maps. These "quad maps," as they are known, cover every parcel of land in this country. They are divided into rectangular maps that are very detailed. Each quad has a name, usually based on a physical feature located within the quad. In this case the hike traverses the quad map named "Rainy Mountain". Quad maps can be obtained online at www.usgs.gov. Next, other helpful maps are included. In this case, "Sumter National Forest—Andrew Pickens Ranger District" map will be helpful.

"Trailhead GPS Coordinates" gives you the latitude and longitude of the trailhead location. Therefore you can simply punch the coordinates into your navigational GPS and reach the trailhead. However, readers can easily access all trailheads in this book by using the written directions given. But for those who prefer using this GPS technology to navigate, the necessary data has been provided.

"Contact Information" gives you mail, phone, and internet modes of learning more about the hike, should your curiosity extend beyond what is given in the book or if you desire information about the destination beyond the scope of hiking.

Following the information box is an overview of the hike. This paragraph or two give you an overall feel of what to expect, what you might see, trail conditions or important information you might need to consider before undertaking the hike, such as permits needed, river fords, or challenging driving conditions. "Getting There" follows the hike overview. Detailed directions from a known and identifiable starting point are given to help hikers reach the trailheads. "The Hike" follows the directions. This gets into the meat and potatoes of the trek. A running narrative of the hike gives detailed descriptions of the trails used in the hike, including trail junctions, stream crossings, interesting human or natural history along the way. This keeps you apprised of your whereabouts as well as making sure you don't miss those features. With the information included in this guide, you can enjoy an informed, better-executed hike, making the most of your precious time.

In writing this book, I had the pleasure of meeting many friendly helpful people: local residents proud of the unique lands around them, as well as state park and national park employees who endured my endless questions. Even better were my fellow hikers, who were eager to share their knowledge about their favorite spots. They already knew what beauty lay on the horizon. As the Carolina mountains become more populated, these lands become that much more precious. Enjoy them, protect them, and use them wisely.

I.

SOUTHWEST NORTH CAROLINA MOUNTAINS

Joyce Kilmer-Slickrock Wilderness Loop

TOTAL DISTANCE: 10.7-mile loop	

HIKING TIME: 6:30

VERTICAL RISE: 1,700 feet

RATING: Difficult due to trail conditions

MAPS: National Geographic #784 Nantahala National Forest—Fontana & Hiwassee Lakes, USGS 7.5' Tapoco TN-NC

TRAILHEAD GPS COORDINATES: N35°25'02.6", W83°58'21.8"

CONTACT INFORMATION: Nantahala National Forest, Cheoah Ranger District, 1070 Massey Branch Road, Robbinsville, NC 28771, (828) 479-6431, www.fs.usda.gov/nfsnc

This circuit explores the ultra-rugged Joyce Kilmer-Slickrock Wilderness, starting at Big Fat Gap and descending to Slickrock Creek, where numerous fords await you along the clear-as-air waterway, enveloped in junglesque primeval woodlands. The challenging fords lead past Wildcat Falls, a series of tiered cataracts ending in a deep, chilly pool. Continue down the valley before climbing from the creek, only to drop into Nichols Cove, where you can view a small pioneer cemetery. Make a final uptick back to Big Fat Gap. You will earn your scenery, because the trails are often overgrown, fallen trees left where they fall—maintained to a wilderness standard. The stream fords can be deep and swift when the water is up. However, trail intersections are clearly signed. Backpackers will find campsites aplenty.

GETTING THERE

From the intersection of NC 143 and US 129 in Robbinsville, take US 129 North for 14 miles to turn left on Forest Road 62, Deep Creek Road (a bridge crosses the Cheoah River here). Follow FR 62 for 0.1 mile, then curve sharply right as gravel FR 445 goes straight. Continue up Deep Creek Road for 6.6 miles to dead end at the Big Fat Gap trailhead.

THE HIKE

Be prepared for rugged conditions on this hike, but you will be amply rewarded for your efforts. You will clamber over, under, and around fallen trees, taking false user-created trails that peter out and work through brushy tunnels of mountain laurel, rhododendron, and doghobble. But you will also gain appreciation for the wilds of the Southern Appalachian Mountains with their

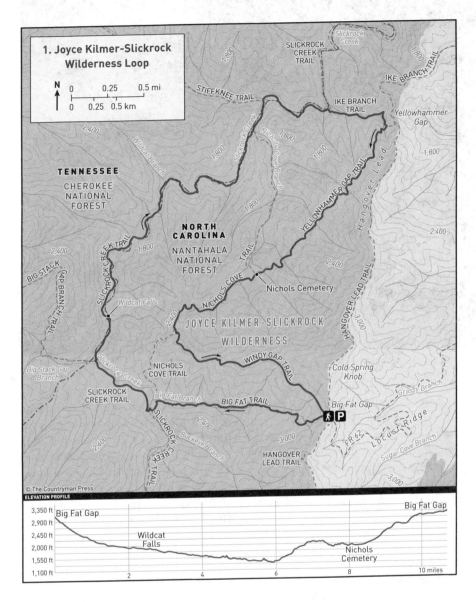

1. Joyce Kilmer-Slickrock Wilderness Loop

N
0   0.25   0.5 mi
0   0.25   0.5 km

SLICKROCK CREEK TRAIL

IKE BRANCH TRAIL

STIFFKNEE TRAIL

IKE BRANCH TRAIL

Yellowhammer Gap

TENNESSEE
CHEROKEE NATIONAL FOREST

NORTH CAROLINA
NANTAHALA NATIONAL FOREST

Nichols Cemetery

JOYCE KILMER-SLICKROCK WILDERNESS

Wildcat Falls

NICHOLS COVE TRAIL

SLICKROCK CREEK TRAIL

WINDY GAP TRAIL

Cold Spring Knob

Big Fat Gap

BIG FAT TRAIL

HANGOVER LEAD TRAIL

Big Stack Gap Branch

Buckeye Branch

Grassy Branch

Locust Ridge

Sugar Cove Branch

© The Countryman Press

ELEVATION PROFILE

3,350 ft — Big Fat Gap
2,900 ft
2,450 ft — Wildcat Falls
2,000 ft
1,550 ft — Nichols Cemetery
1,100 ft

Big Fat Gap

2   4   6   8   10 miles

everywhere-you-look beauty amidst over 19,000 wild acres. Originally Cherokee territory, the rugged mountains were thinly settled. About 65 percent of the forest was logged in the early 1900s, when Babcock Timber Company ran a rail line up Slickrock Creek. The US Forest Service bought up the land in the 1930s, and Joyce Kilmer-Slickrock Wilderness was established in 1975. Combined with adjacent Citico Wilderness, mostly in Tennessee, the two tracts combine to create a contiguous tract of over 35,000 acres and trails galore to explore. I've enjoyed multinight backpacks multiple times in this special swath of the Southern Appalachians.

Start your adventure at Big Fat Gap, elevation 3,100 feet, on Big Fat Trail #41. Windy Gap Trail #400 will be

THIS DROP IS JUST ABOVE WILDCAT FALLS

your return route. Immediately sharply descend west into buckeye and oak rich hardwood coves of Big Fat Branch, along which you sidle at 0.3 mile. It isn't long before you encounter the first of many fallen trees blocking the trail. The wilderness trail management plan leaves most of these down where they lie. Note the abundance of Fraser's sedge, a stalky ground plant, in the cove. Cross the stream a couple of times. The valley widens and you meet Nichols Cove Trail #44 at 1.4 miles. Stay left here to meet and join the Slickrock Creek Trail #42 at 1.5 miles. Head right and work your way through a campsite to ford Slickrock Creek. Navigating through streamside campsites will continue to be a challenge along the stream, as user-created trails spur away in all directions. However, most creek crossings are signed.

Appreciate the clear-as-air, trouty mountain waters of Slickrock Creek as you cross to the left bank. All crossings will be fords—be prepared with hiking sticks and proper footwear—"They don't call it Slickrock Creek for nothin'." The streamside scenery will please, with mossy rocks framing the dashing waterway—at this point forming the North Carolina–Tennessee state line. Overhead, hardwoods canopy the watershed while lush vegetation led by rhododendron fashions a temperate mountain jungle.

At 2.0 miles, the path squeezes past a rugged bluff—it's hard to believe a logging rail went through here, but it did and you follow this grade along Slickrock Creek. Hop over Big Stack Gap Branch, entering from the Volunteer State, then pass Big Stack Gap Branch Trail #139 leaving left. Another crossing of Slickrock Creek and you are back in Carolina. The next crossing—at 2.5 miles—takes place just above multi-tiered Wildcat

TYPICAL SCENE ON SLICKROCK CREEK

Falls. You can explore the upper stages just before the crossing. Squeeze past outcrops as Wildcat Falls tumbles 45 feet in four distinct stages. Ahead, a steep spur leads to the massive plunge pool at the base of the curving cataract.

Ford Slickrock Creek again at 3.0, 3.1, 3.2 and 3.4 miles, losing elevation while soaking in the scenery. Squeeze past another bluff at 4.2 miles, then at 4.4 miles Slickrock Creek narrows while caroming off grey rocks then bending to the left past yet another bluff. At 4.8 miles, ford Slickrock Creek yet again. At 5.1 miles, Nichols Cove Branch enters on your right. At 5.3 miles, signed Nichols Cove Trail #44 leaves acutely right. You can use this trail to shortcut the loop if the fallen trees and dense vegetation of the Slickrock Creek valley have worn you out. Just ahead, ford Slickrock Creek back into Tennessee, then step over gorgeous Little Slickrock Creek to meet the interestingly named Stiffknee

THE LONELY GRAVES IN NICHOLS COVE

Lead, dipping into moist coves with small drainages and over dry ridges. The forest as a whole is less junglesque than down on Slickrock Creek, and the hiking less arduous, despite more elevation variation. Birdsong echoes through the valley of Nichols Cove Branch.

At 8.2 miles, look left for stone fences along the trail. This area was settled. Imagine an isolated mountain farm a century or more back, hand-cleared in this mountain fastness that has once again reclaimed land where corn once grew and livestock grazed—and settlers lived out their lives in an isolation we of the Internet Age can't even imagine. Just ahead, meet the Nichols Cove Trail #44 coming in from your right. At this junction in the cove, you will also see a small cemetery where one of the graves states, "Two Sisters of John & Margret Dotson—Born December 14, 1914—Died December 20, 1914—At Rest."

Stay left, joining the Nichols Cove Trail, making an easy cruise through the upper Nichols Cove, cupped in wooded hills. By 8.8 miles, the climb sharpens, leaving the cove amidst mountain laurel, pine, and sourwood. Auburn needles carpet the trailbed. At 9.2 miles, you reach and join Windy Gap Trail #400. The path turns east, tracing a ridge emanating from Cold Spring Knob, mostly ascending among oaks and pines, bordered with berry bushes. Dip to a gap, then veer right, joining an old logging road. The trailbed is wide here. The walking is easy and level as you curve southeast under the mantle of Cold Spring Knob. Return to Big Fat Gap at 10.7 miles, completing the wilderness circuit.

Trail #106 at 5.4 miles. Continue the gentle downgrade to ford Slickrock Creek again at 5.8 miles. You are on the right-hand bank, heading downstream. Imagine building railroad bridges at these crossings!

At 6.0 miles, join Ike Branch Trail #45, as Slickrock Creek makes a sharp, scenic bend to the left. You are at the hike's low point, just under 1,400 feet. Ascend the narrow, heavily wooded cove, rich with dwarf crested iris and other wildflowers, to reach an intersection at 6.5 miles. Here, head right on single-track Yellowhammer Gap Trail #49. Work along the west slope of Hangover

Joyce Kilmer Memorial Forest

TOTAL DISTANCE: 2.0-mile figure eight double loop	

HIKING TIME: 1:15

VERTICAL RISE: 580 feet

RATING: Easy

MAPS: National Geographic #784 Nantahala National Forest—Fontana & Hiwassee Lakes, USGS 7.5' Santeelah Creek

TRAILHEAD GPS COORDINATES: N35°21'32.1", W83°55'46.4"

CONTACT INFORMATION: Nantahala National Forest, Cheoah Ranger District, 1070 Massey Branch Road, Robbinsville, NC 28771, (828) 479-6431, www.fs.usda.gov/nfsnc

There's something inspiring about massive old-growth trees, giants standing for centuries as silent witnesses to the natural splendor of the Carolina mountains. One such place is Joyce Kilmer Memorial Forest, where you can make an eye-pleasing trek among colossal tulip trees and other massive hardwoods. Named after renowned World War I veteran Joyce Kilmer, who wrote the poem titled "Trees," the old-growth grove honors the man and allows us to hike through the colossal hardwoods situated in the Santeelah Creek valley. You will first leave the parking area with its informative kiosk (worth your time) and then cross Santeelah Creek, heading up one of its tributaries into Poplar Cove, where you can enjoy the big trees up close, standing where they have for hundreds of years.

GETTING THERE

From Robbinsville, take US 129 North 1.1 miles to Massey Branch Road and NC 143. Turn left on Massey Branch Road and follow it 3.4 miles to a "T" intersection. Turn right on Snowbird Road, still NC 143. Follow it 6.8 miles to NC 1127. Turn right on NC 1127, Rattler Ford Campground Road, and follow it 2.2 miles. Turn left on Joyce Kilmer Road and follow it 0.4 mile to dead end at the trailhead.

THE HIKE

Perhaps Joyce Kilmer's famous poem "Trees" was inspired by old-growth tulip trees such as those found along this hike, standing regally for more than 400 years, reaching over 20 feet in circumference, though we do know he never saw these particular trees. His poem goes like this: "I think that I shall never

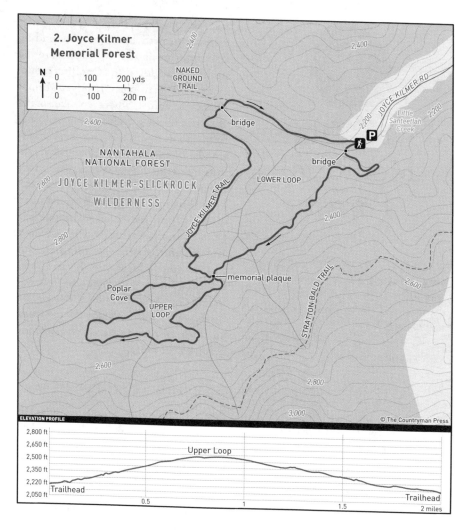

2. Joyce Kilmer Memorial Forest

N

0   100   200 yds
0   100   200 m

NAKED GROUND TRAIL

bridge

JOYCE KILMER RD

Little Santeetlah Creek

NANTAHALA NATIONAL FOREST

JOYCE KILMER-SLICKROCK WILDERNESS

JOYCE KILMER TRAIL

LOWER LOOP

bridge

memorial plaque

Poplar Cove

UPPER LOOP

STRATTON BALD TRAIL

© The Countryman Press

ELEVATION PROFILE

2,800 ft
2,650 ft
2,500 ft
2,350 ft
2,220 ft
2,050 ft

Upper Loop

Trailhead

Trailhead

0.5   1   1.5   2 miles

see / A poem lovely as a tree / A tree whose hungry mouth is prest / Against the earth's sweet flowing breast / A tree that looks at God all day / And lifts her leafy arms to pray / A tree that may in Summer wear / A nest of robins in her hair / Upon whose bosom snow has lain / Who intimately lives with rain / Poems are made by fools like me / But only God can make a tree."

New Jersey native Joyce Kilmer lived but 32 years, tragically killed in France during World War I. Before the conflict, Mr. Kilmer had received accolades for his poetry and journalism and was a staffer at the *New York Times*. After his death, the reputation of Joyce Kilmer lived on in his famous poem "Trees." Thus, when the US Forest Service purchased a 3,600-acre tract of old-growth woodlands in the mountains of western North Carolina, it only seemed fitting to memorialize Mr. Kilmer by naming the grove for him. Interestingly, numerous streets and parks in the northeastern United States are also named for the hero.

Part of the rugged and primitive Joyce Kilmer–Slickrock Wilderness, the trails of this walk—unlike other paths in this wilderness—are maintained for more casual hikers. By the way, restrooms and picnic tables enhance the trailhead, as does the stone shelter, full of informative displays about Joyce Kilmer and old-growth forests.

Your hike makes a double loop, working up Poplar Cove. You'll leave the trailhead to immediately bridge Little Santeelah Creek, draining the high country of Joyce Kilmer-Slickrock Wilderness. Soak in looks up and down this untamed watershed on a sturdy footbridge. Your ascent is made gentle by a prolonged switchback on a thickly vegetated slope growing in profusion after the fall of the hemlocks due to the exotic pest that is the hemlock wooly adelgid. On the plus side, Joyce Kilmer is a verdant wildflower hotspot.

Wood and earth steps lead you through rhododendron, doghobble, and ferns. Trickling streams flow over the trail but you cross them via quaint little bridges. The first old-growth trees you'll see are yellow birch and beech, and though old aren't huge. The big ones are found on the upper loop, which you will reach after a half-mile. Here, you will also find a plaque memorializing Joyce Kilmer.

Now comes the payoff in upper Poplar Cove, where the cool air and moist but well-drained soils are tailor-made for tulip trees. By the way, in earlier times tulip trees were commonly called poplars, hence the name Poplar Cove. And here begins the scattering of giants, rising above the dim forest floor, where visitors are surprised not only by the size of the trees but the overall composition

AUTHOR ADMIRES A PAIR OF MASSIVE TULIP TREES

OLD-GROWTH TULIP TREES ARE THE LARGEST LIVING
THINGS IN THE CAROLINA MOUNTAINS

old-growth forest has trees that are passing through all stages of their existence, incessantly growing then dying from lightning strikes, competition, or disease. A healthy forest will feature trees of all ages within its realm. Other old-growth trees in this forest you will see are red oaks, basswood, and Carolina silverbells, though in their old-growth stage they seem small compared to the mighty tulip trees.

User created paths lead to the base of the tulip trees, where visitors crane their necks skyward and have their picture taken in front of the tulip trees, the largest living things in the Carolina mountains. A pair of oft-photographed trailside twin giants is encountered at 0.9 mile. Here, imagine living on this mountainside cove for more than four centuries—the storms, the sun, the changing seasons, the wildlife passing by . . .

It is such thoughts to which old-growth forests give rise. At 1.2 miles, you will have completed the upper loop. Stay left and complete the lower loop, passing a few more tulip trees and all-around attractive woods. Cross the stream draining Poplar Cove. Wooden steps lead down to Little Santeelah Creek and a second bridged crossing of the stream. Here, the Naked Ground Trail leaves left, but you head right, down the creek, and you are soon back at the trailhead.

of the forest. For most visitors expect nothing but old-growth trees in an old-growth forest, but it just isn't so.

Typical virgin woodland will be populated with giants, but also younger, lesser trees rising where old-growth trees have fallen, creating a light gap. Then, new trees rise quickly in the beneficial sun, to rise up and once again fashion a continuous canopy. A typical

Three Falls of Snowbird Creek

TOTAL DISTANCE: 12.6 mile there-and-back	
HIKING TIME: 6:45	
VERTICAL RISE: 940 feet	
RATING: Difficult due to distance	
MAPS: National Geographic #784 Nantahala National Forest—Fontana & Hiwassee Lakes, USGS 7.5' Santeelah Creek, NC	
TRAILHEAD GPS COORDINATES: N35°16'25.3", W83°54'44.0"	
CONTACT INFORMATION: Nantahala National Forest, Cheoah Ranger District, 1070 Massey Branch Road, Robbinsville, NC 28771, (828) 479-6431, www.fs.usda .gov/nfsnc	

This deep woods adventure heads into the secluded Snowbird Backcountry, where you trek along a wild waterway, visiting three major waterfalls amid a torrent of Carolina mountain splendor. Set in a remote section of the Nantahala National Forest, you will follow an old railroad grade most of the hike, keeping the elevation changes moderate. Lush forests of yellow birch and other highland species accompany your route that leads first past the cataracts of Big Falls, then off the railroad grade to admire impressive and wide Middle Falls, with its outsized plunge pool. Finally, rejoin the railroad grade for a scenic trek to seldom-visited Upper Falls. Nowadays, with hiker bridges and alternate routes, you can undertake this hike year-round without getting your feet wet. Furthermore, if the hike seems long, you can shorten it by visiting just one or two of the first cataracts.

GETTING THERE

From the intersection of NC 143 and US 129 in Robbinsville, take US 129 North for 1.1 miles to Massey Branch Road, NC 143. Follow it for 3.4 miles to a "T" intersection. Turn right here on Snowbird Road, still on NC 143. Follow Snowbird Road for 2.1 miles, then turn left on NC 1115. Follow NC 1115 for 2.0 miles, still on Snowbird Road. Make an acute left on NC 1127 after passing Robinson's Grocery (closed). Follow NC 1127 for 0.9 mile, then turn right on Big Snowbird Road, NC 1120. NC 1120 becomes gravel after 2 miles, then it becomes Forest Road 75, where it dead-ends at the trailhead 4 miles beyond the blacktop.

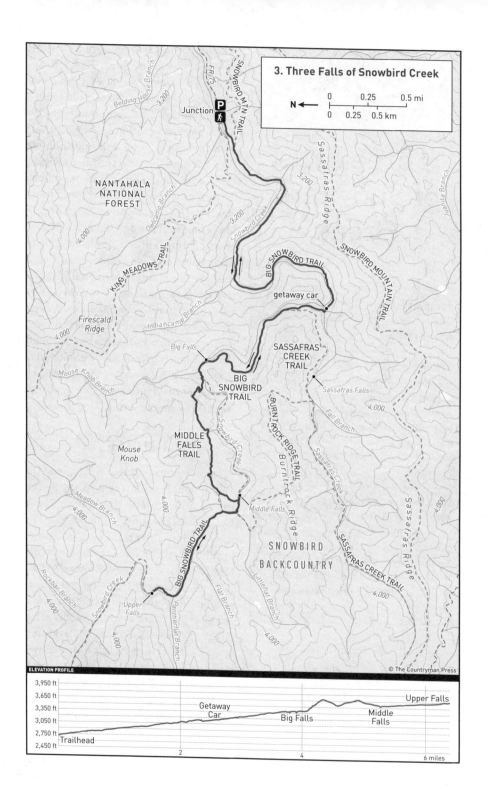

3. Three Falls of Snowbird Creek

N ←

| 0 | 0.25 | 0.5 mi |
| 0 | 0.25 | 0.5 km |

Belding House Branch

3,200

FR 75

SNOWBIRD MTN TRAIL

Junction

P

NANTAHALA NATIONAL FOREST

Oxicamp Branch

3,200

Snowbird Creek

3,200

Sassafras Ridge

Juahita Branch

4,000

KING MEADOWS TRAIL

BIG SNOWBIRD TRAIL

SNOWBIRD MOUNTAIN TRAIL

getaway car

Firescald Ridge

Indiancamp Branch

4,000

SASSAFRAS CREEK TRAIL

Big Falls

BIG SNOWBIRD TRAIL

Sassafras Falls

Mouse Knob Branch

Snowbird Creek

BURNTROCK RIDGE TRAIL

Fall Branch

4,000

MIDDLE FALLS TRAIL

Mouse Knob

Burntrock Ridge

Sassafras Creek

Sassafras Ridge

4,000

Meadow Branch

4,000

Middle Falls

4,000

SNOWBIRD BACKCOUNTRY

SASSAFRAS CREEK TRAIL

4,000

Rockbar Branch

Snowbird Creek

BIG SNOWBIRD TRAIL

Flat Branch

Littleflat Branch

4,000

Upper Falls

Pantherflat Branch

© The Countryman Press

ELEVATION PROFILE

| | | | Upper Falls |

3,950 ft
3,650 ft
3,350 ft
3,050 ft
2,750 ft
2,450 ft

Getaway Car

Big Falls

Middle Falls

Trailhead

2   4   6 miles

THE HIKE

The Snowbird Backcountry encompasses the mountain-rimmed Snowbird Creek watershed, set fast against the state line ridge dividing North Carolina from Tennessee. After exploring the seemingly impenetrable yet regal forests that rise along Snowbird Creek and its tributaries, you will find it hard to believe the area was ever logged. But from 1928 to 1942, the forest was cut down. After four score and more years, the forest has recovered magnificently. A positive legacy of the logging days is the railroad grade you follow almost the entirety of the hike, making a gentle ascent into a resplendent and scenic valley, replete with three worthwhile waterfalls to see in addition to everywhere-you-look splendor. In addition, the Snowbird Creek Trail is part of a well-signed 35-mile trail network

exploring the 8,000-acre Snowbird Backcountry.

Our hike leaves the trailhead on the Big Snowbird Trail as the King Meadows Trail leaves right to bridge Snowbird Creek. The wide and easy railroad grade penetrates a tall forest of birch bordered in rhododendron thickets. At 0.3 mile, the infrequently trod Snowbird Mountain Trail leaves left.

Snowbird Creek bends through rising hills and impenetrable forests, frothing white then slowing in crystalline pools. The doghobble- and rhododendron-lined path turns with the creek, forging deeper into the backcountry to find Sassafras Creek blocking the way at 2.5 miles. Here you'll find a rusting 1930s bullet-riddled jalopy, named the "getaway car" by woodland visitors. A hiker footbridge leads across Sassafras Creek, and you are on your way to pass the Sassafras Creek Trail at 2.8

UPPER FALLS IS LONGER THAN IT IS HIGH

MIDDLE FALLS MAKES A CREEK-WIDE 20-FOOT LEDGE DROP

miles (Sassafras Falls, a high spiller, can be accessed via this trail). Continue with the railroad grade, staying well above crashing Snowbird Creek, where trout hold fast as rising ridges wall you off from the rest of the world. You'll hear Big Falls (also known as Lower Falls though the official USGS name is Big Falls) upon approach and at 3.8 miles, a user-created path drops precipitously to the series of cataracts crashing over slick stone in stages, divided by deep pools. Access is difficult. The best hanging out spot is at the top of the falls.

Ahead, step over old embedded railroad ties in areas where spring seeps

through tall, vine-draped trees. At 5.0 miles, head left with the Middle Falls Trail, as an official shortcut goes right to rejoin Big Snowbird Trail. Quickly rejoin the Big Snowbird Trail downstream, then white noise quickly leads you to an easy spur going to the base of Middle Falls, in my opinion the most scenic of the spillers in the Snowbird Backcountry. Here, the entirety of Snowbird Creek nosedives 20 feet off a stream-wide fractured ledge, slowing in a substantial sun-splashed plunge pool.

From there, continue up the railroad grade that is the Big Snowbird Trail. The tread is much less worn above Middle Falls. Reach an avoidable river crossing and the Burntrock Ridge Trail by Little-flat Branch at 5.4 miles. (You can avoid the crossings by backtracking 0.1 mile on the Middle Falls Trail, then splitting left at the shortcut to Big Snowbird Trail). Stay with the grade, passing through a leveled former logging camp to cross back over to the right-hand bank at 5.5 miles. Walk directly alongside Snowbird Creek under a mantle of cherry and birch trees. Moss grows everywhere in this almost always cool environment. At 6.1 miles, a long straightaway ends and you turn north, briefly leaving the grade before reaching Upper Falls at 6.4 miles. Here, Snowbird Creek pours white on an elongated stone slide into a chilly, shady pool at 3,700 feet. The length of the falls is more than its height of about 30 feet. The deep pool is easily accessible, and the trail goes alongside the slide cascade.

Upper Falls is a satisfactory turnaround point, a remote, well-earned place to appreciate the untamed Snowbird Backcountry. Allow ample time for the substantial backtrack.

cross the path. At 3.9 miles, bridge Snowbird Creek and reach a trail intersection. The old railroad grade keeps straight and level, crisscrossing the creek, but our route takes us on the single-track Middle Falls Trail, climbing and avoiding the fords while undulating

Siler Bald Loop

TOTAL DISTANCE: 3.4-mile loop

HIKING TIME: 1:40

VERTICAL RISE: 1,040 feet

RATING: Moderate

MAPS: National Geographic #784 Nantahala National Forest—Fontana & Hiwassee Lakes, USGS 7.5' Wayah Bald NC

TRAILHEAD GPS COORDINATES: N35°9.244', W83°34.804'

CONTACT INFORMATION: Nantahala National Forest, Cheoah Ranger District, 1070 Massey Branch Road, Robbinsville, NC 28771, (828) 479-6431, www.fs.usda .gov/nfsnc

This loop hike in the Nantahala National Forest combines the world's most famous footpath—the Appalachian Trail—with a closed-to-traffic forest road to create a circuit leading up to the nearly-mile-high meadow of Siler Bald, where you can revel in extensive vistas of the Carolina mountains from commanding heights. Leave Wayah Gap, southbound on the AT, working steadily uphill through rich wildflower-bountiful woods to reach a highland pass and the base of flower-strewn Siler Bald. Here, you ascend to the peak, finding 360-degree views as far as the clarity of the sky allows. You can simply backtrack but I recommend taking the closed forest road used by forest personnel to keep the bald mown, thus adding new trail mileage.

GETTING THERE

From the intersection of US 23/441 and US 64 in Franklin, take US 64 West for 3.8 miles to turn right on Old Murphy Road. Drive for 0.2 mile, then turn left on Wayah Road, NC 1310. Follow NC 1310 for 9.2 miles to Wayah Gap. Forest Road 69 leaves right from the gap. Look on your left just past FR 69 for a left turn uphill to a limited parking area. If it is full, park along the shoulder of NC 1310.

THE HIKE

Leave from the parking locale on stone steps, passing through a partially shaded picnic area, rising into full-blown woods. There used to be a Nantahala National Forest campground hereabouts. Meet the Appalachian Trail at 0.1 mile. Here, turn right and begin your worthwhile climb to Siler Bald. Your return route is dead ahead, a double-track forest road closed to public driving.

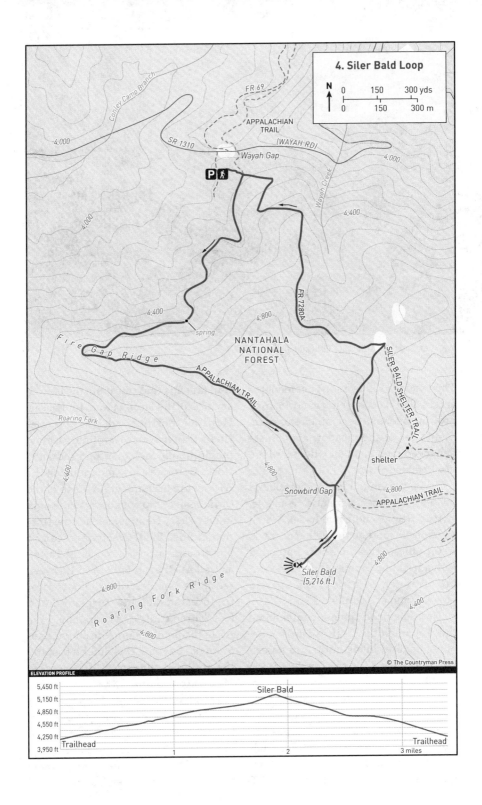

4. Siler Bald Loop

N
| 0 | 150 | 300 yds |
| 0 | 150 | 300 m |

Conley Camp Branch

FR 69

APPALACHIAN TRAIL

-4,000-

SR 1310

[WAYAH RD]

Wayah Gap

4,000

Wayah Creek

4,400

4,000

spring

4,400

4,800

FR 7280A

NANTAHALA
NATIONAL
FOREST

Fire Gap Ridge

APPALACHIAN TRAIL

SILER BALD SHELTER TRAIL

Roaring Fork

shelter

4,400

4,800

Snowbird Gap

4,800

APPALACHIAN TRAIL

Siler Bald
(5,216 ft.)

4,800

4,400

Roaring Fork Ridge

4,800

4,800

© The Countryman Press

ELEVATION PROFILE

	Siler Bald
5,450 ft	
5,150 ft	
4,850 ft	
4,550 ft	
4,250 ft	
3,950 ft	Trailhead

Trailhead

1

2

Trailhead

3 miles

A HOST OF MOUNTAIN STRETCHES OUT FROM SILER BALD

This road is used by forest personnel to access Siler Bald, keeping it mown, from growing over and becoming reforested. The edges of the meadow also create enhanced food plots for wildlife, where blackberries grow.

Trace the white blazes, southbound on the AT under a mantle of maple, striped maple, and witch hazel. Watch for exposed roots on the well-used track. At 0.2 mile, curve into a cove bottomed with a trickling branch. If you are looking for water, be patient, then pass a piped spring at 0.6 mile.

Now is a good time to contemplate the Appalachian Trail in North Carolina. Several hikes in this guide use sections of the AT in the Tar Heel State. Of the AT's 2,200-or-so-mile journey from Georgia to New England (the exact length of the AT changes year to year due to reroutes), 96 miles are exclusively in North Carolina, such as this section. North Carolina also includes an additional 218 miles of AT

trail mileage that run along the boundary of North Carolina and Tennessee. Heading northbound, the Appalachian Trail in North Carolina is a moving highlight reel. Standing Indian is North Carolina's first mountain on the AT and the first mountain north of the Caribbean to top out above a mile high in elevation. Next comes our destination of Siler Bald. Great views can be had from nearby Wesser Bald Tower, as well as Cheoah Bald. And then you reach the Smokies, where lofty spruce–fir–forested heights surpass 6,000 feet. Three trailside towers along the AT in the Smokies provide stellar panoramas. Beyond the Smokies stand the rounded meadows of venerated Max Patch, dubbed the grandstand of the Smokies. Lovers Leap near Hot Springs is another standout destination, looming above the grand, brawling French Broad River. And the balds of Roan Mountain offer unforgettable vistas of ridges near and far as you roll

SILER BALD IS KEPT OPEN BY MOWING THIS FIELD

AUTUMN CAN BE GLORIOUS WHEN VIEWED FROM SILER BALD

through mountain meadows extending for miles.

And then there's the woodland wonderment offered in every footfall as you trek along, such as this segment of the rise from Wayah Gap. You are working around a slope of Fire Gap Ridge, on the top-ten all-time Carolina Appalachians names list. At 0.9 mile, you have reached the crest of Fire Gap Ridge and now turn east along the nose of the ridge. Oaks are more prevalent up here, despite being almost 4,800 feet elevation.

The Appalachian Trail gently rolls into Snowbird Gap, a grassy open area at the base of Siler Bald, at 1.7 miles. Now, head right through a meadow for your final climb. At 1.9 miles, top out on Siler Bald, where a marble slab denotes the peak as 5,216 feet. You have climbed over 1,000 feet from Wayah Gap, here in the Nantahala Mountains. Easterly, look for the stone sentinels of the Fishhawk Mountains. Southward rises Standing Indian, the tower of Albert Mountain and Georgia's highest point of Brasstown Bald. Closer, and to the north, rise the transmission towers of now-wooded Wine Spring Bald. The Great Smoky Mountains and Tennessee stand to the distant northwest. What a view!

From here, descend Siler Bald back to Snowbird Gap. At this point, the AT continues southeast, but you head northeast on a track, where a sign to Snowbird trail shelter indicates the proper direction. Descend the blue-blazed doubletrack to level off in a meadow at 2.6 miles. From here, the blue-blazed trail to Snowbird Shelter leads right, but you head left across the meadow, sticking with the double-track. Reenter the forest and keep descending under a mantle of hardwoods. The downgrade is steady while bisecting a second meadow at 3.0 miles. In summer the meadow grasses can be high. Make a final downgrade in the forest to complete the loop portion of the hike at 3.3 miles. From here it is a simple backtrack through the picnic area to the trailhead.

5

Upper Nantahala River Route

TOTAL DISTANCE: 8.9-mile loop	

HIKING TIME: 4:30

VERTICAL RISE: 975 feet

RATING: Moderate to difficult due to distance

MAPS: National Geographic #784 Nantahala National Forest—Fontana & Hiwassee Lakes, USGS 7.5' Rainbow Springs

TRAILHEAD GPS COORDINATES: N35°4.488', W83°31.645'

CONTACT INFORMATION: Nantahala National Forest, Cheoah Ranger District, 1070 Massey Branch Road, Robbinsville, NC 28771, (828) 479-6431, www.fs.usda .gov/nfsnc

This loop hike begins near the popular Standing Indian campground, nearly encircled by a large backcountry trail network in the Nantahala National Forest. You will first cut through the attractive campground, then join the Nantahala River downstream, a vale of exceptional beauty highlighted by the mountain stream itself. After enjoying river scenes, you will turn up Park Creek, a scenic waterway in its own right. Follow Park Creek to its headwaters, rambling along Middle Ridge on the Park Ridge Trail, eventually returning to the Nantahala River and completing the circuit.

GETTING THERE

From the crossing of US 23/441 and US 64 in Franklin, take US 64 West for 12 miles to West Old Murphy Road. There will be signs for Standing Indian Campground here. Turn left on West Old Murphy Road and follow it for 1.9 miles to the right turn onto Forest Road 67. Follow FR 67 for 2.0 miles to the Backcountry Information Center on your right. The hike starts at the kiosk.

THE HIKE

The headwaters of the Nantahala River are found in the Nantahala National Forest's greater Standing Indian hiking area, backed up against the Georgia state line. Comprised of the 23,000-acre Southern Nantahala Wilderness and the adjacent 10,000-acre-plus Standing Indian Backcountry, the streams draining the high country flow north to form the Nantahala River. Along the ridges, the Appalachian Trail winds its way through the Standing Indian Backcountry. Other pathways, including the ones used for this hike, create a 40-plus-mile

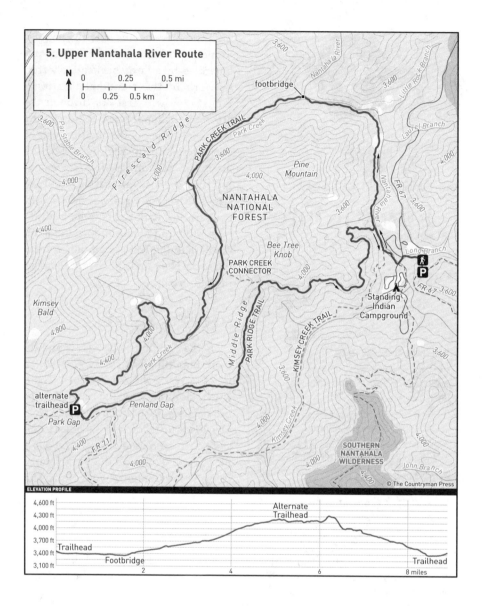

5. Upper Nantahala River Route

ELEVATION PROFILE

trail network. If you enjoy camping and hiking, base out of Standing Indian Campground and explore your heart away.

This particular circuit is one of my favorites hereabouts. Leave the Backcountry Information Center to follow a signed connector trail leading downhill, westerly, to bridge Long Branch, and reach the paved road of Standing Indian

Campground at 0.1 mile. Here, head left, bridging the Nantahala River. From the span, enjoy downstream views of the crystalline, mountain-bred watercourse. Just beyond the road bridge, at 0.2 mile, leave right on a signed path, the Park Creek Trail. You are running along the Nantahala River, with campsites on the far side of the free-flowing watercourse. Black birch, yellow birch, rhododendron, and doghobble line the trail. You are at just under 3,400 feet elevation.

At 0.3 mile, the Kimsey Creek Trail leaves left. Continue straight, down the Nantahala River, enjoying looks at the rock-strewn stream. Navigation is easy from here forward, a simple loop. At 0.5 mile, the Park Ridge Trail, your return route, leaves left. You keep straight on the Park Creek Trail, still wandering the floodplain of the Nantahala River, tracing an old railroad grade. At 0.6 mile, a trail-side outcrop allows access to the bending river near a deep pool. Shortly ahead, leave the old railroad grade, passing through fern gardens amid wooded flats. At 1.2 miles, the trail and river turn west. You are roughly circling Pine Mountain.

At 1.6 miles, come to Park Creek. Turn up this mountain watershed, crossing Park Creek on a hiker bridge to join an old double-track. Initially the trail goes off and on the double-track, switching to standard single-track foot trail where the double-track is washed out or mucky. Park Creek cascades iridescent below. Look for a series of cataracts upstream of its meeting the Nantahala River. Overhead, basswood, buckeye, and maple fashion a green mantle. This is a rich wildflower area. Hop over small marshy tributaries adding their flow to Park Creek. At 2.6 miles, the Park Creek Trail passes below a clearing that may have been an old homesite—the valley is wide and flat here—for a mountain valley. The path crosses Park Creek, without benefit of footbridge, at 3.0 miles. You are now on the left-hand bank heading upstream, and at 3.2 miles the Park Creek Connector leads 0.3 mile left to the Park Ridge Trail, enabling a 5.1-mile loop using this shortcut.

The main hike continues up Park Creek beyond the shortcut, passing through a flat that was likely a former

CROSSING THE FOOTBRIDGE OVER PARK CREEK

THE NANTAHALA RIVER STREAMS PAST BOULDERS BIG AND SMALL

logging camp. At 3.3 miles, cross Park Creek again—no bridge. At 3.7 miles, the gradient increases as you turn up a tributary of Park Creek. Ahead, cross an old forest road and rise into oak, cherry, and maple. Roam the wooded slopes below now-wooded Kimsey Bald to step over now-small Park Creek at 5.0 miles. Rise to reach Park Gap and an alternate trailhead at Forest Road 71 at 5.3 miles.

Now join the signed single-track Park Ridge Trail, heading southeast. This path actually follows Middle Ridge—there is no Park Ridge on the official USGS topo, perhaps a trail namer's mistake. Run below FR 71 a bit, then break away from the gravel forest road in hardwoods to meet Penland Gap at 5.8 miles. Cruise a narrow dry ridge populated with chestnut oak, sourwood, and wild azalea. Ramble over a knob at 6.2 miles, the hike's high point at 4,230 feet. Watch for impressive northern red oaks. It's almost all downhill from here. You are running the highland dividing Park Creek on your left from Kimsey Creek to your right. At 7.0 miles, steps lead you to a gap and the Park Creek Connector. Stay with the blazes heading right and downhill, still on the Park Ridge Trail, as old forest roads spoke out from the gap. Curve through a tulip-tree-filled cove to meet brushy woods growing up from a 2016 wildfire. Look for scarred tree trunks. You are in the Kimsey Creek valley on a side slope well above the waterway and well below Bee Tree Knob. Note the abundance of sassafras and locust in this recovering mountainside.

The Park Ridge Trail turns into the Nantahala River valley at 7.8 miles. The descent continues as you curve in and out of small tributaries of the Nantahala River. Rhododendron thickens as the rushing music of the Nantahala rises to your ears. Step over dashing creeklets to meet the Park Creek Trail at 8.4 miles, completing the loop portion of the hike. From here, backtrack 0.5 mile, returning to the Standing Indian Backcountry Information Center at 8.9 miles.

6

Bartram Trail Vistas

TOTAL DISTANCE: 9.6-mile there-and-back
HIKING TIME: 5:00
VERTICAL RISE: 1,500 feet
RATING: Moderate-difficult due to distance
MAPS: National Geographic #785 Nantahala National Forest—Nantahala and Cullasaja Gorges, USGS 7.5' Scaly Mountain NC
TRAILHEAD GPS COORDINATES: N35°4.561', W83°17.271'
CONTACT INFORMATION: Nantahala National Forest, 90 Sloan Road, Franklin, NC 28734, (828) 524-6441, www.fs.usda .gov/nfsnc

This is an excellent but underused hike on the Bartram Trail visiting several wide granite faces that present stellar panoramas of the Little Tennessee River valley and the Nantahala Mountains beyond. Start up high at remote Jones Gap and trace the Bartram Trail over Jones Knob and a huge stone slope, replete with a glorious panorama. Next pass another overlook, then drop to a gap and backcountry campsite before climbing Whiterock Mountain and finding more inspiring vistas. Additional highlights await, including a side trip to the top of Fishhawk Mountain and an overlook near Wolf Rock.

GETTING THERE

From the intersection of US 23/441 and US 64 in Franklin, take US 64 East for 14.6 miles to Turtle Pond Road, NC 1620. Turn right on Turtle Pond Road, just before the left turn into Cliffside Recreation Area. At 1.0 mile, stay right, now on Dendy Orchard Road. In another mile, the pavement ends. Climb, then 2.3 miles from US 64, turn left on Forest Road 4522. There will be a Bartram Trail access sign here. Follow FR 4522 steeply uphill, dead-ending at Jones Gap and the trailhead at 2.0 miles. Alternate directions: From Highlands, take US 64 West 4.5 miles, just past the entrance to Cliffside Recreation Area, and reach Turtle Pond Road. Turn left and follow the above directions.

THE HIKE

This hike starts high and stays high, rolling atop the ridgeline of the Fish-hawk Mountains, using a part of the Bartram Trail. This long trail winding through the mountains of North Georgia, western North Carolina, and parts

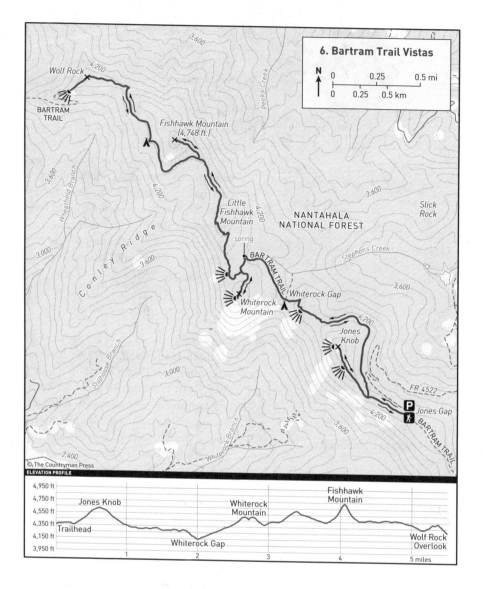

6. Bartram Trail Vistas

of Alabama, Florida and South Carolina, was named for 18th-century naturalist William Bartram. Mr. Bartram, a naturalist, explored what became the southeastern United States shortly before the American Revolution, sojourning for 4 years, after which he wrote a lasting book titled *Travels of William Bartram* In addition to recording the journey, he also discovered and catalogued over 200 plants. Today, the Bartram Trail honors the man.

Do your own self a favor and make this hike. If the distance is a bit long, just go to the first couple of overlooks. The trek leaves northwest from Jones Gap, passing around a metal gate under maples, oak and thick underbrush in the summertime. The path opens onto a former clearing, now growing into

THE LITTLE TENNESSEE RIVER VALLEY AS SEEN FROM WHITEROCK MOUNTAIN

successional forest. Look for blackberries here in late July. At 0.3 mile, come to your first spur trail. Here, head left for Jones Knob. Rise on a rocky path bordered by stunted trees and mountain laurel. A preliminary view opens to your left, but at 0.6 mile, you open onto the rock dome of Jones Knob, pocked with squat pines and oaks. Slip left through some brush where you can look west a very, very long way. Here, the valley of the Little Tennessee River runs north–south, backed by the Nantahala Mountains. Nearby, Whiterock Mountain shows its stone face.

Return to the Bartram Trail, circling around the east side of Jones Knob. Drop to a gap at 1.7 miles before curving around a small knob only to descend again to Whiterock Gap at 2.0 miles. You are at the low point of the hike and still above 4,000 feet. Find a small campsite here and a signed spur trail descending to Stephens Creek, the water source for this remote and infrequently used camp. Beyond the camp, the single-track trail works up the slope of the ridge and turns into the headwaters of Stephens Creek. At 2.4 miles, pass by a short path leading right to a spring, nestled under brush. Continue working for Whiterock Mountain and at 2.5 miles, take the 0.2-mile spur left, up to the apex of Whiterock Mountain.

NAKED ROCK FACES CHARACTERIZE THE FISHHAWK MOUNTAINS

THE FISHHAWK MOUNTAINS WELCOME THE MORNING SUN

Top out over the 4,500 foot peak, then descend a bit, through partially vegetated rock, before opening onto a naked rock slab. The views are enormous here—to the northwest stands Trimont Ridge and behind that the Smokies. Westward rise the Nantahalas. To the southwest, the rolling wooded ramparts of Georgia's Chattahoochee National Forest stand out in relief. Jones Knob and nearer peaks rise proudly as part of the Fishhawk Mountains. This is what hiking in the Carolina mountains is all about.

Backtrack and return to the Bartram Trail, where more panoramas open as you pass through partially wooded rock outcrops. At 3.3 miles, the path skirts around the steep west side of Little Fishhawk Mountain in mountain laurel. At 4.0 miles, take the signed spur to the top of Fishhawk Mountain. The trail is faint; most hikers skip the climb. But don't. It's a short steep challenge, but at the top elevation, 4,748 feet, at 4.0 miles, stands

a plaque on a rock with this inscription, "For the glory of God who created the beautiful heavens and Earth and in memory of William Bartram who, in the year of our Lord 1775, passed through the valley below." This is the hike's high point, but views are limited.

Backtrack and return again to the Bartram Trail. Circle the west side of Fishhawk Mountain, passing a campsite at 4.7 miles. The hike continues along the ridge, and you surmount mostly wooded Wolf Rock at 5.3 miles, expecting a view, but not getting much of one. However, the trail descends the rocky ridge and comes to a signed lookout at 5.5 miles. Here, you can scan southwesterly into the Tessentee Creek Valley below and a host of hills around it.

This is a good place to turn around. If you take just the Bartram Trail back without taking the side trails, it is 4.1 miles back to the trailhead, making your hike 9.6 miles.

Chinquapin Mountain and Glen Falls

TOTAL DISTANCE: 1.6-mile and 3.4-mile there and backs, respectively

HIKING TIME: 2:30

VERTICAL RISE: 580 feet and 750 feet respectively

RATING: Moderate

MAPS: National Geographic #785 Nantahala National Forest—Nantahala and Cullasaja Gorges, USGS 7.5' Highlands NC-GA

TRAILHEAD GPS COORDINATES: N35°1.9978', W83°14.1511'

CONTACT INFORMATION: Nantahala National Forest, 90 Sloan Road, Franklin, NC 28734, (828) 524-6441, www.fs.usda .gov/nfsnc

Take on two rewarding yet dissimilar hikes from one trailhead. Here, in the Nantahala National Forest just outside of the town of Highlands, you can first walk along a well-maintained and very popular path beside East Fork Overflow Creek to view Glen Falls, a series of wild cataracts several hundred feet long crashing time and again to fashion photogenic waterfalls. Three observation decks deliver aquatic views, and a final locale allows water access at the base of the falls. Next, take the lesser-used route to the top of Chinquapin Mountain, where open rock faces allow distant panoramas of the mountainlands around you.

GETTING THERE

From the intersection of US 64 and NC 106 in Highlands, take NC 106 South for 1.8 miles, then turn left on Glen Falls Road. The access road to Chinquapin Mountain and Glen Falls veers right, just after the left turn from NC 106. Follow Glen Falls Road for 1.0 mile and dead end at the trailhead. Parking is limited so be considerate about how and where you park your vehicle.

THE HIKE

These two treks start from the same trailhead; therefore, they are often hiked together. However, if you feel like having an easy day, just do one hike. The Glen Falls Trail is vastly more popular and is often busy with waterfallers viewing the nearly continuous cataracts tumbling south to meet the fabled Chattooga River. Chinquapin Mountain gets 5 percent of the traffic as Glen Falls despite not only leading to a series of overlooks but also providing a contrast to the watery adventure of Glen Falls.

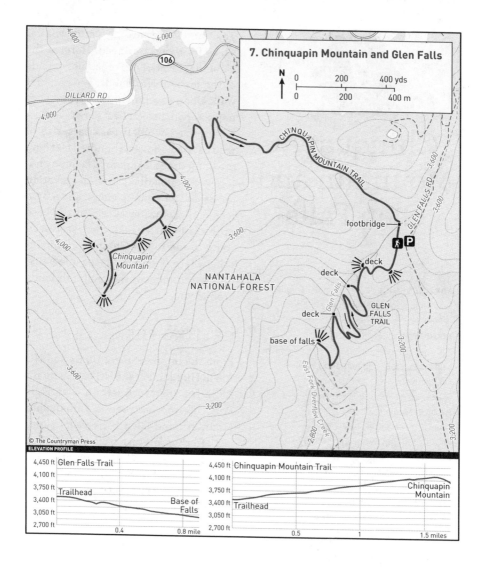

ELEVATION PROFILE

Glen Falls Trail

Chinquapin Mountain Trail

© The Countryman Press

Almost everyone starts with the hike along Glen Falls. The Glen Falls Trail leaves south on a level, wide track amidst bushy mountain laurel and fragrant white pines. Reach a cleared view to the southeast into Georgia, then start dropping into the East Fork Overflow Creek watershed on a wide trail with many wood steps, reaching the first viewing deck at 0.2 mile. Here, you see the stream dive away from you out of sight but gain vistas of mountains beyond.

Ahead, the trail splits. Head acutely right to find the second observation deck and a better view. The falls dash from a stone ledge then down a wide rock chute and onward below, leaving sight once again. The main trail switchbacks down to make the third observation deck at 0.7 mile. Here, you gain another rewarding view of the white tumbler bashing and crashing over a rock falls, briefly gathering itself before once again spilling and sliding out of sight. Calculating

LOOKING TOWARD RABUN BALD AND GEORGIA FROM THE TOP OF GLEN FALLS

the height of each individual fall is nigh well impossible—they have no definitive beginning or end!

Continue down, making one last switchback where the Glen Falls Trail leads left to its south trailhead on Forest Road 79C. Our hike takes one final spur to the base of Glen Falls, where a pool forms below a final visible cataract, though the pool is often cluttered with wood debris, because this is the first slow water where tree limbs and such can collect. The pool is fun for kids' play.

After backtracking 0.8 mile and regrouping, start the Chinquapin Mountain Trail. You turn up East Fork Overflow Creek, bridging it in a pretty spot where tall trees shade the bubbling

sandy stream, quite unlike the crashing creek below. From here, ascend a snaking tributary of East Fork Overflow Creek, where you will find a huge old-growth tulip tree at 0.2 mile. At 0.4 mile, step over the small creek. This is the first of several successive creek crossings, all simple rock hops. Pyrite in the stone makes the stream sparkle and the footing on the rocks hold fast to your shoes.

At 0.7 mile, an official spur trail leaves right for NC 106. Stay left with the Chinquapin Mountain Trail. Climb away from the creek, rising into oak woods complemented with mountain laurel, wild azalea, and berry bushes. Switchbacks make the climb easier. Galax lines the path. At

GLEN FALLS IS AN UNDENIABLY PICTURESQUE CASCADE

LOOKING SOUTH FROM CHINQUAPIN MOUNTAIN

1.1 miles, an unofficial trail leaves right for Little Scaly and is part of an unofficial signed trail network here. Stay left here and head for the signed spurs to overlooks atop Chinquapin Mountain. By 1.4 miles you are atop the broad crown of the peak. Ahead, pass a spur to your left and a fine view to the southeast. Here, an open rock outcrop reveals mountain scenes across East Fork Overflow Creek valley, southeast toward the Chattooga River, South Carolina and Georgia. Stone-sided Whiteface Mountain rises near to your left, all framed in stunted oaks. Resume the main trail. The next lookout is somewhat limited.

Continuing on, you will reach the spur to the third lookout at 1.6 miles. You are now at the top of Chinquapin Mountain. However, this third lookout descends a quarter-mile due south, and you lose hard-earned elevation, but the third vista is worth it. Here, the Blue Valley below is topped by Georgia's Rabun Bald rising proudly into the sky, bordered by pines. After backtracking to the main trail again, the next lookout takes you through a laurel thicket to a below average view to the southwest. The final and fifth view is a disappointment. Beyond this last overlook, you can work your way to make a loop atop the mountain using the unofficial trails, but my recommendation is to go to the first three views then backtrack. Otherwise you are at the mercy of the unofficial trails. A GPS or your smart phone may come in handy here if you decide to make a loop atop Chinquapin Mountain using the unofficial trails.

8

Panthertown Valley Highlight Hike

TOTAL DISTANCE: 12.3-mile loop

HIKING TIME: 6:00

VERTICAL RISE: 2,000 feet

RATING: Difficult due to distance

MAPS: National Geographic #785 Nantahala National Forest—Nantahala and Cullasaja Gorges, USGS 7.5' Big Ridge NC

TRAILHEAD GPS COORDINATES: N35°09'28.4", W82°59'56.8"

CONTACT INFORMATION: Nantahala National Forest, 90 Sloan Road, Franklin, NC 28734, (828) 524-6441, www.fs.usda.gov/nfsnc

This hike explores most of Panthertown Valley Backcountry's highlights in one grand loop. And there is a lot to see. You'll enter this 6,300-acre land of waterfalls, granite domed mountains, crystalline stream and varied forests—all connected with a fine, well-marked trail network—to first visit Macs Falls and Greenland Creek Falls before climbing to multiple vistas from Big Greenland Mountain. Next, turn down Panthertown Creek to view Granny Burrell Falls. After that comes Frolictown Falls and Wilderness Falls. Soak in the view from Salt Rock before making your way up to Little Green Mountain and its granite sloped panoramas. Finally, dip to popular Schoolhouse Falls and its big swimming pool. A final ascent returns you to the trailhead. Be apprised the trails are mostly easy and climbs are never long or arduous, gaining 2,000 feet in aggregate over the entire circuit. These many highlights attract plenty of visitors, therefore solitude seekers should hike here during off periods.

GETTING THERE

From the town square in Brevard, take US 64 West for 15.7 miles to NC 281. Turn right onto NC 281 North and follow it for 0.8 mile, then turn left on Cold Mountain Road, just after passing the Lake Toxaway Fire and Rescue Station, on your right. Follow Cold Mountain Road for 5.6 miles, then turn left on a marked gravel road just before reaching Canaan Land residential development. Follow this marked gravel road 0.1 mile, then turn right on a signed gravel road. Follow it 0.1 mile to dead end at the trailhead.

THE HIKE

Give yourself all day to savor this hike, or backpack overnight, or simply do

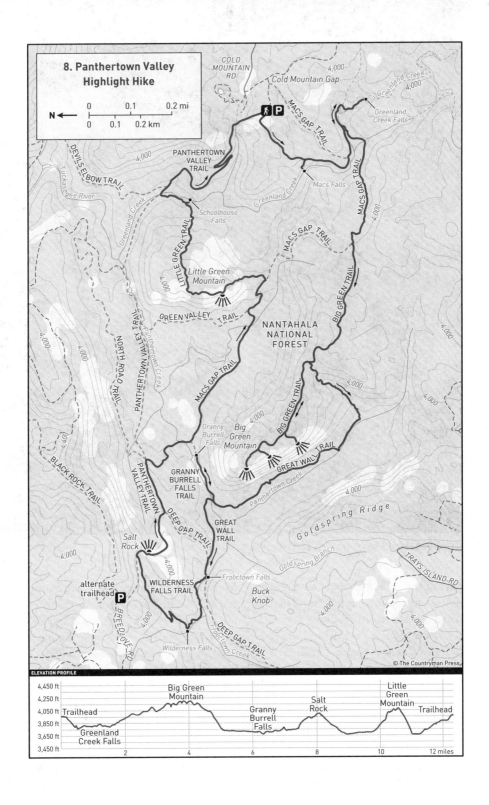

8. Panthertown Valley Highlight Hike

N ←

0   0.1   0.2 mi
0   0.1   0.2 km

COLD MOUNTAIN RD

Cold Mountain Gap

4,000

Greenland Creek

4,000

Greenland Creek Falls

DEVILS ELBOW TRAIL

PANTHERTOWN VALLEY TRAIL

MACS GAP TRAIL

4,000

Tuckasegee River

Greenland Creek

Schoolhouse Falls

Macs Falls

MACS GAP TRAIL

BIG GREEN TRAIL

4,000

LITTLE GREEN TRAIL

Little Green Mountain

MACS GAP TRAIL

GREEN VALLEY   TRAIL

NANTAHALA NATIONAL FOREST

4,000

PANTHERTOWN VALLEY TRAIL

NORTH ROAD TRAIL

Panthertown Creek

MACS GAP TRAIL

4,000

BIG GREEN TRAIL

4,000

Granny Burrell Falls

Big Green Mountain

GREAT WALL TRAIL

4,000

BLACK ROCK TRAIL

4,000

GRANNY BURRELL FALLS TRAIL

Panthertown Creek

Goldspring Ridge

TRAYS ISLAND RD

PANTHERTOWN VALLEY TRAIL

DEEP GAP TRAIL

GREAT WALL TRAIL

4,000

Salt Rock

Goldspring Branch

Buck Knob

4,000

alternate trailhead

WILDERNESS FALLS TRAIL

Frolictown Falls

4,000

BREEDLOVE RD

DEEP GAP TRAIL

Frolictown Creek

Wilderness Falls

© The Countryman Press

ELEVATION PROFILE

		Big Green Mountain			Salt Rock		Little Green Mountain	

4,450 ft
4,250 ft
4,050 ft   Trailhead   Trailhead
3,850 ft
3,650 ft   Greenland   Granny
3,450 ft   Creek Falls   Burrell
                                   Falls

        2   4   6   8   10   12 miles

FROLICTOWN FALLS IS AN EYE CATCHING CATARACT WITH AN EAR CATCHING NAME

part of the trek, shortcutting the loop if it seems too long. But do it no matter what. Panthertown Valley Backcountry is one of the best hiking destinations in western North Carolina. The hike leaves Cold Mountain Gap on the Greenland Creek Trail, immediately passing under a powerline to then enter cool ferny woods. Descend to Greenland Creek, and at 0.4 mile follow the spur right to Macs Falls, where you see Greenland Creek spill 12 feet over a creek-wide ledge into a plunge pool.

Backtrack to the main trail, continuing toward Greenland Creek in thickets of mountain laurel, meeting it and the Macs Gap Trail at 0.7 mile. From here, keep straight on the Greenland Creek/ Macs Gap Trail. At 0.8 mile, Macs Gap Trail leaves right, but for now you keep straight on Greenland Creek Trail, winding along the water under fragrant pines and clingy mountain laurel. Come to lesser-visited Greenland Creek Falls at 1.1 miles. Here, a boulder garden stands across a plunge pool as the

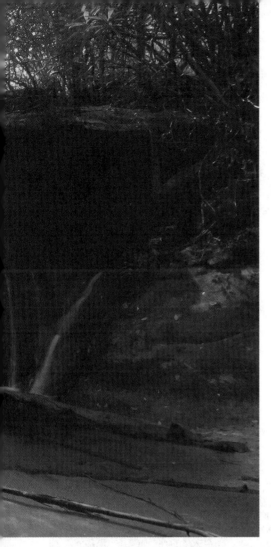

and the greater backcountry beyond. Some of the spurs fight through brush before opening onto rock. Patient and persistent view-seekers will be amply rewarded atop Big Green Mountain. Also scan for evidence of past fires.

At 4.6 miles, begin descending the Great Wall Trail, paralleling a small stream. Steps have been cut into potentially slippery stone slabs. Other spots have been bridged. Come to and turn down clear Panthertown Creek at 5.1 miles. Enjoy the wide valley backed by a huge stone wall to your right and beaver-dam slowed Panthertown Creek, all under a thick forest. The Great Wall Trail passes a busy backpacker shelter just before reaching the Granny Burrell Falls Trail at 6.1 miles. Turn right here, staying along Panthertown Creek among evergreen thickets to reach Granny Burrell Falls at 6.3 miles. A huge and popular pool—bordered by a sand beach—lies below the cataract after it slides 15 feet down a rock face.

Backtrack to the Great Wall Trail, fording Panthertown Creek then climbing a bit to meet the Deep Gap Trail at 6.9 miles. Stay left joining the Deep Gap Trail, descending to Frolictown Creek, Frolictown Falls and a trail intersection at 7.0 miles. Check out Frolictown Falls as it makes a 14-foot curtain spill over a ledge into a dim, dusky pool, a lesser-visited and photography-friendly spiller. Turn right on the Wilderness Falls Trail, working through brushy woods along Frolictown Creek, only to turn up a tributary at 7.2 miles. Here, begin switchbacking uphill as Wilderness Falls slides 80 or so feet down a granite slide. Unfortunately, the cataract is difficult to view in its entirety due to excessive vegetation.

Reach drier pine oak lands and a trail intersection at 8.0 miles. Head

dashing 40-foot cataract bounces down a widening rock face.

From Greenland Creek Falls backtrack to the Macs Gap Trail, joining Macs Gap Trail to rock hop Greenland Creek at 1.5 miles. Here, you rise in pines to a gap at 2.2 miles. Stay straight, joining the Big Green Trail, enjoying a high elevation flat under stately oaks. Rise to another intersection. Here, stay straight with the Big Green Trail, heading out to various user-created spur trails leading to open rock faces availing vistas into Panthertown Creek valley below

GREENLAND CREEK FALLS DROPS IN TWO TIERS

Little Green Mountain, Big Green Mountain, and Boardcamp Ridge. The walking is easy on a double-track. And you soon meet the Deep Gap Trail again at 8.3 miles. Stay straight, still with the now-narrower Panthertown Valley Trail. The hiking remains easy, and you soon turn right onto the Macs Gap Trail at 8.6 miles, descending over rock slabs to level out at a former homesite. Watch here as the trail winds through a pine grove with spurs passing campsites. Bridge Panthertown Creek at 8.9 miles and quickly pass the other end of the Granny Burrell Falls Trail. You were very near here earlier. Continue through level pine woods on the Macs Gap Trail. Step over a tributary of Panthertown Creek, then climb to meet the Little Green Trail at 9.9 miles. Up you go again, but the highlights are worth it.

right on the Panthertown Valley Trail to quickly open onto Salt Rock with its open stone slabs and stunted trees and a stellar view. Here, you can longingly look east down the Panthertown Creek Valley framed by Blackrock Mountain,

Ascend north on Little Green Mountain. Short steep sections lead to an open rock slab and jaw-dropping views

THE CURTAIN DROP OF SCHOOLHOUSE FALLS

MISTY PANTHERTOWN VALLEY AS SEEN FROM SALT ROCK

that continue off and on for the next quarter mile. Here, Panthertown Valley opens to the west with distant ridges rising beyond. Look for Salt Rock, where you were earlier. Ahead, be watchful; the path winds through little groves of vegetation amid the rock slabs. At points, blazes are painted on the rock slabs. The views keep on coming. Yield to the temptation to explore the rock slab, seeking cool hangout spots and other vistas. Look for berry bushes and watch out for spring seeps. The trail turns east and surmounts Little Green Mountain, then descends east for Greenland Creek and famed Schoolhouse Falls. Here, at 11.1 miles, an ultra large pool—attracting scads of summertime swimmers—fronts the vertical pourover as it makes a clean, crisp curtain-style drop—a prototypical waterfall.

From Schoolhouse Falls, head left, crossing a boardwalk to reach the Panthertown Valley Trail at 11.3 miles. Here, turn right, bridging Greenland Creek. Ahead, the Devils Elbow Trail leaves left while you ascend a wide gravel doubletrack. This road-like trail can handle the crowds drawn by Schoolhouse Falls and also allows access to the falls for emergency workers after the all-too-frequent accidents that occur here in summertime. From here, work your way up to the trailhead, using switchbacks, returning to the trailhead at 12.3 miles.

Black Balsam Knob

TOTAL DISTANCE: 4.9-mile loop

HIKING TIME: 2:30

VERTICAL RISE: 800 feet

RATING: Moderate, trail can be brushy and difficult to follow

MAPS: National Geographic #780 Pisgah National Forest—Pisgah Ranger District, USGS 7.5' Shining Rock NC

TRAILHEAD GPS COORDINATES: N35°19'33.0", W82°52'54.9"

CONTACT INFORMATION: Pisgah National Forest, Pisgah Ranger District, 1001 Pisgah Highway, Pisgah Forest, NC 28768, (828) 877-3265, www.fs.usda.gov/nfsnc

This view-laden highlight reel highland trek starts over a mile in elevation and gets higher to crest over Black Balsam Knob, standing proud at 6,214 feet. First trace an old railroad grade beneath Black Balsam Knob, offering views aplenty as you make your way toward Ivestor Gap. Next, join the single-track Art Loeb Trail climbing to Tennant Mountain, where outcrops deliver first-rate panoramas of Pisgah Ridge and adjacent valleys in the rear, as well as Carolina mountains stretching to the horizon. Stay with the Art Loeb Trail, crossing open Black Balsam Knob, with more marvelous panoramas. Finally, descend among rock outcrops, then wind through dark and rare spruce-fir forests before returning to the trailhead.

GETTING THERE

From the intersection of NC 280 and US 276 in Brevard, take US 276 North for 15 miles to the Blue Ridge Parkway. Follow the Blue Ridge Parkway southbound 8.4 miles to Forest Road 816, on your right. Turn right on FR 816 and follow it for 1.2 miles to dead end at the Black Balsam trailhead.

THE HIKE

First-time visitors to the Shining Rock high country are stunned by the treeless open peaks like Black Balsam Knob amid the otherwise forested expanses of the Pisgah National Forest. The views from the clearings are legendary. However, it wasn't always so, for the name *Black Balsam Knob* denoted the once dusky spruce and fir forests that grew so thick that day seemed night. These very forests attracted timber interests in the early 1900s, and the forests of the Balsam Mountains were taken down

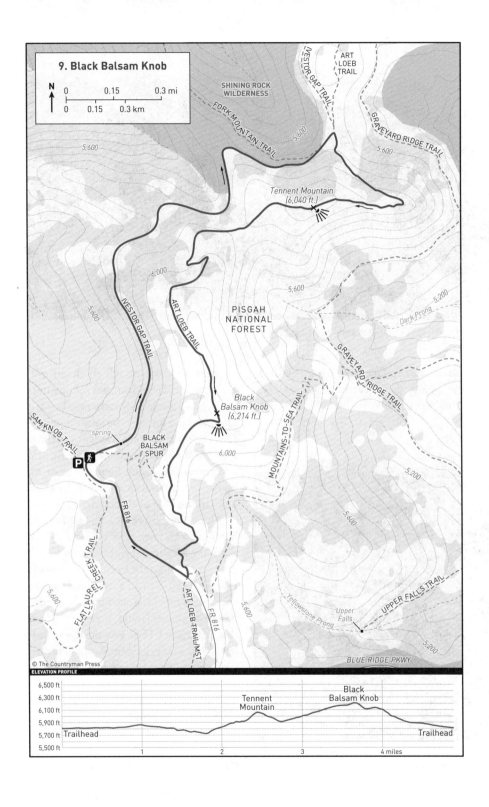

9. Black Balsam Knob

N
0   0.15   0.3 mi
0   0.15   0.3 km

SHINING ROCK
WILDERNESS

ART
LOEB
TRAIL

IVESTOR GAP TRAIL

FORK MOUNTAIN TRAIL

GRAVEYARD RIDGE TRAIL

5,600

5,600

5,600

Tennent Mountain
(6,040 ft.)

6,000

5,600

Dark Prong

5,200

PISGAH
NATIONAL
FOREST

IVESTOR GAP TRAIL

ART LOEB TRAIL

5,600

GRAVEYARD RIDGE TRAIL

Black
Balsam Knob
(6,214 ft.)

MOUNTAINS-TO-SEA TRAIL

5,200

SAM KNOB TRAIL

spring

BLACK
BALSAM
SPUR

6,000

5,600

FR 816

FLAT LAUREL CREEK TRAIL

5,600

ART LOEB TRAIL/MST

FR 816

5,600

Yellowstone Prong

Upper
Falls

UPPER FALLS TRAIL

5,200

BLUE RIDGE PKWY

© The Countryman Press

ELEVATION PROFILE

6,500 ft
6,300 ft
6,100 ft
5,900 ft
5,700 ft
5,500 ft

Trailhead

Tennent
Mountain

Black
Balsam Knob

Trailhead

1   2   3   4 miles

THE VIEW EAST OF THE BLUE RIDGE AND BEYOND

nearly to the last tree, from the highest peaks down to the lower valleys. The barren hillsides were littered with

THE MONUMENT TO TRAIL BUILDER AND HIKING LEGEND GEORGE TENNENT

unwanted cuttings, which dried out, then caught fire and burned the cuttings down to bedrock. Still more fires burned later, leaving an infertile landscape still recovering from that unpleasant time. And yet today, with grasses, brush, and returning trees, the locale is now an attraction, with its views and cool air, even in the heat of summer.

This hike traverses these former burned-over, now scenic lands. Leave the busy FR 816 parking area and walk around a pole gate to follow the wide Ivestor Gap Trail, a railroad grade used to remove the vast stands of timber from the Balsams. Look left down the Little East Fork Pigeon River valley while Black Balsam Knob rises on your right. Quickly walk by a splashing spring. Other springs flow across the trail ahead, leaving a seeping path in places, with mountain ash, yellow birch and brush growing along its side. Walk the easy grade north. At 1.2 miles, watch for a user-created trail rising right to the

Art Loeb Trail in a gap between Tennant Mountain and Black Balsam Knob.

At 1.4 miles, the seldom-canopied path rolls over a ridge between non-native planted stands of red pine. At 1.7 miles, the signed but easily missed Fork Mountain Trail leaves left, reaching Sunburst Campground after a long descent. Come to a gap at 1.8 miles. The Ivestor Gap Trail continues left on the railroad grade while the single-track Art Loeb Trail crosses the gap. Here, cut right, turning sharply back south and climbing on the rutted Art Loeb Trail. You are walking among low tight-knit brush mountain ash trees rise from. Angle up the north side of Tennant Mountain, still in close-knit brush, then gain the crest of Tennant Mountain. At 2.3 miles, open onto a rock outcrop with astonishing views to the southeast of the Graveyard Fields valley below, the Blue Ridge Parkway, Black Balsam Knob, and waves of mountains stretching all the way to the Piedmont. A plaque honoring George Tennant, an early hiking enthusiast and supporter of the Pisgah National Forest, stands here atop the mountain named for him. If the conditions are favorable, this is a place to linger, though a wealth of views continues ahead.

The Art Loeb Trail descends off 6,040 foot Tennant Mountain, still running through brush to reach a gap at 2.7 miles. Now make the not-difficult, 300-foot climb to the top of Black Balsam Knob. User-created spur trails splinter off here and it can be difficult to stay on the correct path. Look for waterbars and other evidence of trail construction. It is also hard to keep your eyes on the trail, with all the eye-popping panoramas opening. You can look in all directions at the wealth of Carolina mountains. The wind is often blowing here, so be prepared for all sorts of weather. By the way,

LOOKING OUT FROM TENNENT MOUNTAIN

shoot for clear days to get the maximum payoff on this hike.

Reach the top of Black Balsam Knob at 3.7 miles. Dip just a bit, then come to an area of extensive rock outcrops from which vistas open all around. Sam Knob, the Graveyards Fields, the trailhead parking area, and Shining Rock Wilderness, as well as distant lowlands—and just about everywhere is lower than the top of 6,240 foot Black Balsam Knob. Here stands yet another plaque, this one to Art Loeb, another man who made hiking a popular activity in the Carolinas.

Continue on the Art Loeb Trail, passing the spur to the parking area. Views continue as you descend naked outcrops. At 4.4 miles, the trail enters recovered spruce-fir forest, giving you an idea of what this area looked like before the fires, and is the reason for taking this part of the route. Golden needles cover the dim forest floor. Smell the evergreens. This area is popular with campers. At 4.5 miles, come to paved Forest Road 816. Turn right here, road walking mostly downhill to the trailhead, completing the highland loop at 4.9 miles.

10

Waterfalls of the Graveyard Fields

TOTAL DISTANCE: 3.4-mile loop including out-and-back	
HIKING TIME: 1:20	
VERTICAL RISE: 440 feet	
RATING: Easy-moderate	
MAPS: National Geographic #780 Pisgah National Forest—Pisgah Ranger District, USGS 7.5' Shining Rock NC	
TRAILHEAD GPS COORDINATES: N35°19.220', W82°50.821'	
CONTACT INFORMATION: Pisgah Ranger District, 1001 Pisgah Highway, Pisgah Forest, NC 28768, (828) 877-3265, www.fs .usda.gov/nfsnc	

This is a neat little adventure in an intriguing valley among the highlands of the Pisgah National Forest, where it adjoins the Blue Ridge Parkway. Enjoy high-mountain vistas and brash waterfalls amidst everywhere-you-look beauty. Start over 5,000 feet high, then descend into the perched valley of Yellowstone Prong. After bridging the creek, turn downstream to discover Lower Falls, a froth of water and rock. Next, turn up the Yellowstone Prong, scanning upward at majestic spruce- and fir-covered peaks, as well as streamside scenery nearby. Make your way to two overlooks of Upper Falls, a tall tiered cascade. After backtracking, bridge Yellowstone Prong a second time to loop back to the parking area. Be apprised this hike can be crowded on weekends, especially the first part leading to Lower Falls.

GETTING THERE

From the intersection of NC 280 and US 276 in Brevard, take US 276 North for 15 miles to the Blue Ridge Parkway. Follow the Blue Ridge Parkway 7 miles south to the Graveyard Fields Overlook, on your right at milepost 418.8. Here you will find a large parking lot and a restroom.

THE HIKE

The name Graveyard Fields is a real attention-getter, conjuring up images of a grassy mountain internment. But the moniker actually came from a storm a century back, where trees in the flats along Yellowstone Prong were over-turned in a devastating storm. Over time the fallen trees eroded. Their remaining root balls resembled gravestones in the grassy meadows. Since then, the mead-ows have been slowly re-growing, but

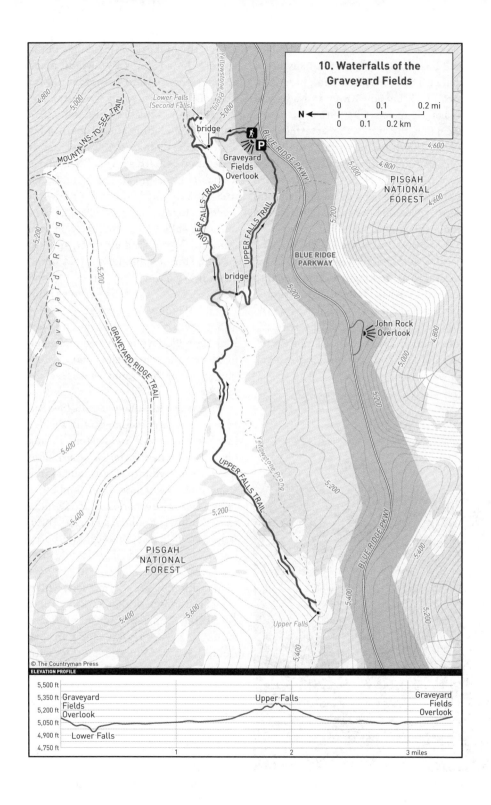

10. Waterfalls of the Graveyard Fields

N ←   0   0.1   0.2 mi
       0   0.1   0.2 km

Lower Falls
(Second Falls)

Yellowstone Prong

bridge

Graveyard
Fields
Overlook

BLUE RIDGE PKWY

P

MOUNTAINS-TO-SEA TRAIL

Graveyard Ridge

GRAVEYARD RIDGE TRAIL

LOWER FALLS TRAIL

UPPER FALLS TRAIL

bridge

PISGAH
NATIONAL
FOREST

4,800

5,000

4,600

5,200

4,600

4,800

BLUE RIDGE
PARKWAY

5,200

John Rock
Overlook

4,800

5,000

5,200

BLUE RIDGE PKWY

5,400

5,200

UPPER FALLS TRAIL

Yellowstone Prong

5,200

5,200

PISGAH
NATIONAL
FOREST

5,600

5,400

5,400

5,600

5,200

5,400

5,400

Upper Falls

© The Countryman Press

ELEVATION PROFILE

5,500 ft			
5,350 ft	Graveyard	Upper Falls	Graveyard
5,200 ft	Fields		Fields
5,050 ft	Overlook		Overlook
4,900 ft	Lower Falls		
4,750 ft	1	2	3 miles

the vegetation of the Graveyard Fields still has ample open and brushy areas that still deliver views of mighty 6,214-foot Black Balsam Knob and adjacent peaks. No matter what lures you here—the name, the vistas, the waterfalls—do come. The drive along the Blue Ridge Parkway to the trailhead will be your first highlight. Note: the Graveyard Fields area has been closed to camping due to repeated bear encounters. Please honor this regulation.

Leave the Graveyard Fields Overlook parking area near the restroom building, joining an asphalt path descending into a tangle of rhododendron under stunted birch and spruce. You are nearly a mile high. Soak in trailside interpretive information. Bridge Yellowstone Prong, gaining looks at this alluring stream,

among the highest watercourses in the eastern United States. At 0.2 mile, reach an intersection. Here, turn right toward Lower Falls. This is easily the most heavily used part of the hike, and the trail is built for it, including sturdy boardwalks with handrails taking you over wet or vegetation-sensitive areas. Ahead, pass a spur connecting to the Mountains-to-Sea Trail then descend a series of wooden steps to find yourself at the base of Lower Falls at 0.3 mile. Here, absorb a face-on look at the cataract, spilling 50 feet, stair-stepping over gold tinted stone into a chilly, plunge pool. Craggy boulders below the falls serve as vantage points for casual walkers going for a short jaunt off the Blue Ridge Parkway. Interestingly, despite the common name of Lower Falls, it is officially named Second Falls, per the United States Geological Survey.

Backtrack from Lower Falls/Second Falls and begin heading up the slender mountain valley of Yellowstone Prong, one of the prettiest in the Carolina mountains. The crowds are mostly left behind. Cherry, spruce, yellow birch, and other vegetation more common in Canada than Carolina populate the locale. Ferns fields, small grassy glades, and berry bushes grow in places, allowing hikers looks beyond the trees. Above you, Pisgah Ridge rises to your left, which is where the Blue Ridge Parkway runs. Ahead, Black Balsam Knob and Tennant Mountain tower over 6,000 feet. To your right, Graveyard Ridge looms thick with vegetation. Boardwalks escort you over messy areas. When the rains have been falling, this trail can get a bit mucky. After all, the path wanders through an almost level valley riddled with little streamlets flowing from the adjacent ridges feeding Yellowstone Prong.

TREKKING A BOARDWALK IN THE GRAVEYARD FIELDS

Watch out for user-created paths

LOWER FALLS

leading to the stream or to old campsites. The Graveyard Fields were once heavily camped, but the sites are now growing over. At 0.9 mile, reach an official trail intersection. You will return here later. For now, head right, continuing toward Upper Falls, deeper into the Yellowstone Prong. Weave through dense evergreen thickets, small open glades, and forest, all changing from one moment to the next. The grassier-than-average understory is a relic from when the Graveyard Fields were truly fields.

The trail climbs and becomes rockier, the closer you get to Upper Falls. Note the trail stonework, where native stones were fashioned into steps. At 1.8 miles, the pathway splits. Head left here and you can walk directly to the lower portion of Upper Falls. Here, the cataract is executing a long angled slide almost as wide as it is high. Many hikers turn around here, thinking they have seen the Upper Falls. However, they are only

getting part of the picture. From here, backtrack a bit and climb more stone stairs, and there you find upper Upper Falls. Overhead, a towering sky and a tall evergreen lord over golden tan rock over which plummets foaming whitewater, dashing a good 60 feet, widening as it descends. The waterfall almost levels out before making a final shorter jump over a wide ledge. Upper Falls easily meets the high standards expected of such a pretty vale.

Backtrack a mile to the junction you were at earlier. Here, head right, crossing Yellowstone Prong on a hiker bridge. Stop on the bridge and gaze upstream at the rocky waterway some of the highest terrain in the Tarheel State rises from. Beyond the bridge the hike enters dark rhododendron copses. Boardwalks lead across wet areas. Gently climb to emerge at the far end of the Graveyard Fields Overlook parking area at 3.4 miles, completing the highland valley hike.

Cat Gap Loop

11

TOTAL DISTANCE: 5.6-mile loop
HIKING TIME: 2:20
VERTICAL RISE: 1,301 feet
RATING: Moderate, does have steady climb
MAPS: National Geographic #780 Pisgah National Forest—Pisgah Ranger District, USGS 7.5' Shining Rock NC
TRAILHEAD GPS COORDINATES: N35°17'03.2", W82°47'26.2"
CONTACT INFORMATION: Pisgah Ranger District, 1001 Pisgah Highway, Pisgah Forest, NC 28768, (828) 877-3265, www.fs.usda.gov/nfsnc

This cool hike rises from the Pisgah Center for Wildlife Education (worth a visit) up to a granite dome towering above the Davidson River Valley. Here, resplendent views open onto Looking Glass Rock and the Blue Ridge crest. Start out at the wildlife center and adjacent fish hatchery, trekking alongside the Davidson River before climbing to the open stone slab that is John Rock. Soak in the views, then descend to Cedar Rock Creek, where you can visit the tiers of Cedar Rock Falls before returning to the trailhead. Be apprised that the area as a whole is popular, therefore off times will produce solitude if desired.

GETTING THERE

From the intersection of NC 280 and US 276 in Brevard, take US 276 North for 5.2 miles, then turn left on Forest Road 475 toward the Pisgah Center for Wildlife Education. Follow FR 475 for 1.4 miles, then turn left across the bridge over the Davidson River to the wildlife center and fish hatchery. The hike starts at the lower end of the parking area, away from the wildlife center.

THE HIKE

If John Rock weren't situated literally within sight of celebrated Looking Glass Rock, it would receive more acclaim itself. However, this can be a good thing, because it leaves John Rock less visited. Nevertheless, the trailhead parking lot below John Rock is often full of cars. However, many people are also visiting the wildlife education center, fishing, picnicking, and hiking other trails. In fact, I've never been atop John Rock when other visitors were there. And the views are worthy. You can look down on the fish hatchery below, across at Looking Glass

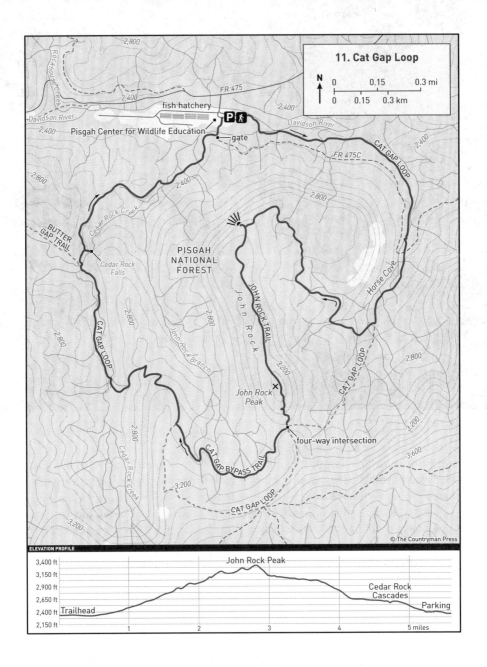

11. Cat Gap Loop

N

| 0 | 0.15 | | 0.3 mi |
| 0 | 0.15 | 0.3 km | |

fish hatchery

FR 475

Davidson River

Pisgah Center for Wildlife Education

gate

FR 475C

CAT GAP LOOP

BUTTER GAP TRAIL

Cedar Rock Creek

Cedar Rock Falls

PISGAH NATIONAL FOREST

Horse Cove

John Rock

JOHN ROCK TRAIL

John Rock Branch

CAT GAP LOOP

John Rock Peak

CAT GAP LOOP

four-way intersection

CAT GAP BYPASS TRAIL

Cedar Rock Creek

CAT GAP LOOP

© The Countryman Press

ELEVATION PROFILE

John Rock Peak

3,400 ft
3,150 ft
2,900 ft
2,650 ft
2,400 ft — Trailhead
2,150 ft

Cedar Rock Cascades

Parking

1   2   3   4   5 miles

Rock and beyond to the Blue Ridge, with a wealth of mountains added to the mix. And this hike also has a first-rate tiered waterfall, so one could argue it's a better destination than is Looking Glass Rock, but maybe not as known a destination among your social network followers.

The hike leaves the lower end of the large parking area on the Cat Gap Loop. Travel east along the wooded flats of the Davidson River, spying for anglers clad in waders and other accouterments. Bridge Cedar Rock Creek and keep along the flats of the Davidson River, passing

THE UPPER CATARACT OF CEDAR ROCK FALLS

campsites in re-growing post-hemlock woods mixed with rhododendron thickets shading streamlets flowing over the trail.

At 0.5 mile, turn up the valley of Horse Cove, where a tributary of the Davidson River gurgles past wildflower-rich lands overlorded by ranks of arrow straight tulip trees. Horse Cove closes and you rock hop the tributary at 0.9 mile and begin the steady climb, crossing an old forest road. Intersect the John Rock Trail at 1.2 miles as the Cat Gap Loop keeps straight. You will rejoin it later. Pick up the John Rock Trail as it works through xeric hickory/oak forest divided by rhododendron-shrouded streamlets.

At 2.0 miles, the trail curves left, now atop the ridgecrest of John Rock, flanked by tightly knit mountain laurel after you cross a spring outflow. Now, the open rock slab of John Rock is to your right, on the far side of low-slung trees and blueberry bushes. At 2.1 miles, the first spur trail leads right to the open granite. If you take this trail, you can continue walking up the open granite to higher views, where the mile-high Blue Ridge frames a sea of mountains in the distance, with Looking Glass Rock in the fore. Below, look for the individual holding tanks of the fish hatchery. Nearby, flat mosses and nutrient-stunted pines cleave to granite fissures. Be watchful for seeps running over the face of John Rock. People and pets are at risk.

After clambering around John Rock, return to the woods and the trail. Climb still through hardwoods, southbound now, to top out on John Rock at 2.4

miles. Briefly descend then climb still more, reaching the high point of the hike at 2.9 miles. From there it's a steep drop on an eroded trail. Hiking sticks come in handy here. At 3.1 miles, level off at a four-way trail intersection. Turn right on the Cat Gap Bypass Trail while the Cat Gap Loop keeps straight.

Cruise north facing coves among the headwaters of John Rock Branch. Intersect the Cat Gap Loop at 3.7 miles and rejoin this path yet again. Quickly descend to cross over Cedar Rock Creek at 4.2 miles. Enter a pretty forest of pines with golden needles carpeting the ground. Ahead, you will find campsites amidst a planted pine grove. At 4.5 miles, cross Cedar Rock Creek again.

At 4.7 miles, bridge Cedar Rock Creek among boulders to reach an intersection near what once were the Picklesimer Fields, now all but grown over. Head right here, still with the Cat Gap

REHYDRATING ATOP JOHN ROCK

Loop, paralleling Cedar Rock Creek as it begins a waterfall extravaganza. At 4.8 miles, drop right with a user-created

THE LOWER CATARACT OF CEDAR ROCK FALLS

HIKER LOOKS DOWN ON THE FISH HATCHERY FROM THE OPEN SLAB OF JOHN ROCK

spur trail and follow it carefully to reach the two primary tiers of Cedar Rock Falls. These two main spillers drop about 15 and 20 feet respectively, flanked by a host of lesser cascades. After exploring the cataracts, maybe trying your hand at a few photos, resume downhill on the trail, running past fences of the fish hatchery. At 5.3 miles, bridge Cedar Rock Creek a final time before coming to a gated road just a few feet away from the back of the wildlife center. Turn left here, completing the hike. You are now so close to the wildlife center it's difficult not to visit. Don't worry—they're used to sweaty hikers stopping by!

Looking Glass Rock

TOTAL DISTANCE: 5.6-mile there-and-back

HIKING TIME: 2:40

VERTICAL RISE: 1,700 feet

RATING: Moderate, does have steady uphill grade

MAPS: National Geographic #780 Pisgah National Forest—Pisgah Ranger District, USGS 7.5' Shining Rock NC

TRAILHEAD GPS COORDINATES: N35°17.445', W82°46.580'

CONTACT INFORMATION: Pisgah Ranger District, 1001 Pisgah Highway, Pisgah Forest, NC 28768, (828) 877-3265, www.fs .usda.gov/nfsnc

Named for the reflective sheen from winter's frozen seeps running down the enormous rock slopes of the eye-catching mountain, Looking Glass Rock is a Carolina mountain legend that should be on your must-do list of peaks to summit. This highland protuberance rises almost 2,000 feet from the Davidson River Valley outside of Brevard, a conspicuous combination of naked granite and forest. The hike to the peak is about as user-friendly as a climb such as this can be. The Forest Service has constructed and continues to improve the heavily used trail, using seemingly innumerable switchbacks to ease the uptick. Once up top, you actually descend a short distance to reach the view—and it is worth every step. The open granite slope reveals panoramic vistas of the Blue Ridge forming a green wall to the northwest, as well as endless forest below. Once up here, feel free to explore beyond the main slope for additional views.

GETTING THERE

From the intersection of NC 280 and US 276 in Brevard, take US 276 North for 5.2 miles, then turn left on Forest Road 475 toward the Pisgah Center for Wildlife Education. Follow FR 475 for 0.3 mile and the trailhead will be on your right. Be considerate while parking, because the trail can be busy.

THE HIKE

Interestingly, the mountain of 3,969 feet elevation stands out whether you are scanning upward from the Davidson River or down from the crest of Pisgah Ridge. As mountains do, Looking Glass Rock attracts climbers who first started scaling it the hard way back in the 1960s,

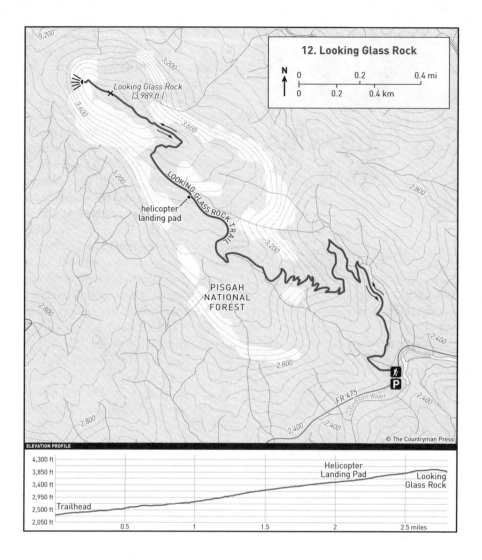

12. Looking Glass Rock

Looking Glass Rock
(3,989 ft.)

helicopter
landing pad

PISGAH
NATIONAL
FOREST

FR 475

Davidson River

© The Countryman Press

ELEVATION PROFILE

Helicopter
Landing Pad

Looking
Glass Rock

Trailhead

thus increasing the legendary status of this exceptional peak. We hikers will be fully satisfied with the standard foot trail to the top of Looking Glass Rock. It starts off Forest Road 275, a single-track trail attacking the crag's south slope.

Leave the parking area as the Looking Glass Rock Trail rises into forest. The trail uses wood and earth steps to check erosion. A couple of bridges lead over a dribbling streamlet, and by 0.2 mile you are working your way up the vale of the mountain's only significant stream, and even that is small, just a trickle in late summer.

Cruise the mountainside cloaked with pine, tulip trees, sourwood and black gum. At 0.5 mile, the nearby stream is flowing in tinkling slides, more evident during heavier springtime flows. In other places it spills underneath tangles of rhododendron. At 0.6 mile, make your first switchback. The Forest Service greatly appreciates your

THESE STONE SLOPES WHEN COVERED IN RAIN OR ICE REFLECT LIGHT, GIVING THE MOUNTAIN ITS NAME

not shortcutting the switchbacks; that undermines and erodes the constructed path.

By 1.6 miles, the trail comes near the last of the moving water. You have been navigating a steep slope, but from here on out the slope eases. Hickories and oaks stand above an understory of blueberry and huckleberry bushes. Mountain laurel becomes more common on the drier slopes. The trail is often sandy and crisscrossed with roots. By 2.1 miles, the terrain is barely sloping as you tunnel under mountain laurel and step over hard rock slabs. At 2.2 miles, walk beside an open rock slab to your left. This slab is used as a helicopter landing pad and has a faded "H" on it. In days gone by, the forest service had a loop trail atop the mountain. You can still see the faded blazes on the far side of the slab. Hikers are lured in by the

THE TRAIL TO LOOKING GLASS ROCK IS WELL GRADED AND WELL MAINTAINED

slab, thinking it is the trail or using it as a break spot. However, the hike keeps straight beyond the slab, continuing up the mountain. At 2.5 miles, a spur path goes right to a smaller rock slab but you turn left here, continuing up the balance of the mountain, along its crest, westbound. The terrain drops off both to your left and right as you rise through a mix of hardwoods and evergreens.

You may notice some healthy hemlocks up here. These are the endangered Carolina hemlocks and are being treated to prevent infestation from the dreaded exotic pest, hemlock wooly adelgid, that is killing the Eastern hemlock. The Carolina hemlock is a compact, conical evergreen with needles spreading in all directions, unlike the needles of an Eastern hemlock, which spread in two rows on either side of the branch. Carolina hemlocks occur—not surprisingly—in western North Carolina, as well as East Tennessee and southwest Virginia. The tree grows on dry slopes like this, unlike the moisture-loving Eastern hemlock, which is usually found in moist valleys near creeks.

Reach Looking Glass Rock's high point at 2.7 miles. Campsites are found

A DISTANT VIEW OF LOOKING GLASS ROCK FROM THE BLUE RIDGE PARKWAY

in the vicinity. You are almost there. Descend through brushy woods, then reach the huge granite slab that is your personal Carolina mountain viewing theater. Here, stunted cedars and pines desperately grasp their roots onto the granite slope where thin soils have gathered. Seeping water waxes and wanes with the seasons—and freezes in winter, giving the peak its name. Below you the bare granite drops beyond view, dropping so steeply as to prohibit access by all but expert climbers. Forested ridges and valleys vein out below. Above, Pisgah Ridge, home of the Blue Ridge Parkway, reaches for the sky. Scan the ridgecrest for the scenic road and its overlooks, as well as peregrine falcons that nest along the slopes of Looking Glass Rock. By the way, I highly recommend viewing Looking Glass Rock from the Parkway. It will raise your appreciation of this Carolina mountain. A word of caution: be careful traipsing the granite mountainside, because it can be steep and even slick, especially when temperatures drop below 32 degrees.

FLOWERS AND A SMILING HIKER GRACE LOOKING GLASS ROCK

Twin Falls

TOTAL DISTANCE: 5.8-mile loop

HIKING TIME: 3:10

VERTICAL RISE: 650 feet

RATING: Moderate

MAPS: National Geographic #780 Pisgah National Forest—Pisgah Ranger District, USGS 7.5' Shining Rock NC

TRAILHEAD GPS COORDINATES: N35°18.967', W82°45.136'

CONTACT INFORMATION: Pisgah Ranger District, 1001 Pisgah Highway, Pisgah Forest, NC 28768, (828) 877-3265, www.fs .usda.gov/nfsnc

Although your destination is the cataracts of the Twin Falls, you actually get to see a third thrilling spiller in Avery Creek Falls. The aquatic hike makes a loop combining trails in the Pisgah National Forest's upper Avery Creek valley. These pathways are a mix of well-used and lesser-used tracks. First, descend to Avery Creek, then shortly pass by the classic curtain drop and pool of Avery Creek Falls. Next, turn up Henry Branch where you will discover Twin Falls, a pair of parallel cataracts on adjacent streams. After exploring each of these side-by-side 80-foot ribbon-like spillers, climb away to join a gated forest road before descending into narrow Clawhammer Cove, returning to Avery Creek and the trailhead. The climbs and descents are moderate, with the variety of forest scenes exceeding the effort to view it.

GETTING THERE

From the intersection of NC 280 and US 276 in Brevard, take US 276 North for 2.1 miles, then turn right on Forest Road 477. You will see a sign here directing you toward Pisgah Riding Stables. Follow FR 477 for 2.5 miles, and the trailhead will be on your right, 0.8 mile beyond the Pisgah Riding Stables. Trailhead parking is limited so be courteous.

THE HIKE

This hike is best enjoyed when the mountain waters are flowing—spring, after summer thunderstorms, or winter. By the way, footbridges enable dry-footed passage the duration of the hike, with just a few rock hops over smaller creeklets. Begin the wide and easy Buckhorn Gap Trail, flanked by evergreens. Avery Creek rushes below, flanked by

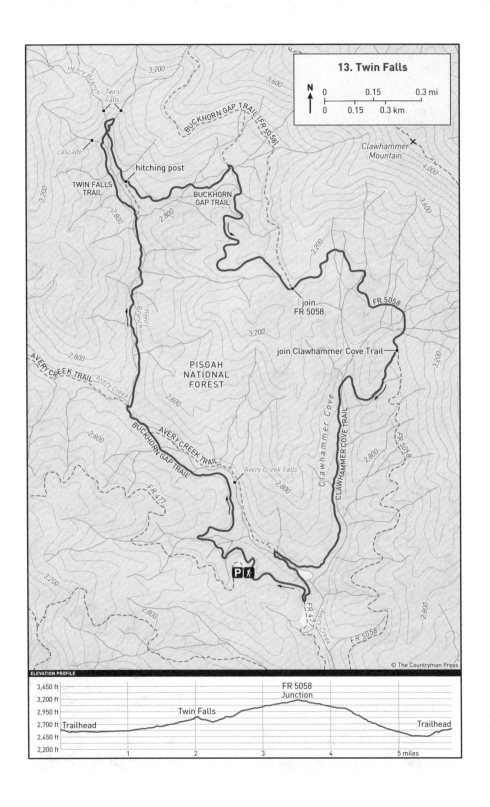

13. Twin Falls

N

| 0 | 0.15 | 0.3 mi |
| 0 | 0.15 | 0.3 km |

Henry Branch

3,200

3,600

Twin Falls

BUCKHORN GAP TRAIL (FR 5058)

Clawhammer Mountain

4,000

cascade

hitching post

TWIN FALLS TRAIL

2,800

2,800

BUCKHORN GAP TRAIL

3,200

3,600

3,200

join FR 5058

FR 5058

3,200

join Clawhammer Cove Trail

Henry Branch

3,200

AVERY CREEK TRAIL

2,800

Avery Creek

PISGAH NATIONAL FOREST

2,800

Clawhammer Cove

CLAWHAMMER COVE TRAIL

2,800

FR 5058

2,800

BUCKHORN GAP TRAIL

AVERY CREEK TRAIL

FR 477

Avery Creek Falls

2,800

3,200

2,800

FR 477

FR 5058

Avery Creek

2,800

© The Countryman Press

ELEVATION PROFILE

3,450 ft				FR 5058 Junction		
3,200 ft						
2,950 ft			Twin Falls			
2,700 ft	Trailhead					Trailhead
2,450 ft						
2,200 ft		1	2	3	4	5 miles

THIS CATARACT ON HENRY BRANCH IS ONE OF THE TWIN FALLS

AVERY CREEK FALLS IS UNDESERVINGLY OVERLOOKED

rhododendron and black birch. At 0.3 mile, step over a feeder branch of Avery Creek, easing downhill. Come to Avery Creek Falls at 0.6 mile. Most hikers access the 10-foot curtain-style pou-rover from the other side of the stream via the Avery Creek Trail. However, you can access the cataract from here, though the falls is about 100 feet down-hill of the Buckhorn Gap Trail.

Continue cruising up the valley beyond the falls to meet the Avery Creek Trail. The Buckhorn Gap Trail and Avery Creek Trail run in conjunction before splitting 0.1 mile ahead. Here, we stay with the Buckhorn Gap Trail to cross Avery Creek right on a hiker bridge, while the Avery Creek Trail splits left. The path turns up Henry Creek, where a series of hiker bridges span the creek while equestrians use fords. Work up the steep-sided mountain valley rife with birch and beech, with fern fields rising on the hillsides.

At 1.7 miles, split left with the Twin Falls Trail while the Buckhorn Gap Trail stays straight. Bridge Henry Branch yet again. The mountain walls rise and Twin Falls looms. At 2.0 miles, a user-created trail splits left to a lesser heralded cas-cade that dives about 20 feet from a stone lip. Resuming Twin Falls Trail, the two waterfalls soon come into view. Take in the whole scene: here, Henry Branch makes its swan dive, while the tributary dives as well, their collective white noise reverberating throughout the steep wooded mountainside. Closer to you, the two ribbons of white dash and crash around perpetually wet stones, merging at your feet.

Individually, the fall on the left is more easily visible. Here, Henry Branch makes its downward gambit in four dis-tinct stages, widening each step, drop-ping easily 100 or more feet. To the right, the tributary of Henry Branch drops even more, but heavy vegeta-tion makes the tapered spiller difficult to see in its entirety. A user-created trail works up the tributary to a ledge, where you can get close to a portion of the cataract, where it pours off an overhanging ledge.

To continue the loop, backtrack to a campsite just below the Twin Falls, then bridge Henry Branch heading downstream on the left bank. Reach a horse hitching post and trail intersection at 2.3 miles. Head left, rejoining the Buckhorn Gap Trail, curving into another tributary of Henry Branch on a nicely graded track under sourwood, mountain laurel and maples. Step over the tributary at 2.6 miles, where at one time concrete was laid to check erosion. The path rises into a mountain cove. Overhead, straight trunked tulip trees dominate the forest. Rise to a junction at 2.7 miles. Here an arm of the Buckhorn Gap Trail splits left 0.2 mile to Forest Road 5058 while we turn right, still on the main arm of the Buckhorn Gap Trail. Moderately climb along upper coves and ridges shaded by oaks and tulip trees.

Emerge at gated Forest Road 5058 at 3.7 miles. You are at the hike's high point of 3,174 feet. Head right here, continuing in and out of more coves on an easy gravel track. Small streams drain the highlands. At 4.4 miles, leave Forest Road 5058 right, back on footpath, picking up the slender hiker-only Clawhammer Cove Trail as it descends past impressive tulip trees on its upper end. Bridge the stream of Clawhammer Cove at 4.7 miles. The forest here is transitioning away from hemlock, victims of the hemlock wooly adelgid. Fire cherries are rising in their place in the

A FACE ON VIEW OF AVERY CREEK FALLS

DAPPLED LIGHT GRACES THE BUCKHORN GAP TRAIL

short term. Nobody knows the future forest composition in these moist valleys after the hemlocks are gone. Pines find their place at the lower end of the narrow defile. The stream of Clawhammer Cove serenades you downstream.

Come to Avery Creek at 5.2 miles. The path turns up Avery Creek and you meet the Avery Creek Trail at 5.3 miles. Head left to bridge the clear, rock-bottomed stream. The path takes you down along Avery Creek with boardwalks laid over the sloppiest spots. You are at the hike's lowest elevation of 2,440 feet. Ascend to meet Forest Road 477 at 5.6 miles. From here, trace FR 477 right, reaching the trailhead at 5.8 miles, completing the watery adventure.

14

Mount Pisgah

TOTAL DISTANCE: 3.2-mile there-and-back

HIKING TIME: 1:30

VERTICAL RISE: 940 feet

RATING: Moderate

MAPS: National Geographic #780 Pisgah National Forest—Pisgah Ranger District, USGS 7.5' Cruso NC

TRAILHEAD GPS COORDINATES: N35°24'48.8", W82°45'04.2"

CONTACT INFORMATION: Pisgah National Forest, Pisgah Ranger District, 1001 Pisgah Highway, Pisgah Forest, NC 28768, (828) 877-3265, www.fs.usda.gov/nfsnc

Make this very doable climb to the top of iconic Mount Pisgah, starting a little below 5,000 feet on the Blue Ridge Parkway at a high country picnic area, an attraction in its own right. Take the Mount Pisgah Trail through northern hardwoods, ascending toward Little Mount Pisgah. Cruise through a rocky highland cove, hopping over the headwaters of Pisgah Creek. Gain a rib ridge of Mount Pisgah, then execute the rocky ascent to the top of the peak, where a transmission tower rises high while a viewing platform delivers views you would expect from a regal summit, standing 5,720 feet in elevation.

GETTING THERE

From exit 33 on I-26 south of downtown Asheville, take NC 191 South for 2.4 miles, then turn right onto the short signed spur road to the Blue Ridge Parkway. Follow the parkway right, southbound, for 14.0 miles to milepost 407.8, turning right at the sign for Mount Pisgah Picnic Area.

THE HIKE

Although this hike isn't long, it packs a punch from beginning to end and can be part of a Blue Ridge Parkway/Pisgah National Forest experience. Save it for a clear day. And you can even check for cloud cover by checking the Mount Pisgah Lodge cam online before your adventure. The name Mount Pisgah has a familiar ring to more than just Carolina mountain hiking enthusiasts. In the Christian Bible, the book of Deuteronomy, Mount Pisgah was the mountain climbed by Moses, where he viewed the territory labeled the "land of milk and honey," the land promised by God to the Israelites on the map. Proud Carolinians

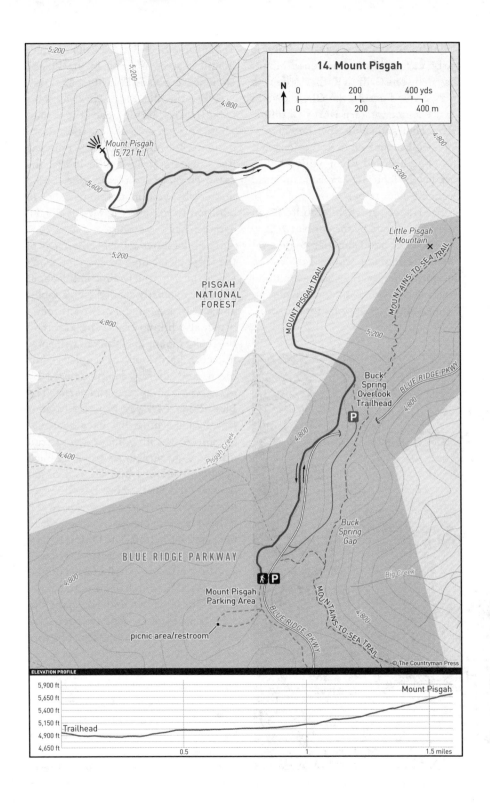

14. Mount Pisgah

0   200   400 yds
0   200   400 m

N

Mount Pisgah
(5,721 ft.)

5,200

4,800

5,200

4,800

PISGAH
NATIONAL
FOREST

Little Pisgah
Mountain

MOUNTAINS-TO-SEA TRAIL

MOUNT PISGAH TRAIL

5,200

Pisgah Creek

4,400

4,800

Buck
Spring
Overlook
Trailhead

BLUE RIDGE PKWY

4,800

Buck
Spring
Gap

Big Creek

BLUE RIDGE PARKWAY

4,800

Mount Pisgah
Parking Area

MOUNTAINS-TO-SEA TRAIL

4,800

picnic area/restroom

BLUE RIDGE PKWY

© The Countryman Press

ELEVATION PROFILE

	0.5	1	1.5 miles
5,900 ft			Mount Pisgah
5,650 ft			
5,400 ft			
5,150 ft	Trailhead		
4,900 ft			
4,650 ft			

still think of their land as such, but this particular peak was christened Mount Pisgah by one Griffith Rutherford—who in 1776 was fighting the Cherokees in what became western North Carolina. A preacher and soldier by the name of John Hall suggested to Rutherford that the French Broad River Valley below recalled the Biblical Promised Land, and the name came to be.

The ridgecrest where Mount Pisgah stood was owned by former North Carolina senator and Confederate general Thomas Clingman, who in turn sold it to George Vanderbilt, who was to build the iconic Biltmore Estate, accumulating a staggering 125,000 mountain acres.

Today, much of Vanderbilt's former holdings are contained in the Pisgah National Forest and Blue Ridge Parkway.

When the Blue Ridge Parkway came to be, the Park Service made the greater Mount Pisgah area a recreation destination, with trails aplenty, the parkway itself, a campground, the lodge, the camp store, and a picnic area. So no matter what your mountain passion—in addition to hiking—the Mount Pisgah complex has something for you.

The hike starts at the northern end of the large picnic area parking lot. Don't follow the loop trail leading uphill about 80 yards to mostly shaded picnic tables and a restroom. Instead, drop through brush at a hiking trail sign, and then the rocky Mount Pisgah Trail will enter northern hardwoods of maple, yellow birch, and cherry, complemented by evergreen red spruce and ferns. The Blue Ridge Parkway runs off to your right. At 0.2 mile, bridge a seasonal stream. At 0.5 mile, meet a spur trail leading a short distance from the Buck Springs Overlook trailhead. The hiking is easy on a much more heavily used gravel track bordered by rocks. At 0.6 mile, pass a conspicuous rock outcrop to the right of the trail. The hiking is very level and you are expecting some uphill.

At 0.7 mile, cross tributaries of Pisgah Creek. The climb begins at 1.0 mile. The ridge narrows and you gain the ridgecrest. Huge stones have been strategically placed, making steps of a sort underneath mountain ash and bush-like beech trees. The path is rocky to the extreme, made rockier still by continual use over the decades. Somewhere along the way you have left Blue Ridge Parkway property and entered Pisgah National Forest.

At 1.5 miles, you are almost there, having passed plenty of out-of-shape

VIEW OF THE "PROMISED LAND" FROM MOUNT PISGAH

parkway drivers who decided to tackle Mount Pisgah. The transmission tower that looms on the distant horizon and can be seen throughout the vicinity, being an easily identifiable focal point, now looms near. Note the stunted, gnarled trees as you approach the pinnacle. At 1.6 miles, reach the scene-dominating communication tower. However, a wooden deck stands wide and is your viewing platform from the commanding height. Here, the Blue Ridge runs north–south, a dark line amidst forest ridges. To the west, the Pigeon River flows into Tennessee. But the best view is to the east, across the French Broad valley—the Promised Land envisioned by John Hall where you can see all the way to the Piedmont. Downtown Asheville is visible to the northeast. The Balsam Mountains, home to Shining Rock Wilderness, rise to the south. Looking Glass Rock and Cedar Rock, both destinations in this guide, are visible in the south as well. Nearby, Frying Pan Mountain Tower, a short trek, beckons. Enjoy.

15

South Fork Mills River Loop

TOTAL DISTANCE: 8.4-mile loop	
HIKING TIME: 4:30	
VERTICAL RISE: 580 feet	
RATING: Moderate	
MAPS: National Geographic #780 Pisgah National Forest—Pisgah Ranger District, USGS 7.5' Pisgah Forest. NC	
TRAILHEAD GPS COORDINATES: N35°20'33.5", W82°39'33.3"	
CONTACT INFORMATION: Pisgah National Forest, Pisgah Ranger District, 1001 Pisgah Highway, Pisgah Forest, NC 28768, (828) 877-3265, www.fs.usda.gov/nfsnc	

This watery hike, ideal for summer, takes you along South Fork Mills River and its tributaries, making a loop in the Pisgah National Forest. From the Turkeypen Gap trailhead, descend to the South Fork Mills River, heading downstream amid streamside flats. Eventually turn up Bradley Creek, also enveloped in mountain valley beauty. Smaller still Pea Branch leads you to upland hill hiking before descending back to the river, completing the circuit. Several fords make this well-signed loop a warm weather proposition. Also consider starting your circuit in the morning to avoid afternoon thunderstorms.

GETTING THERE

From exit 40 on I-26 south of Asheville, take NC 280 West for 10.2 miles to Turkeypen Road, on your right, just after Boylston Creek Church (Turkeypen Road is signed on the highway but the entrance looks like a gravel driveway). Follow Turkeypen Road for 1.2 miles to dead end at the trailhead.

THE HIKE

When I think of summertime hiking in the Carolina mountains, South Fork Mills River comes to mind. You will enjoy this loop during the warm season—hiking, fishing and perhaps swimming or camping out. The Turkeypen area of the Pisgah Ranger district has lots of trails for lots of different users and you will see not only hikers but also mountain bikers and equestrians. Nevertheless, don't let its popularity dissuade you, for a summertime afternoon spent on the South Fork Mills River is not counted against the days of your life.

Leave the trailhead on the South Mills River Trail, descending north toward the

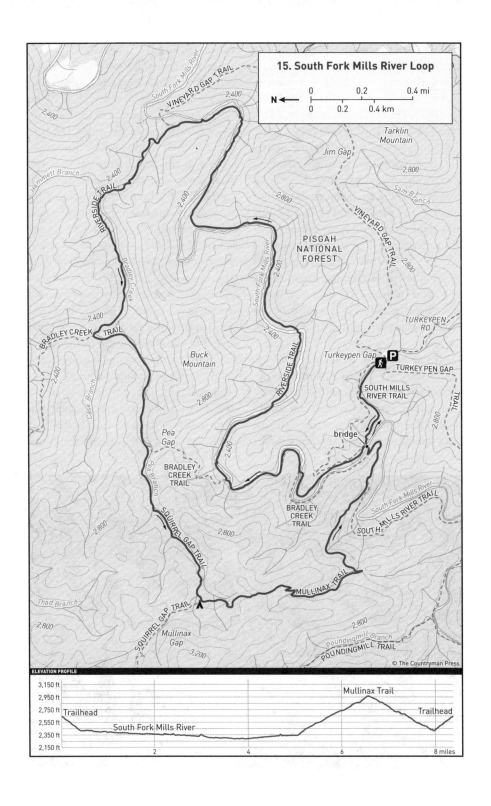

15. South Fork Mills River Loop

N ←

| 0 | | 0.2 | | 0.4 mi |
| 0 | 0.2 | | 0.4 km | |

South Fork Mills River

VINEYARD GAP TRAIL

2,400

2,400

Tarklin Mountain

Jim Gap

2,800

Sam Br Branch

Hammett Branch

2,400

RIVERSIDE TRAIL

2,400

VINEYARD GAP TRAIL

2,800

PISGAH NATIONAL FOREST

2,800

Bradley Creek

South Fork Mills River

2,400

TURKEYPEN RD

BRADLEY CREEK

TRAIL

2,400

Case Branch

Buck Mountain

2,800

2,400

RIVERSIDE TRAIL

Turkeypen Gap

P

🚶

TURKEY PEN GAP

SOUTH MILLS RIVER TRAIL

TRAIL

2,800

bridge

2,400

Pea Gap

Pea Branch

BRADLEY CREEK TRAIL

BRADLEY CREEK TRAIL

South Fork Mills River

SOUTH MILLS RIVER TRAIL

SOUTH MILLS RIVER TRAIL

SQUIRREL GAP TRAIL

2,800

2,800

Thad Branch

2,800

SQUIRREL GAP TRAIL

MULLINAX TRAIL

⛺ ▲

Mullinax Gap

3,200

2,800

Poundingmill Branch

POUNDINGMILL TRAIL

© The Countryman Press

ELEVATION PROFILE

3,150 ft	
2,950 ft	Mullinax Trail
2,750 ft	Trailhead — Trailhead
2,550 ft	South Fork Mills River
2,350 ft	
2,150 ft	2 4 6 8 miles

water. Reach the South Fork Mills River at 0.4 mile, near a trail bridge spanning the watercourse. This is your return route. For now head right on the Bradley Creek Trail, downstream, passing a wide old forest road leading back up to the trailhead and a horse ford crossing the river. Keep downstream, tracing an old railroad grade on the righthand bank of the river amid rhododendron and tree cover on the Bradley Creek Trail. At 0.8 mile, make your first ford of South Fork Mills River. This is a good gauge—if you can make this ford, then you will be fine the entire circuit. Hiking sticks or a stout limb will aid your crossings. Additionally, avoid this trek if heavy rains are forecast, potentially causing the waterways to rise to unsafe levels.

Cruise the left bank amid everywhere-you-look beauty—nearly jungleesque forest rising around a clear mountain stream, with beard cane and mossy rocks all about. However, the trail will have muddy spots here and there. At 1.3 miles, the Bradley Creek Trail leaves left to rise through Pea Gap. Stay right here, now on the Riverside Trail. Continue along the South Fork Mills River, fording at 1.4, 1.8 and 2.2 miles. Pass frequent campsites. At 2.9 miles, the rhododendron-shrouded path cuts across a bend in the South Fork Mills River. Fern fields and doghobble add more greenery. At 3.4 miles, ford South Fork Mills River one last time. You are now on the left-hand bank heading downstream. The valley widens. At 3.7 miles, the Vineyard Gap Trail enters on your right but you stay straight. Ahead, curve left toward Bradley Creek, to cross the stream at 3.9 miles. Here, an unofficial trail leads right down South Fork Mills River but you stay left, still on the Riverside Trail, turning up the Bradley Creek valley. Cruise big flats populated with tall, straight-trunked tulip trees rising over ferns and rhododendron copses. Ford Bradley Creek at 4.1 miles and at 4.3 miles. At 4.6 miles, the trail cuts

IF YOU CAN MAKE THIS FIRST FORD THEN THE REST ARE DOABLE

BACKPACKER FORDING SOUTH FORK MILLS RIVER

through a long, narrow meadow that can be overgrown in late summer.

Make your final crossing of Bradley Creek at 4.9 miles to intersect the Bradley Creek Trail. Here, the Bradley Creek Trail goes right, continuing up Bradley Creek, while our route heads left, also on the Bradley Creek Trail. Head briefly downstream along Bradley Creek only to cross Case Branch then turn up the slender Pea Branch valley. The easy level hiking is over, yet the climb ahead is by no means arduous. The path may be rutted and brushy as you come to another intersection at 5.6 miles. Here, the Bradley Creek Trail splits left for Pea Gap and can be a shortcut if you want to cut off the loop. Instead, stay straight, joining the Squirrel Gap Trail. Continue climbing along the forested headwaters of Pea Branch, stepping over small tributaries dancing amid mountain laurel and rhododendron thickets.

At 6.3 miles, reach a trail intersection and small campsite. Head left here, now southbound on the Mullinax Trail, as the Squirrel Gap Trail goes right. A little more climbing is in order beneath arbors of mountain laurel and oak. Bisect a gap at 6.6 miles, and your climbing is over. You are running a ridgeline, then you drop right, following a stream valley on a wide, easy track shaded by maples. At 7.3 miles, the Mullinax Trail drops to a gap, then splits left as an old forest road leads right. Cross the stream you've been following, working deeper into the South Fork Mills River valley. The sounds of the watercourse drift into your ears.

At 7.7 miles, come to a signed intersection. Here, split left with the South Mills River Trail, tracing the watercourse downstream as it makes a hairpin bend. At 8.0 miles, very near the river, the area gets confusing as a horse ford and user-created trails lead to the water. Still, one of the paths leads to a tall hiker bridge over the South Fork Mills River. Take this bridge across the river, then stay right, backtracking on the South Mills River Trail. Climb 0.4 mile back to the Turkeypen trailhead, completing the watery hike.

16

DuPont State Forest Waterfall Hike

TOTAL DISTANCE: 6.2-mile loop	

HIKING TIME: 3:15

VERTICAL RISE: 200 feet

RATING: Moderate, has no prolonged ups or downs

MAPS: National Geographic #504 DuPont State Recreational Forest, DuPont State Recreational Forest, USGS 7.5' Standingstone Mountain

TRAILHEAD GPS COORDINATES: N35°12.546', W82°36.918'

CONTACT INFORMATION: DuPont State Recreational Forest, P.O. Box 300, Cedar Mountain, NC 28718-0300, (828)877-6527, www.dupontstaterecreationalforest.com

One of North Carolina's premier mountain destinations, large and popular DuPont State Forest is a land of rich forests, cool streams, and waterfalls aplenty. This hike leads past four of the six primary cataracts found in the forest, including massive High Falls and swimming destination Hooker Falls. The trek uses well marked and maintained double-track trails winding through the preserve. First, pass small Lake Imaging, then discover lesser-visited Grassy Creek Falls. From there view momentous High Falls from multiple vantages, then admire Triple Falls from near and far. Finally, visit Hooker Falls and perhaps take a dip. The final part of the hike leads you through a quiet part of the forest to close the loop. Consider executing this hike during off times to avoid the crowds.

GETTING THERE

From the intersection of NC 280 and US 276 in Pisgah Forest, just north of Brevard, take US 64 East for 3.5 miles to a light at Crab Creek Road. Turn right on Crab Creek Road and follow it 4.2 miles to turn right on DuPont Road. Follow DuPont Road as it soon becomes Staton Road for a total of 2.5 miles to the large Lake Imaging trailhead parking area on your left.

THE HIKE

The large parking area at Lake Imaging gives you an idea of DuPont's popularity. Try to hit the trails during the week, in the morning, or during cooler times of the year for solitude. Also be apprised that the trails are popular with mountain bikers, but they usually stick to less popular paths for speed. Nevertheless, keep your eyes peeled and ears open

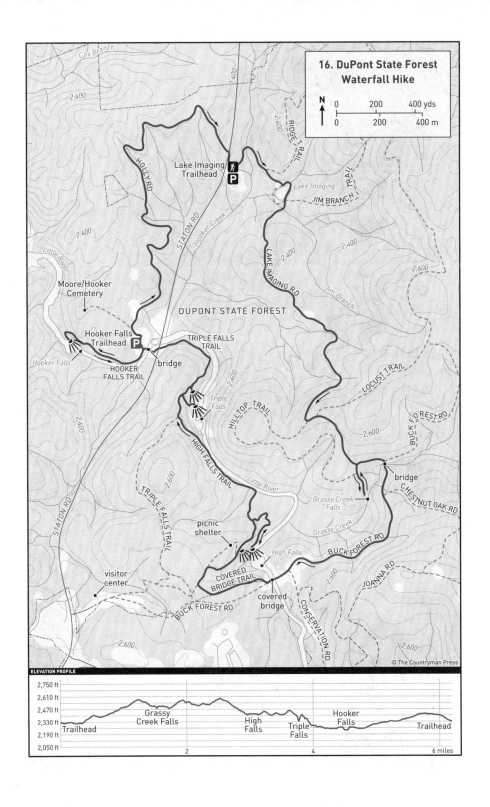

N

| 0 | 200 | 400 yds |
| 0 | 200 | 400 m |

Cox Branch

2,400

2,400

HOLLY RD

STATON RD

Hooker Creek

Little River

Moore/Hooker
Cemetery

Hooker Falls
Trailhead

Hooker Falls

HOOKER
FALLS TRAIL

bridge

TRIPLE FALLS
TRAIL

DUPONT STATE FOREST

Lake Imaging
Trailhead

RIDGE T RAIL

2,400

Lake Imaging

JIM BRANCH

2,400

LAKE IMAGING RD

TRAIL

Jim Branch

2,400

2,600

LOCUST TRAIL

BUCK FOREST RD

2,400

Triple
Falls

HILLTOP TRAIL

2,600

HIGH FALLS TRAIL

Little River

Grassy Creek
Falls

bridge

CHESTNUT OAK RD

STATON RD

TRIPLE FALLS TRAIL

2,600

picnic
shelter

Grassy Creek

High Falls

BUCK FOREST RD

visitor
center

COVERED
BRIDGE TRAIL

covered
bridge

CONSERVATION RD

JOANNA RD

BUCK FOREST RD

2,600

2,600

2,600

© The Countryman Press

ELEVATION PROFILE

| 2,750 ft |
| 2,610 ft |
| 2,470 ft |
| 2,330 ft |
| 2,190 ft |
| 2,050 ft |

Trailhead

Grassy
Creek Falls

High
Falls

Triple
Falls

Hooker
Falls

Trailhead

2

4

6 miles

TRIPLE FALLS LIVES UP TO ITS NAME, CRASHING 125 AGGREGATE FEET IN THREE STAGES

for the two-wheel set. Join Lake Imaging Road, passing around the pole gate. Remember, the roads are closed to public vehicular travel. Enter lush attractive forest and at 0.2 mile, the Ridgeline Trail, head left. Stay straight to reach small but scenic Lake Imaging at 0.3 mile. The waterside shelter makes for an ideal picnicking spot. Stay left around the pond-like impoundment and pass the Jim Branch Trail to your left and the path around the lake to the right. Climb into pines, holly, and mountain laurel on Lake Imaging Road, taking note that no single climb on this hike exceeds 200 feet, making the trek not difficult at all by Carolina mountain standards.

At 0.8 mile, slice through a former clearing, now filling with maturing pines. At 1.2 miles, the trail takes you over open rock slabs, then you pass the Hilltop Trail leading right, then the Locust Trail leading left. The number of intersections here can be dizzying, but the paths are clearly marked, easing the navigational challenge. At 1.4 miles, turn right on Grassy Creek Trail, quickly passing the other end of the Hilltop Trail. Just ahead you reach the top of Grassy Creek Falls, a long slide-type cataract frothing 60 vertical feet down a long granite slab. Thick waterside vegetation inhibits a straight-on view.

Resume Lake Imaging Road, as Buck Forest Road leads left at 1.8 miles. Stay right here, bridging Grassy Creek to pass Chestnut Oak Road leading left. Go to the top of a hill, then drop to pass Conservation Road leading left at 2.4 miles. Keep straight to walk across the quaint covered bridge over Little River. High Falls roars below, and you will have your chance to view it head-on. Split right on the Covered Bridge Trail just after

HIKERS LOOK ON THE SECOND OF THE THREE TRIPLE FALLS

passing through the covered bridge to meet yet another intersection at 2.7 miles. Here, split right on the High Falls Loop, then descend right yet again, as a short trail loops left past a picnic shelter. Then, at 2.9 miles, meet a cleared view of High Falls. What a vista! What a waterfall! High Falls crashes, wide and loud, long and strong, 120 feet to gather in a swirling mist above the gathering Little River. Whoa.

Now, continue down the trail then split right at the spur leading to the base of High Falls, where you reach a waterside flat then walk upstream for a closer view. High Falls towers in the fore and spills mighty! Backtrack and rejoin the High Falls Trail, walking alongside a calmer part of clear, trouty Little River.

Anglers are often seen in this section. At 3.8 miles, turn right on the Triple Falls Trail and shortly come wooden steps leading right, to the middle tier of Triple Falls. Hear the roar of white as Triple Falls lives up to its name, crashing 125 aggregate feet in three stages of power, slashing over granite rock. Backtrack to the Triple Falls Trail and shortly come to more distant views of the spilling trio.

Once again, travel a bucolic segment of the two-faced Little River, reaching Staton Road. The trail passes under the road at 4.2 miles. Ahead, a sturdy iron bridge quickly leads you over Little River and to the very large Hooker Falls parking area. You will soon see why the parking area is so big as you take the 0.3-mile Hooker Falls Trail downstream

HOOKER FALLS IS WIDE, LOW AND WITH A PLUNGE POOL ATTRACTING SWIMMERS

HIGH FALLS CREATES A POWERFUL WHITE ROAR

along the Little River. Walk above the curtain drop of Hooker Falls, gaining a sidelong look, then descend to reach a massive plunge pool and the base of Hooker Falls. This is a very popular swimming spot, hence the large parking area. Hooker Falls creates a 15-foot river-wide translucent curtain, flowing past a rocky spot where sunbathers and swimmers gather in large numbers on hot summer days.

Return to the Hooker Falls parking area, crossing the lot to pass around a pole gate and join Holly Road. Just ahead, stay right at the road leading left to the Moore/Hooker Cemetery at 4.9 miles. Holly Road is as quiet as Hooker Falls Trail is busy. Meander through piney woods. The path includes interpretive information about forestry practices. Curve toward Staton Road to reach the blacktop at 6.2 miles. Here, walk right along the public road for a very short piece and return to the Lake Imaging trailhead, completing the scenic waterfall tour.

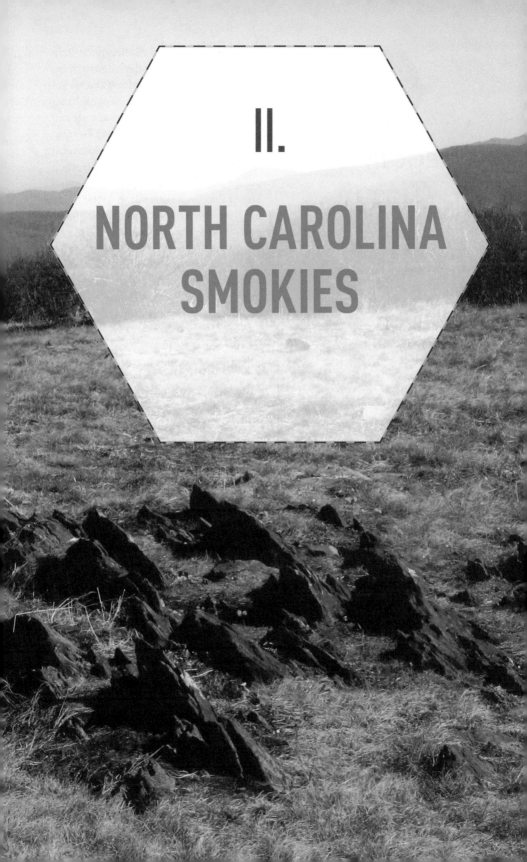

II.

NORTH CAROLINA
SMOKIES

Gregory Bald Circuit

TOTAL DISTANCE: 15.6-mile figure balloon loop

HIKING TIME: 8:45

VERTICAL RISE: 3,570 feet

RATING: Difficult due to distance and elevation gain

MAPS: National Geographic #229 Great Smoky Mountains National Park, USGS 7.5' Tapoco, Fontana Dam, Cades Cove, Calderwood

TRAILHEAD GPS COORDINATES: N35°28'03.8", W83°52'35.9"

CONTACT INFORMATION: Great Smoky Mountains National Park, 107 Park Headquarters Road, Gatlinburg, TN 37738, (865) 436-1200, nps.gov/grsm

This is a classic—and challenging—loop hike on the western end of the Smokies. There is plenty to see along the way. I recommend this as a backpack hike; four backcountry campsites are strung out along the way. Leave remote Twentymile Ranger Station, climbing along the cascades of Moore Springs Branch before joining Wolf Ridge. Reach fabled Sheep Pen Gap, then climb to the fields of Gregory Bald, with its stellar views and world-famous azalea displays. From there, ramble the high country before dropping to Twentymile Creek, another sightly Smokies stream, passing Twentymile Cascades before completing the circuit that entails over 3,500 feet of elevation gain.

GETTING THERE

From the intersection of NC 143 and US 129 in Robbinsville take US 129 north for 18 miles to turn right onto NC 28 South and follow it for 2.9 miles to turn left into the Twentymile area of the Smokies; follow the access road a short distance past the ranger station to the trailhead parking on your right.

THE HIKE

This is easily one of my favorite hikes in the Smokies. In addition to views and waterfalls—and challenge—the trek presents national-park-level scenery, as well as backpacking possibilities. The circuit can be done as a very long and strenuous day hike, especially during the extended daylight hours of summer. Allow yourself plenty of time to stop and enjoy the sights. Leave Twentymile Ranger Station on the wide double-track Twentymile Trail in lush woods with Moore Spring Branch crashing below to your right. Bridge the stream before

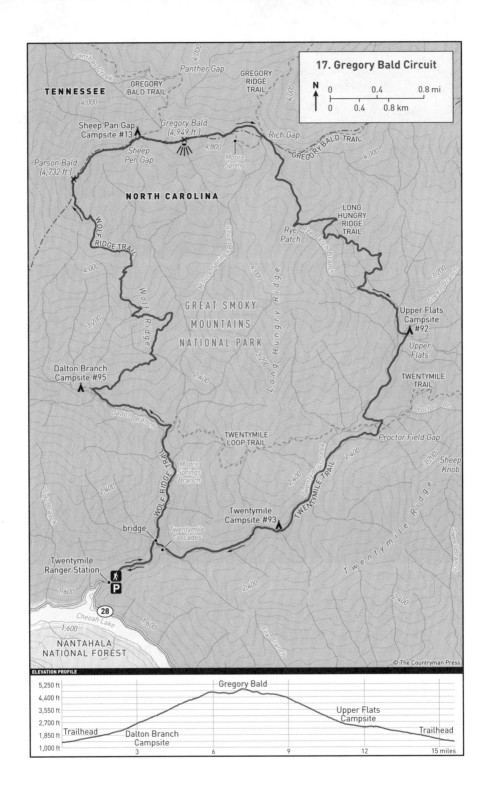

TENNESSEE

Panther Creek

Panther Gap

GREGORY BALD TRAIL

GREGORY RIDGE TRAIL

Sheep Pan Gap Campsite #13

Gregory Bald (4,949 ft.)

Sheep Pen Gap

Rich Gap

GREGORY BALD TRAIL

Parson Bald (4,732 ft.)

4,800

Moore Spring

NORTH CAROLINA

WOLF RIDGE TRAIL

Moore Springs Branch

LONG HUNGRY RIDGE TRAIL

Rye Patch

Rye Patch Branch

Green Branch

Wolf Ridge

Long Hungry Ridge

GREAT SMOKY MOUNTAINS NATIONAL PARK

Upper Flats Campsite #92

Upper Flats

Dalton Branch Campsite #95

Dalton Branch

TWENTYMILE TRAIL

Proctor Br.

TWENTYMILE LOOP TRAIL

Proctor Field Gap

Sheep Knob

Moore Springs Branch

WOLF RIDGE TRAIL

Twentymile Creek

TWENTYMILE TRAIL

Twentymile Ridge

Sweet Branch

Twentymile Campsite #93

bridge

Twentymile Cascades

Twentymile Ranger Station

1,600

28

Cheoah Lake

1,600

Cody Branch

Fox Branch

NANTAHALA NATIONAL FOREST

© The Countryman Press

ELEVATION PROFILE

		Gregory Bald			
5,250 ft					
4,400 ft				Upper Flats	
3,550 ft				Campsite	
2,700 ft					
1,850 ft	Trailhead	Dalton Branch			Trailhead
1,000 ft		Campsite			
	3	6	9	12	15 miles

TWENTYMILE CASCADES

reaching an intersection at 0.5 mile. Here, head left, joining the Wolf Ridge Trail as it turns up along still-cascading Moore Spring Branch. At 0.9 mile, cross the trouty, clear-as-air stream twice on elevated footlog bridges, allowing first-rate looks at the watercourse, bordered with mossy bluffs, ferns and rhododendron. Three more log bridges lie ahead, as you pass slide cascades and deep pools amid junglesque growth.

At 1.7 miles, the Twentymile Loop Trail leaves right but we head left as the Wolf Ridge Trail turns west up the serene, wildflower-rich Dalton Branch valley. At 2.6 miles, a spur trail goes a quarter-mile up Dalton Branch to the less-than-level, lesser-used Dalton Branch campsite (a pre-park path once kept west to Dalton Gap and the Tennessee state line), which is your first camping option. We stay right with the Wolf

cruising over what once was Parson Bald. At 6.2 miles, pass a sign indicating Parson Bald, staying in an abundance of yellow birch on the state line, around 4,700 feet. Stinging nettles can be thick and troublesome here in summer. At 6.9 miles, come to Sheep Pen Gap campsite, located in a long, wooded flat. The camp has been renowned for bear/camper encounters through the decades. Here, the Gregory Bald Trail goes left and right. Stay right with the Gregory Bald Trail, still on the state line, ascending the wooded slopes of lower Gregory Bald.

At 7.3 miles, open onto the slopes of Gregory Bald. This field has been open since before Cades Cove was settled. Farmers drove their cattle up here to graze, keeping it grassy. Today, the park service keeps it open through cutting and burning. The 360-degree views here are stupendous. Cades Cove and Tennessee stretch north while Fontana Dam and waves of Carolina mountains expand to the horizon. Nearby, flame azaleas cluster in the world's largest bloom concentration, while blackberries and blueberries ripen in summer.

Find a seat and revel in this special swath of the Smokies. I've spent many an hour here. After all, you have climbed over 3,500 feet! Reenter woods and descend, passing the spur to Moore Spring at 7.7 miles. A trail shelter once stood here long, long ago, yet the spring's waters are—in my opinion—the finest aqua in the Carolinas. At 8.0 miles, come to Rich Gap and a four-way intersection. Here, the Gregory Ridge Trail heads left to Cades Cove and Tennessee while the other end of the Moore Spring spur goes right. We stay straight on the Gregory Bald Trail, hiking just 0.1 mile farther then splitting right on the Long Hungry Ridge Trail, leaving the Volunteer State

Ridge Trail as it leaves Dalton Branch, steepens and enters hardwoods of hickory, sourwood, and oaks mixed with rock outcrops, mountain laurel, and azalea. Make a big switchback to the left at 3.8 miles. You are now scaling Wolf Ridge. The uptick is steady but well graded.

At 5.0 miles, reach a gap and head left, still pushing up Wolf Ridge. At 6.0 miles, level off in woods with widely branched trees and a grassy forest floor. You are on the state line with Tennessee,

THIS FOOTLOG BRIDGE SPANS MOORE SPRINGS BRANCH

for good. The path was said to have been named by two hunters stuck up here by flooded streams all around the ridge. Begin a prolonged downgrade on a narrow, much less used track. Relic grasses thicken under trees. At 9.0 miles, drop off Long Hungry Ridge at a level spot known as Rye Patch. Descend into high coves. At 10.8 miles, come to Rye Cove Branch and cut down through its valley thick with tulip trees, crossing Twentymile Creek to make the Upper Flats campsite at 11.4 miles. This desirable camp is situated in woods bordered with waterways all around.

Continue down the rhododendron heavy Twentymile Creek valley before turning away from the stream to make now-wooded Procter Field Gap at 12.6 miles. Note the preserved hemlocks in the gap. Here, the Twentymile Loop Trail comes in on the right and the Twentymile Trail climbs left to Sassafras Gap and the AT. Descend right with the Twentymile Trail, now on an old double-track originally constructed to access the Shuckstack fire tower. The walking is easy in rich woods and you soon come back along crashing and dashing Twentymile Creek. Bridge the creek twice before spanning it one more time to find Twentymile campsite at 14.0 miles. This smallish site is on a slope near the stream. The wide trail traces Twentymile Creek, allowing you fine watery views of cataracts, bridging the stream twice more. At 15.0 miles, the signed spur to Twentymile Cascades leads left. The 30-foot spiller drops in a series of slide cataracts. Use care in reaching its base. From there it is but 0.1 mile to the intersection with the Wolf Ridge Trail. You have been here before. From this junction it is but a 0.5-mile backtrack to the trailhead, completing the stellar Carolina Smokies hike.

18

Shuckstack Fire Tower

This Smokies hike takes you to one of the two still-standing metal fire towers in the park. Situated at the western end of the state line ridge dividing Tennessee and North Carolina, this trek starts near Fontana Lake and uses the Appalachian Trail to rise from the lake waters to over 4,000 feet where fantastic 360-degree views await of the crest of the Smokies, Fontana Lake, and the cornucopia of montane splendor that is Great Smoky Mountains National Park.

TOTAL DISTANCE: 6.6-mile there-and-back

HIKING TIME: 3:30

VERTICAL RISE: 2,100 feet

RATING: Moderate-difficult, does have big climb

MAPS: National Geographic #229 Great Smoky Mountains National Park, USGS 7.5' Fontana Dam

TRAILHEAD GPS COORDINATES: N35°27'37.9", W83°48'39.7"

CONTACT INFORMATION: Great Smoky Mountains National Park, 107 Park Headquarters Road, Gatlinburg, TN 37738, (865) 436-1200, nps.gov/grsm

GETTING THERE

From the intersection of NC 143 and US 129 in Robbinsville, take NC 143 East for 8.8 miles to turn left onto NC 28 North and follow it for 9.9 miles to turn right onto Fontana Dam Road and follow it for 1.5 miles to cross Fontana Dam. Stay with the main road here and follow it for 0.7 mile to dead end at the trailhead for both the Appalachian Trail and the Lakeshore Trail.

THE HIKE

The trek, though uphill almost the entire way, isn't too difficult; the ascent is steady but moderate on a well-tended track. Join the Appalachian Trail as it leaves the parking area north as a single-track path while the Lakeshore Trail follows a wide track east. The Appalachian Trail was rerouted in 1944 to here after Fontana Dam was constructed. The new, changed route took hikers to Shuckstack. We essentially follow this route today. Ascend a dry slope of pine, chestnut oak, black gum, and hickory, xeric species you would expect to find on this south-facing incline. Make your first switchback and gain the nose of the ridge. At 0.5 mile, you make a big switchback to the right. Pass occasional

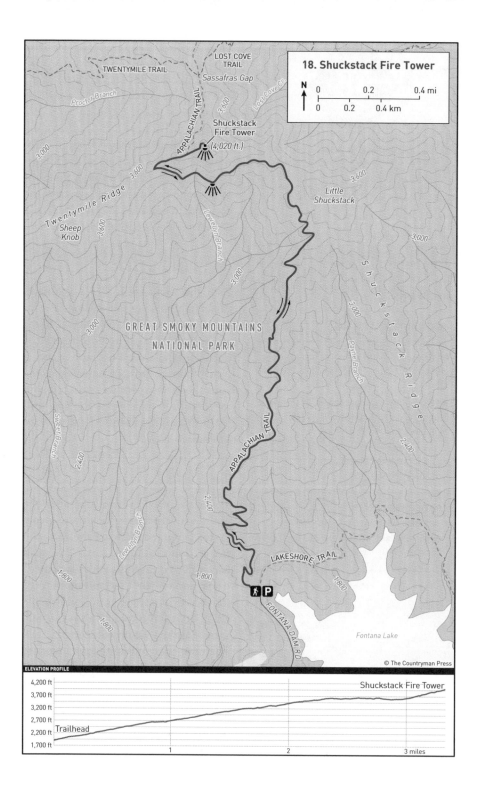

18. Shuckstack Fire Tower

TWENTYMILE TRAIL

LOST COVE TRAIL

Sassafras Gap

Proctor Branch

APPALACHIAN TRAIL

Shuckstack Fire Tower (4,020 ft.)

Lost Cove Cr.

Little Shuckstack

Twentymile Ridge

Sheep Knob

Llewellyn Branch

Shuckstack Ridge

GREAT SMOKY MOUNTAINS NATIONAL PARK

Payne Branch

Sweet Branch

APPALACHIAN TRAIL

Llewellyn Branch

LAKESHORE TRAIL

Fontana Dam Rd.

Fontana Lake

N
0   0.2   0.4 mi
0   0.2   0.4 km

© The Countryman Press

ELEVATION PROFILE

Shuckstack Fire Tower

Trailhead

4,200 ft
3,700 ft
3,200 ft
2,700 ft
2,200 ft
1,700 ft

1   2   3 miles

CLOUDS SWEEP ACROSS THE SMOKIES AS SEEN FROM SHUCKSTACK FIRE TOWER

outcrops. By 0.8 mile, Fontana Lake can be seen through the screen of trees. At 1.0 mile, enjoy a short reprieve as the AT levels off and then resumes trekking up the nose of the ridge. Keep a steady uptick among blueberry, sassafras, mountain laurel, and oak.

At 2.1 miles, the path curves left under the knob of Little Shuckstack. Here, it enters a hollow and crosses a trickling branch, your only source of water, and even that can run dry in autumn. At 2.4 miles, the AT surprisingly goes downhill before drifting into a gap separating the mountain of Little Shuckstack from Shuckstack. You are now a little over 3,600 feet. Here, the AT curves west along the south slope of Shuckstack. The hiking is easy here as you cross seams of slate on the mountainside. At 2.9 miles, a particular slate outcrop opens a view to the south, into the wooded ridges of the Nantahala National Forest. Note the stunted oaks, sourwood and other

species, barely scratching out a living on this barren rock nearly devoid of soil.

At 3.0 miles, make a big switchback to the right. You are now scaling Shuckstack as the climb resumes. At 3.2 miles, the Appalachian Trail splits left for Sassafras Gap and onward 2,000 or so miles to the state of Maine and its terminus at Mount Katahdin while we take the spur right, to the top of Shuckstack. Keep working uphill; ahead there is more sky and less land. You are almost there. At 3.3 miles, reach the base of the metal fire tower and the foundation of the ranger quarters perched on top of the 4,020 foot crag. The name is derived from the mountain peak rising like a pile of corn stalks. Trails come from all four directions to Shuckstack but our route is the most direct.

Look around. You can see the base of the one-room log ranger cabin, chimney, and cistern where rainwater was stored for use. It is difficult to imagine

THE STRANGE FLOWER CALLED INDIAN GHOST PIPE RISES ALONG THE TRAIL

living on this scarp. The 60-foot tower and ranger quarters were constructed in 1934 by the Works Progress Administration, a Civilian Conservation Corps offshoot that was a government works program during the Great Depression of the 1930s. The tower was in use for over three decades until fire watching was done by air during fire season, eliminating the need for towers and the men stationed at them.

After ascending the tower stairs, vistas open before you, everywhere you look. The state line ridge and the Smokies crest rise to the northeast. In the other direction, southeast, Fontana Lake stretches its main body and narrow bays where the Little Tennessee River and its tributaries once flowed (while paddling Fontana Lake, Shuckstack is easy to spot because of the fire tower). Across the Twentymile Creek Valley rises Gregory Bald. To the south, range after range of highlands forms the Nantahala National Forest, an imposing rampart. The ranger cabin chimney below provides perspective for this implausibly beautiful natural tableau.

19

Waterfalls of Deep Creek

TOTAL DISTANCE: 2.4-mile loop

HIKING TIME: 1:20

VERTICAL RISE: 390 feet

RATING: Easy

MAPS: National Geographic #229 Great Smoky Mountains National Park, USGS 7.5' Bryson City

TRAILHEAD GPS COORDINATES: N35°27'52.2", W83°26'03.0"

CONTACT INFORMATION: Great Smoky Mountains National Park, 107 Park Headquarters Road, Gatlinburg, TN 37738, (865) 436-1200, nps.gov/grsm

This excellent family hike takes you by three waterfalls as it loops through the lower Deep Creek area of the Smokies. Convenient to national park camping, picnicking and tubing, the circuit first heads up Juney Whank Branch then leads you through the middle of cascading Juney Whank Falls. Next climb a bit through woods to reach Deep Creek, then Indian Creek where you find Indian Creek Falls with its plunge pool. Finally, make a cruise down Deep Creek, passing tall Tom Branch Falls before returning to the trailhead.

GETTING THERE

From Cherokee, take US 19 South to Bryson City. Turn right at the Swain County Courthouse onto Everett Street and carefully follow the signs through town to Deep Creek campground. Inside the park, veer left toward "Trailhead, Waterfalls." Juney Whank Falls Trail starts at the upper end of the Deep Creek Trail parking area.

THE HIKE

Be apprised though this hike is rated easy, it does entail a modicum of climbing. After all, the trek takes place in Great Smoky Mountains National Park. Nevertheless, even the least able hikers can make this loop, given a little extra time. To families with young kids: go for it! You will find ample highlights and water play opportunities to keep younger hikers engaged. Solitude seekers and hardcore waterfallers will want to come here during winter and spring, when the crowds are down and the cataracts are at their fullest.

The adventure begins on the Juney Whank Trail. The gravel path heads left from the busy-in-the-summertime

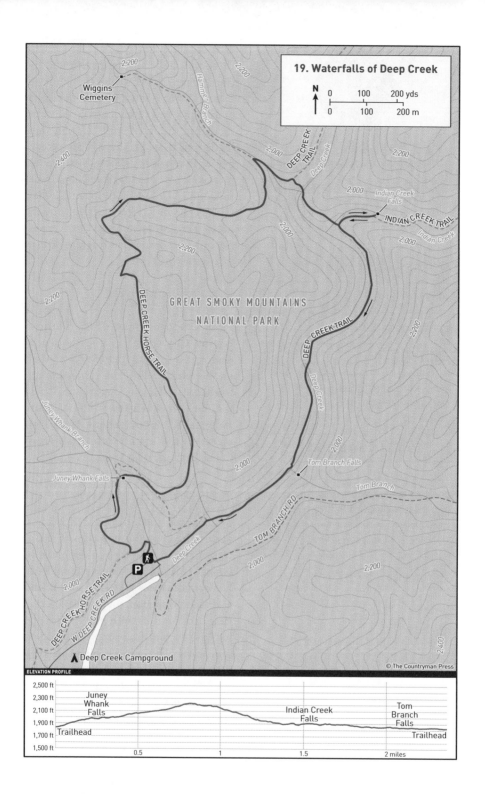

19. Waterfalls of Deep Creek

N

| 0 | 100 | 200 yds |
| 0 | 100 | 200 m |

Wiggins Cemetery

2,200

2,200

2,400

DEEP CREEK TRAIL

Deep Creek

Hammer Branch

2,000

2,200

2,000

Indian Creek Falls

INDIAN CREEK TRAIL

Indian Creek

2,000

GREAT SMOKY MOUNTAINS
NATIONAL PARK

2,200

DEEP CREEK HORSE TRAIL

DEEP CREEK TRAIL

Deep Creek

2,200

2,000

Juney Whank Branch

2,200

Juney Whank Falls

2,000

Tom Branch Falls

Tom Branch

TOM BRANCH RD.

2,000

2,200

Deep Creek

DEEP CREEK HORSE TRAIL

W DEEP CREEK RD.

P

2,000

2,400

Deep Creek Campground

© The Countryman Press

ELEVATION PROFILE

2,500 ft				
2,300 ft	Juney			
2,100 ft	Whank			Tom
1,900 ft	Falls		Indian Creek	Branch
1,700 ft	Trailhead		Falls	Falls
1,500 ft				Trailhead

0.5   1   1.5   2 miles

INDIAN CREEK FALLS MAKES ITS WIDE DROP

trailhead up along smallish Juney Whank Branch, a tributary of Deep Creek, then meets the wide Deep Creek Horse Trail at 0.1 mile. At 0.2 mile, take the hiker-only spur to Juney Whank Falls. The path leads to the sheet spiller, dropping 18 feet and sliding onward below the observation bridge that allows a close-up look at the waterfall. Ahead, reunite with the Deep Creek Horse Trail and stay with it as the Juney Whank Trail descends right, returning to the trailhead.

But we are pushing on for two additional waterfalls and a little Smoky Mountain scenery along the way. Make a gentle uptick along an unnamed tributary of Deep Creek in mountain laurel, galax, and dogwoods. Top out in a little gap at 0.9 mile. It is almost all downhill from here. You've done your work on the front end. The path descends into a hollow and curves left to meet Hammer Branch at 1.3 miles. Here, a spur leads left around a half mile up to the homesite of Moses and Mary Wiggins and the Wiggins Cemetery, where five young children are buried. Infant mortality was staggering when this area was settled, before the park came to be. Other parts of the Deep Creek valley were once settled, including along Juney Whank Branch, Tom Branch, along lower Indian Creek, and along lower Deep Creek. Deep Creek School was located just a mile downstream from the trailhead for this hike. Now, much of this pioneer history has been lost to time and elements.

Our hike turns down Hammer Branch to meet the Deep Creek Trail at 1.4 miles. It you went left, you could trace Deep Creek over 14 miles up to its headwaters near Newfound Gap. But we turn right down Deep Creek Trail, where the trail is a wide double-track path. Bridge Deep Creek and continue downstream. The trail is open to bicycles from here down to the trailhead. Also, in summertime you will see tubers walking up to this point and floating downstream on Deep Creek. The hiking is easy, and you bridge Indian Creek at 1.5 miles. Just ahead, turn left on the

TALL TOM BRANCH FALLS SPILLS 60 FEET

Indian Creek Trail and follow it 200 feet to Indian Creek Falls. This wide 24-foot sheet drop rains down an angled slope to form a large plunge pool. Not many dare to swim its chilly waters, despite the fact that the pool is open to the sun in summertime. By the way, you can gain a top-down view of Indian Creek Falls by continuing up the Indian Creek Trail.

Backtrack to the Deep Creek Trail. Enjoy the still deep pools and singing shoals, where Deep Creek displays national-park-level scenery. Cross Deep Creek on a wide bridge then come to 60-foot Tom Branch Falls at 2.2 miles. Here, across Deep Creek, the slim, faucet-style spiller dives in stages over horizontally layered rock to eventually give its waters up to Deep Creek. Tom Branch Falls in winter can be a frozen sight to see. From here it is a short walk back to the trailhead.

20

Andrews Bald

TOTAL DISTANCE: 3.4-mile there-and-back

HIKING TIME: 1:40

VERTICAL RISE: 590 feet

RATING: Easy–moderate

MAPS: National Geographic #229 Great Smoky Mountains National Park, USGS 7.5' Clingmans Dome NC-TN

TRAILHEAD GPS COORDINATES: N35°33'24.4", W83°29'46.4"

CONTACT INFORMATION: Great Smoky Mountains National Park, 107 Park Headquarters Road, Gatlinburg, TN 37738, (865) 436-1200, nps.gov/grsm

This is a hike of superlatives. Not only do you start at the highest trailhead in the Smokies, but you hike to the highest bald in the Southern Appalachians. Here, you will reach this open meadow and revel in views of the Carolina mountains as far as the eye can see. In addition, you have a chance to bag Clingmans Dome, the highest point in the Smokies and in Tennessee at 6,643 feet, a scant 40 feet less than Mount Mitchell, the highest point east of the Mississippi River.

GETTING THERE

From the intersection of US 441 and US 19 in Cherokee, NC, take US 441 North for 20 miles to Newfound Gap in Great Smoky Mountains National Park. From there, join Clingmans Dome Road left and follow it 7.1 miles to the large parking area below Clingmans Dome. The Forney Ridge Trail starts at the southwestern end of the parking area, just before the parking area loop road curves away from Clingmans Dome. Note: to access the trailhead Clingmans Dome Road must be open. This road, the park's highest, is generally open from April through November. Call ahead at (865) 436-1200 then go to road conditions, if hiking during the shoulder seasons, or check the park website.

THE HIKE

Andrews Bald is one of those mysterious grassy clearings found in the Southern Appalachians, the origins of which are unclear, whether it was from fire, grazing, or who knows what. We do know that since cattle grazing has ceased in places like the Smokies, balds have grown over in the fourscore and more years since the Smokies became a national park. Looking at topographic maps of the

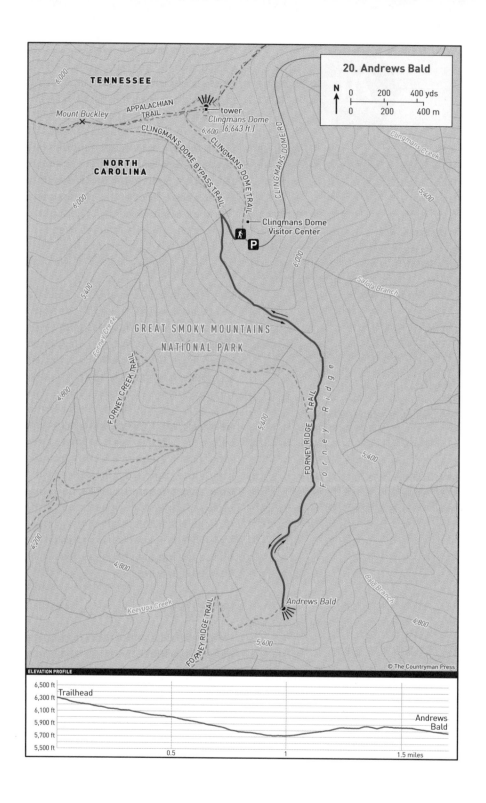

20. Andrews Bald

N

| 0 | 200 | 400 yds |
| 0 | 200 | 400 m |

TENNESSEE

Mount Buckley ✕

APPALACHIAN TRAIL

tower
Clingmans Dome
(6,643 ft.)

CLINGMANS DOME RD

Clingmans Creek

NORTH CAROLINA

CLINGMANS DOME BYPASS TRAIL

CLINGMANS DOME TRAIL

6,600

Clingmans Dome
Visitor Center

P

Salola Branch

GREAT SMOKY MOUNTAINS

NATIONAL PARK

Forney Creek

FORNEY CREEK TRAIL

FORNEY RIDGE TRAIL

Forney Ridge

Bald Branch

Keeyuga Creek

FORNEY RIDGE TRAIL

Andrews Bald

© The Countryman Press

ELEVATION PROFILE

| 6,500 ft |
| 6,300 ft | Trailhead |
| 6,100 ft |
| 5,900 ft | Andrews Bald |
| 5,700 ft |
| 5,500 ft |

0.5   1   1.5 miles

Smokies, you will find balds that are bald no more, retaining only a name— Parson Bald, Newton Bald, Jerry Bald, Big Chestnut Bald and on and on. In fact, all but two balds are fully grown over— Gregory Bald and Andrews Bald. These are being kept open by the park service through cutting and mowing. The park service does this clearing yet tries to leave a natural quality, not resembling a freshly mown square front yard.

Furthermore, a fine display of wild flame azaleas and Catawba rhododendron blooms here in June at 5,800 feet and is part of the natural landscape, along with a plethora of blueberry and blackberry bushes. Along the way you can also enjoy the spruce-fir forests that thrive in these majestic highlands. That is the advantage of starting your hike at 6,400 feet. If the 3.4-mile there-and-back trek to Andrews Bald leaves you wanting more trail miles to travel, make the half-mile walk up to Clingmans Dome with its tower offering unexcelled panoramas. You can also take a stroll on the highest stretch of the entire 2,300-plus mile Appalachian Trail as it travels by Clingmans Dome.

Yet the hike to Andrews Bald stands on its own. When pulling up to the parking area, you may be startled at the number of vehicles and people milling about. Worry not, for most of them are making their way up to Clingmans Dome or simply soaking in the atmosphere from the highest point you can drive to here in Great Smoky Mountains National Park.

Join the gravel Forney Ridge Trail descending. Most hikers will be heading up the wide asphalt path to Clingmans Dome. Walk downhill bordered by scattered Fraser fir and red spruce, along with small brushy openings populated with wildflowers in the summertime. This area receives upwards of 90 inches of precipitation per year, mostly in the form of rain but also from copious snowfalls starting in mid-fall and going through mid-spring.

THE MEADOW OF ANDREWS BALD IS BEING MAINTAINED BY THE NATIONAL PARK SERVICE

CASCADING WAVES OF RIDGES STRETCH OUT FROM ANDREWS BALD

At 0.2 mile, come to a trail intersection. Here, the Clingmans Dome Bypass Trail heads right to meet the Appalachian Trail but we go left, still descending on the Forney Ridge Trail. Sturdy stone steps with built-in water drainages leads you past massive stone outcrops. Brush and round leaf viburnum rise thick. Yellow birch grows in weather stunted shapes. Mountain ash rises from the crags. The sheer labor involved in constructing the stone stairs will amaze, and have improved the trail greatly. Conditions are tough on trails here in the highest of the high.

By 0.8 mile, you are hiking through a deep dark cool copse of spruce and fir. Moss and ferns grow green against the brown needles of the spruce and fir on the forest floor. On wetter level areas, narrow boardwalks help keep your feet dry. At 1.0 mile, the Forney Creek Trail leaves right for the lowlands, heading 12 miles down to Fontana Lake. We have reached the low point of our hike and now gently climb along Forney Ridge, switching over to the west side of the knob named Andrews Bald, though the only open area that remains is our destination. Watch for big outcrops to your left.

At 1.7 miles, open onto the first grassy spots of Andrews Bald, shared with rhododendron, red spruce and Fraser fir. The sloping meadow opens ahead into a magnificent panorama of the Carolina mountains to the south. Interestingly, Andrews Bald should actually be named Andres Bald, the original name received after a herder by the name of Andres Thompson grazed cattle in the 1830s on this parcel of Forney Ridge that he owned. Along the way an errant mapmaker changed the moniker to Andrews. Look out, the arms of Fontana Lake can be seen below, lying 1,710 feet in elevation. Cascading waves of ridges stretch as far as the eye can see. It is a truly inspiring overlook. Grab a seat on the grass or a rock and absorb the scene.

21

Charlies Bunion

TOTAL DISTANCE: 8.4-mile there-and-back

HIKING TIME: 4:30

VERTICAL RISE: 1,086 feet

RATING: Moderate-difficult

MAPS: National Geographic #229 Great Smoky Mountains National Park, USGS 7.5' Mount Guyot TN-NC

TRAILHEAD GPS COORDINATES: N35°36'40.1", W83°25'31.3"

CONTACT INFORMATION: Great Smoky Mountains National Park, 107 Park Headquarters Road, Gatlinburg, TN 37738, (865) 436-1200, nps.gov/grsm

This popular and busy Smoky Mountains hike is popular and busy for good reasons. The hike along the Appalachian Trail from Newfound Gap to the incredible views at Charlies Bunion offers multiple highlights along the way. Climb from the large parking lot at Newfound Gap, and it isn't long before you are rewarded with views into North Carolina while traipsing through the rare spruce-fir forest that only graces the park's highest locales. Another vista opens before you top out then come to iconic Icewater Springs shelter, with its own vistas into the Tarheel State. Hike a slender rocky spine dividing North Carolina from Tennessee before coming to Charlies Bunion, a naked rock outcrop with wide open looks at Mount LeConte and the hills of East Tennessee.

GETTING THERE

From the intersection of US 441 and US 19 in Cherokee, NC, take US 441 North for 19.2 miles to Newfound Gap parking area. The lot is big. Look for the wall-like Rockefeller Memorial near the restrooms. Here you will find the Appalachian Trail heading northbound.

THE HIKE

Newfound Gap, before the Smoky Mountains National Park came to be, was a little-used pass between North Carolina and Tennessee, with Indian Gap, a little way to the west, being the primary trans-mountain state passage, used by American Indians, settlers, and Civil War fighters. But after the Smokies park was developed, the primary road crossing the stateline ridge was routed through Newfound Gap. In 1926, President Calvin Coolidge signed a bill establishing Great Smoky Mountains National Park.

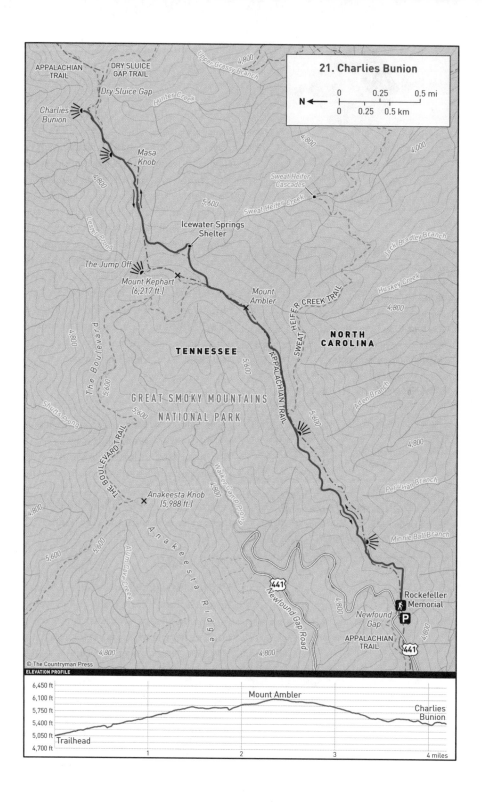

21. Charlies Bunion

N ←

| 0 | 0.25 | 0.5 mi |
| 0 | 0.25 | 0.5 km |

APPALACHIAN TRAIL
DRY SLUICE GAP TRAIL
Dry Sluice Gap
Upper Grassy Branch
4,800

Charlies Bunion

Masa Knob
Hunter Creek
4,800

Sweat Heifer Cascades
4,800
4,000

5,600
Sweat Heifer Creek

Jack Bradley Branch

Icewater Springs Shelter

The Jump Off
Mount Kephart (6,217 ft.)
Mount Ambler
SWEAT HEIFER CREEK TRAIL
Huskey Creek
4,800

NORTH CAROLINA

The Boulevard
TENNESSEE
5,600
APPALACHIAN TRAIL
5,600
Aden Branch

5,600
GREAT SMOKY MOUNTAINS NATIONAL PARK
5,600
4,800

Shutts Prong
THE BOULEVARD TRAIL
4,800
Peruvian Branch

Anakeesta Knob (5,988 ft.)
Walker Camp Prong
Anakeesta Ridge

Minnie Ball Branch

4,800
5,600
Alum Cave Creek

441
Newfound Gap Road
4,800
Rockefeller Memorial
P
Newfound Gap
APPALACHIAN TRAIL
441
4,800

4,800
5,600
4,800

© The Countryman Press

ELEVATION PROFILE

6,450 ft				
6,100 ft		Mount Ambler		
5,750 ft				Charlies Bunion
5,400 ft				
5,050 ft				
4,700 ft	Trailhead			
	1	2	3	4 miles

But it took a while to get things going. Money was raised and land was purchased from timber companies and simple farmers. Trails, roads and facilities were built and it wasn't until September 2, 1940 at Newfound Gap that Franklin Delano Roosevelt officially dedicated Great Smoky Mountains National Park.

From what is known as the Rockefeller Memorial (to honor David Rockefeller's $5 million dollar gift to purchase park properties), in front of a gathered crowd of thousands of local Carolinians and Tennesseans, most of whom had waited for hours, FDR quoted, "There are trees here that stood before our forefathers ever came to this continent; there are brooks that still run as clear as on the day the first pioneer cupped his hand and drank from them. In this park, we shall conserve these trees, the pine, the red bud, the dogwood, the azalea, the rhododendron, the trout and the thrush for the happiness of the American people."

You start this hike at the base of the Rockefeller Memorial. Join the Appalachian Trail, climbing away from Newfound Gap. On busy days throngs of casual strollers will be found on this first quarter mile of trail, but there's nothing like an ascent to weed out walkers with no particular destination. The Appalachian Trail straddles the state line dividing North Carolina from Tennessee, rising from 5,000 feet to above a mile quickly. At 0.6 mile, the narrow spine and limited tree cover allow southbound looks into North Carolina. Newfound Gap Road is visible below. Continue to rise in spruce-fir forest mixed with exposed rock and brush growing where

AUTHOR LOOKS OUT FROM THE CUSP OF CHARLIES BUNION

DURING WINTER ENJOY SOLITUDE AND THIS VIEW OF MOUNT LECONTE

rock isn't. Keep a steady uptick among seeps running across the trail. Mount LeConte can be seen at times through the trees. At 1.5 miles, another view opens on your right with waves of Carolina ridges extending outward like the waves on an ocean. Enjoy a respite from the climb, cruising in deep evergreen woods, nearly always cool. At 1.7 miles, come to a trail intersection. Here, the Sweat Heifer Trail descends past Sweat Heifer Cascades and on down to Kephart Shelter, named for Smokies park proponent Horace Kephart.

At 2.6 miles, reach the high point of the hike as you roll over 6,100 feet on Mount Ambler. Problem is, the climb to the wooded peak is so gradual that it doesn't seem like you are atop a particular mountain on this undulating ridge. However, your legs and lungs will appreciate the forthcoming descent. At 2.7 miles, come to the first of many trail intersections. Here, The Boulevard Trail leaves left and is also the route to the Jump Off, a half-mile spur right off The Boulevard Trail, where you can get a fine look at Charlies Bunion, among other Smokies peaks and lands beyond. Consider adding this as a side hike on your return.

Our hike stays right on the Appalachian Trail, descending to reach another trail split. The trail going left bypasses Icewater Springs shelter. Go right to check out the shelter and enjoy the views east into Carolina. The wood and stone shelter has bunks, a fireplace, a sitting area, and a bathroom nearby. From here, descend past the famed

FROM CHARLIES BUNION CLOUDS SWEEP ACROSS CRAGGY RIDGES

HIKER RELAXES ON THE ROCK OUTCROP THAT IS CHARLIES BUNION

gravelly Icewater Springs, then drop more sharply until you are on a narrow ridge with precipitous drop-offs on both sides, straddling the state line.

At 3.6 miles, reach a gap then angle over to the left side of Masa Knob, named for early Smokies advocate and photographer George Masa. At 3.9 miles, another view opens to your left as the Tennessee side of the stateline ridge falls away extremely steeply. At 4.1 miles, come to a trail intersection. Here, a spur leads left to the mostly rock face that is Charlies Bunion. The Appalachian Trail goes right. Stay left. Continue on a blasted track to reach Charlies Bunion at 4.2 miles. Here, an outcrop rises to astounding views north into Tennessee. The ground below you drops almost vertically. Mount LeConte rises proudly to the fore while Porters Creek drains the lands below. Beyond, the hills of East Tennessee extend as far as the clarity of the sky allows. From this vantage it is easy to understand the popularity of this hike and the reasons for the conservation of this park, as Roosevelt advocated.

22

Sweat Heifer Creek Cascades

TOTAL DISTANCE: 7.2-mile there-and-back	
HIKING TIME: 3:40	
VERTICAL RISE: 1,768 feet	
RATING: Moderate–difficult	
MAPS: National Geographic #229 Great Smoky Mountains National Park, USGS 7.5' Smokemont NC	
TRAILHEAD GPS COORDINATES: N35°35'09.2", W83°21'30.4"	
CONTACT INFORMATION: Great Smoky Mountains National Park, 107 Park Headquarters Road, Gatlinburg, TN 37738, (865) 436-1200, nps.gov/grsm	

This hike won't be found on any typical top-ten Smokies hikes lists but it is an unsung trek to a pretty cool waterfall. And there is plenty to see and enjoy on the way. Leave Newfound Gap Road, bridging uppermost Oconaluftee River, then turn up Kephart Prong, with which you will become familiar, bridging it several times to find Kephart shelter, a backcountry refuge set at a stream confluence. From there wind through wonderful forest to join an old railroad grade, then discover 30-foot Sweat Heifer Cascades, an angled, low-flow spiller draining Mount Kephart above.

GETTING THERE

From the intersection of US 441 and US 19 in Cherokee, NC, take US 441 North for 10.5 miles to the Kephart Trail, parking on your right.

THE HIKE

This hike takes you to an unheralded waterfall in Great Smoky Mountains National Park. It is unheralded because there are higher and more dramatic cataracts within the confines of the park, but Sweat Heifer Cascades presents not only an elongated, sloped scenic cascade but also relative solitude much of the way. In fact, I would be surprised if anyone else was at Sweat Heifer Cascades at the same time as you. And the hike to it is a winner.

The adventure starts with a bridged crossing of the Oconaluftee River. The waterway is formed just upstream of this bridge, where Kephart Prong—the stream along which we will be hiking—and Beech Flats Prong, draining the waters below Newfound Gap at the North Carolina–Tennessee state line, meet.

Kephart Prong was named for famous

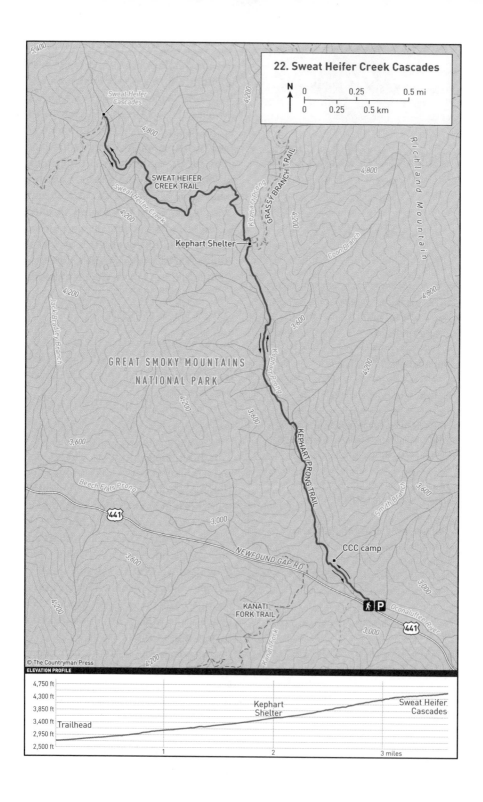

22. Sweat Heifer Creek Cascades

N

0   0.25   0.5 mi

0   0.25   0.5 km

Sweat Heifer
Cascades

5,400

4,200

4,800

SWEAT HEIFER
CREEK TRAIL

Sweat Heifer Creek

4,200

Kephart Prong

GRASSY BRANCH TRAIL

4,800

Richland Mountain

4,200

Kephart Shelter

Coon Branch

4,800

Jack Bradley Branch

4,200

GREAT SMOKY MOUNTAINS
NATIONAL PARK

Kephart Prong

3,600

4,200

3,600

4,200

3,600

Beech Flats Prong

441

3,000

NEWFOUND GAP RD

KEPHART PRONG TRAIL

Smith Branch

3,600

CCC camp

3,600

KANATI
FORK TRAIL

3,600

Kanati Fork

4,200

3,000

441

Oconaluftee River

3,000

© The Countryman Press

ELEVATION PROFILE

4,750 ft			
4,300 ft			Sweat Heifer
3,850 ft		Kephart	Cascades
3,400 ft		Shelter	
2,950 ft	Trailhead		
2,500 ft			
	1	2	3 miles

Smokies park advocate, naturalist, and all-around outdoorsman Horace Kephart whose book *Camping and Woodcraft* was one of the original classics covering outdoor skills. It is one of my all-time favorite tomes and contains several quotes still applicable since the century ago it came out, including one of my mottos: "In the school of the woods there is no graduation day."

The Kephart Prong Trail turns up its namesake stream, after crossing Smith Branch, soon reaching the site of a Civilian Conservation Corps Camp to your right at 0.3 mile. You can still see an old drinking fountain, rusted barrels, a concrete chimney, and more. User-created trails go to other parts of the camp that once housed men from 1933–1942 who built roads, trails, and a fish hatchery in this parcel of the park. Yellow birch, lots of maple, and rhododendron shade the sky.

The walking is easy on a wide, gently rising trail and you cross Kephart Prong on a signature Smoky Mountain log bridge at 0.4 mile. Look down on the translucent waterway flowing among mossy rocks. At 0.9 mile, cross over to the right-hand bank above, made attractive by modest cascades. Each crossing has an equestrian ford and hiker bridge with handrails that separate and come together. Bridge again over to the left bank at 1.0 mile. At 1.7 miles, bridge over to the right-hand bank near the confluence of Sweat Heifer Creek and Kephart Prong. The next time you will see Sweat Heifer Creek will be at Sweat Heifer Creek Cascades. By the way, the name

SECLUDED SWEAT HEIFER CASCADES CAN RUN LOW IN AUTUMN

A CHANNEL OF SWEAT HEIFER CASCADES

bunks, a fireplace, and a sitting area of sorts. A fire ring stands nearby. It is a great place to camp. Reservations and a fee are required, but as Horace Kephart put it, "There are no friendships like those that are made under canvas and in the open field."

We head left from the shelter, joining the Sweat Heifer Trail, bridging Kephart Prong again. You will leave any potential crowds behind at the shelter. Rise along and cross an unnamed stream rising through hardwoods dominated by cherry trees. Leave the water for a while, winding upward. Curve in and out of coves, then turn back into the Sweat Heifer Creek watershed at 2.7 miles. Ahead, the sounds of the stream will enter your ears ahead, as you pick up an old logging grade that makes the hiking easy. Look for bits of coal in the trailbed. Scan for other metal railroad relics.

At 3.7 miles, the trail curves to reach the top of 30-foot Sweat Heifer Creek Cascades, a Smokies highlight you can call your own. It flows over an irregular angular rock slab leaving it longer than tall. Sweat Heifer Creek has limited flow. Amusingly, the fabled waters of Icewater Springs Shelter on the Appalachian Trail contribute their aqua to unsung Sweat Heifer Creek. This cascade will be bold in winter and spring, but will slow to a trickle by autumn. It is what it is. As Horace Kephart himself wrote, "I love the wilderness because there are no shams in it."

is derived from pre-park mountaineers driving their cattle from the lower valleys to certain grassy ridges known as balds to graze them during the summer months, so the farmers could grow hay and other crops in the lowland fields.

Continue your uptick to make Kephart Shelter, just beyond the confluence with the Grassy Branch Trail. Here, a small sloped clearing houses the three-sided stone and wood refuge, with

23

Big Fork Ridge Loop

TOTAL DISTANCE: 9.2-mile loop

HIKING TIME: 5:00

VERTICAL RISE: 1,220 feet

RATING: Moderate–difficult, does have two distinct ascents

MAPS: National Geographic #229 Great Smoky Mountains National Park, USGS 7.5' Cove Creek Gap

TRAILHEAD GPS COORDINATES: N35°36'58.3", W83°07'15.0"

CONTACT INFORMATION: Great Smoky Mountains National Park, 107 Park Headquarters Road, Gatlinburg, TN 37738, (865) 436-1200, nps.gov/grsm

This hike in the Cataloochee area of the Smokies not only features impressive old-growth trees but also a historic homestead and other signs of prepark pioneers. The circuit also includes gorgeous highland waterways, two distinct climbs (and descents), and two recommended backcountry campsites that can turn this loop into an overnight extravaganza. It can also easily be done as a day hike. The circuit uses the Rough Fork Trail, climbing to 4,000 feet before dropping to Caldwell Fork, where you can see the Big Poplars. Onward, cruise once-settled Caldwell Fork. From here, ascend an old pioneer path over Big Fork Ridge then drop back to the trailhead.

GETTING THERE

From Exit #20 on I-40, head south a short distance on US 276. Turn right onto Cove Creek Road and follow it nearly 6 miles to enter the park. Two miles beyond the park boundary, turn left onto Cataloochee Road. Follow it 4.6 miles to dead end at the trailhead.

THE HIKE

Start on the Rough Fork Trail. This path deserves added appreciation when you consider that it was slated to become a park road. Back in the 1960s, Smokies personnel worried that Cataloochee Valley would become so popular that it would need an outlet beyond the current one-way-in, one-way-out setup. Alas, the road was never constructed—and never will be. Leave the wide western end of Cataloochee Valley on a double-track trail. The valley closes in, forcing bridged crossings of Rough Fork at 0.5 mile and 0.8 mile. Continue under a mantle of pines, hardwoods, and rhododendron, soon making a third crossing.

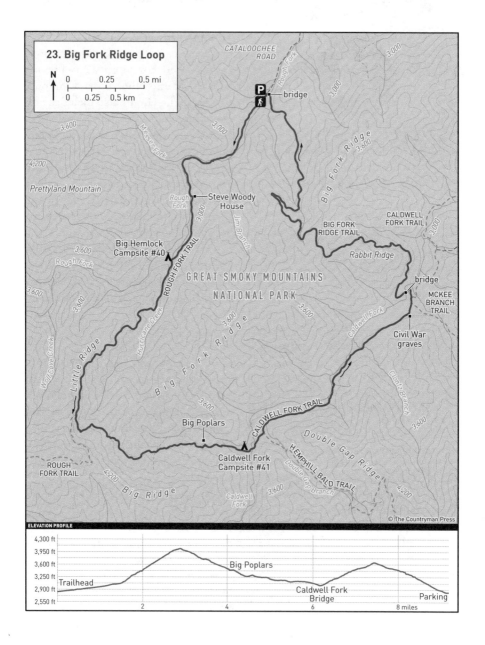

23. Big Fork Ridge Loop

Map labels:

CATALOOCHEE ROAD

bridge

N

0   0.25   0.5 mi
0   0.25   0.5 km

Mosser Fork

3,600

4,200

Prettyland Mountain

3,000

Rough Fork

Steve Woody House

Jim Branch

Big Fork Ridge

3,600

ROUGH FORK TRAIL

Big Hemlock Campsite #40

BIG FORK RIDGE TRAIL

CALDWELL FORK TRAIL

Rabbit Ridge

3,600

3,000

bridge

MCKEE BRANCH TRAIL

GREAT SMOKY MOUNTAINS NATIONAL PARK

Hurricane Creek

Little Ridge

Wolf Cove Creek

Caldwell Fork

Civil War graves

3,600

Big Fork Ridge

3,600

Clontz Branch

3,600

Big Poplars

CALDWELL FORK TRAIL

Double Gap Ridge

ROUGH FORK TRAIL

Caldwell Fork Campsite #41

HEMPHILL BALD TRAIL

Double Gap Branch

4,200

Big Ridge

4,200

Caldwell Fork

3,600

© The Countryman Press

ELEVATION PROFILE

4,300 ft
3,950 ft
3,600 ft
3,250 ft
2,900 ft
2,550 ft

Trailhead

Big Poplars

Caldwell Fork Bridge

Parking

2   4   6   8 miles

At 1.0 mile, emerge into a clearing and the Steve Woody Place. Take the time to examine the wood home of one of the Smokies' earliest tourist enclaves. If you look inside, note the varied heights of the ceiling, indicating that different parts of the structure were built at different times. After all, at one point, 14 children resided under that roof when Steve Woody's father, Jonathan Woody, wed a widow with her own children. Note the nearby springhouse.

In the 1920s, tourists made their way into Cataloochee Valley and Steve Woody acted as a guide of sorts, stocking Rough Fork with trout for them to catch, then charged by the fish as well as providing accommodations. Later, the Woodys were bought out along with everyone else in what became the park.

The Rough Fork Trail becomes more primitive, yet the hiking is still easy. Reach the spur right to Big Hemlock campsite, at 1.5 miles. The site is set beside Rough Fork in small clearings between wooded thickets. Now, the path begins a steady climb up Little Ridge. Look for some sizeable tulip, northern red oak, and chestnut oak trees before intersecting the Caldwell Fork Trail at 2.9 miles. Here, stay left with Caldwell Fork Trail, descending a single-track rhododendron-bordered path. Water noise drifts into your ears on the decline. At 4.1 miles, take the spur trail left to the Big Poplars. Actually they are tulip trees, which were once commonly known as poplars. One huge specimen stands out while others are nearby. After rejoining the Caldwell Fork Trail you will drift into

Caldwell Fork, a backcountry campsite, at 4.5 miles, set in a streamside flat along Caldwell Fork. I've enjoyed a few nights here and recommend it.

Cross the stream by bridge and resume easy hiking through formerly cultivated land, as the Hemphill Bald Trail leaves right at 4.7 miles. Keep down the yellow birch– and Carolina silverbell–rich valley of crystalline Caldwell Fork, crossing Double Gap Branch flowing from the highlands above. The valley has widened considerably by the time you cross Clontz Branch at 5.7 miles. From here down, Caldwell Fork was once heavily settled. At 6.0 miles, a spur leads right to the location where three Union soldiers are buried. At 6.1 miles, the McKee Branch Trail leaves right for Cataloochee Divide while we go a bit farther to head left on the Big Fork Ridge Trail, spanning Caldwell Fork on a high trail bridge.

After bridging Caldwell Fork, reach a thickly wooded flat where Caldwell Fork

BACKPACKER STANDS ON THE PORCH OF THE PRESERVED STEVE WOODY PLACE

THIS ELK WAS SPOTTED AT THE THIS HIKE'S TRAILHEAD

School once stood. It is hard to picture the school now, plainly shown on the 1934 topographic map of the Smokies. From here you gradually climb, circling around Rabbit Ridge to make a gap on Big Fork Ridge at 7.4 miles. Ease your way downhill through rich coves on a fine path.

Ahead you will pass along the site of elk acclimation pens. Elk were reintroduced into Great Smoky Mountains National Park in 2001, brought in from Land Between The Lakes National Recreation Area, astride the Tennessee–Kentucky border hundreds of miles from here. Elk were once common in the Smokies. There is even an area on the Tennessee side of the park known as Elkmont. But these large and majestic ungulates were extirpated from the Smokies due to unregulated hunting and loss of habitat. In past years, elk have also been reintroduced into eastern Kentucky and the Cumberland Mountains of East Tennessee. These, along with ones from the successful Smoky Mountain reintroduction project, have been a resounding success. The park had a second reintroduction of elk, brought from Canada, in 2002. Today, the ungulates are closely watched, and the estimated 200 animals have mostly stayed in the southeastern area of the park but do occasionally stray into neighboring areas. Note: willfully approaching within 50 yards (150 feet), or any distance that disturbs or displaces elk, is illegal in the park.

After wandering through the final cove, cross Rough Fork on a footbridge, emerging on the main road through Cataloochee. Here, turn left to walk the road briefly and reach the Rough Fork Trailhead, completing your hike at 9.2 miles.

24

Little Cataloochee Hike

TOTAL DISTANCE: 8.2-mile there-and-back

HIKING TIME: 4:40

VERTICAL RISE: 1,060 feet

RATING: Moderate–difficult

MAPS: National Geographic #229 Great Smoky Mountains National Park, USGS 7.5' Cove Creek Gap

TRAILHEAD GPS COORDINATES: N35°37'36.3", W83°06'45.3"

CONTACT INFORMATION: Great Smoky Mountains National Park, 107 Park Headquarters Road, Gatlinburg, TN 37738, (865) 436-1200, nps.gov/grsm

One of my favorite hikes in the Carolina Smokies, this history-based adventure offers a little bit of everything—historic structures, beautiful streams, wildlife viewing possibilities, and a little challenge. Start where the elk roam in Cataloochee Valley, taking the Pretty Hollow Gap Trail along scenic Palmer Creek before turning up Davidson Branch on lesser-trod Little Cataloochee Trail. Ascend to a gap, then drop to find the preserved Cook Cabin before delving further into Little Cataloochee Valley to reach pastoral Little Cataloochee Church, open to view both inside and out.

GETTING THERE

From Exit #20 on I-40, head south a short distance on US 276. Turn right onto Cove Creek Road and follow it nearly 6 miles to enter the park. Two miles beyond the park boundary, turn left onto Cataloochee Road. Follow it to 3.7 miles to the trailhead parking on your right, a little beyond the Palmer Chapel on your left and at the gate leading right to Cataloochee Horse Camp.

THE HIKE

Cataloochee is a wonderful area of the park. Allow time to explore the valley's historical structures and spot some elk, perhaps picnicking or camping before embarking on this rewarding hike. The best time for this adventure is when the leaves are off the trees, allowing you to better see homesites and relics of when this area was settled, though any time of year is rewarding. Start by walking around a pole gate and following the double-track Pretty Hollow Gap Trail. This section is used by equestrians to seasonally access Cataloochee Horse

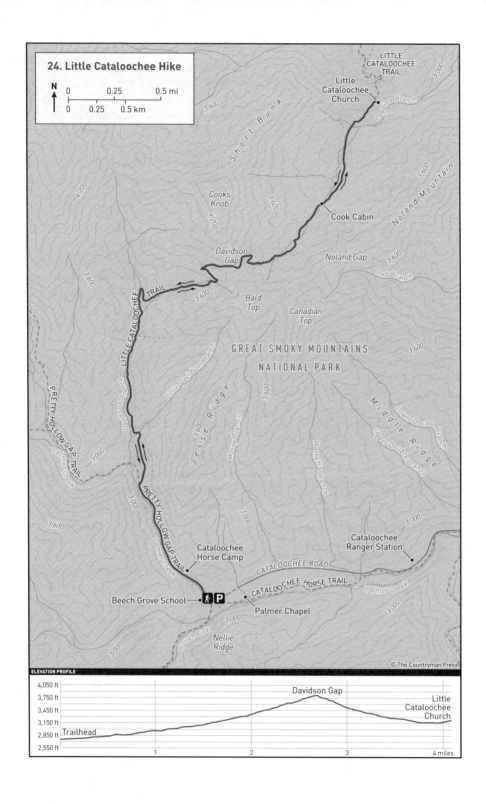

24. Little Cataloochee Hike

N

0   0.25   0.5 mi
0   0.25   0.5 km

LITTLE CATALOOCHEE TRAIL

Little Cataloochee Church

Short Bunk

Cook Cabin

Noland Mountain

Cooks Knob

Davidson Gap

Noland Gap

Hall Branch

LITTLE CATALOOCHEE TRAIL

Bald Top

Canadian Top

GREAT SMOKY MOUNTAINS

NATIONAL PARK

PRETTY HOLLOW GAP TRAIL

Davidson Branch

Little Davidson Branch

Jesse Ridge

Massey Branch

Mathews Branch

Middle Ridge

Lower Double Branch

Upper Double Branch

Palmer Creek

Palmer Creek

Cataloochee Horse Camp

Cataloochee Ranger Station

Beech Grove School

Palmer Chapel

CATALOOCHEE ROAD

CATALOOCHEE HORSE TRAIL

Palmer Creek

Rough Fork

Nellie Ridge

© The Countryman Press

ELEVATION PROFILE

4,050 ft
3,750 ft
3,450 ft
3,150 ft
2,850 ft
2,550 ft

Davidson Gap

Little Cataloochee Church

Trailhead

1   2   3   4 miles

Camp at 0.2 mile. After this, leave any vehicle traffic behind as you walk up the still-wide trail parallel to Palmer Creek, a classic, clear Smoky Mountain waterway, teeming with trout and aquatic life, shaded by black birch, yellow birch, rhododendron, moss, and ferns.

At 0.8 mile, head right on the more primitive Little Cataloochee Trail. It turns up Davidson Branch. Ahead, cross Little Davidson Branch and the hollow narrows. The path becomes very rocky, and in places you are heading directly up braids of Davidson Branch. Cross over to the left bank of the stream at 1.7 miles, rising all the while. At 1.9 miles, the trail curves right in a cove. Step over what's left of Davidson Branch, then climb easterly along a lesser stream in a wide cove full of hardwoods. At 2.4 miles, look for rock walls of an old homestead left of the trail. The stream gives way before reaching Davidson Gap, 3,804 feet, at 2.8 miles. Switchback downhill, reaching the headwaters of Coggins Branch, the stream

along which the community of Little Cataloochee was centered. Look for rock walls, broken glass and metal artifacts, relics of a time when this was a backwater, passed by and left behind as American expansion kept its westward push beyond the Appalachians. This area was settled in the 1850s, when Cataloochee got a little too crowded for some folk.

At 3.5 miles, come to the Cook Cabin, originally the home of Dan and Harriet Cook. Dan survived service in the Civil War and came back to father 11 children. Constructed in 1856, the cabin stood here after the park came to be and was finally dismantled in the 1970s after repeated vandalism. The cabin was restored in 1999 and has graced this piece of paradise ever since. It received a second restoration in 2017. Today the historic structure is in fine shape. The home is bordered with a wraparound porch and has a stone fireplace. The roof is wooden shingles. You can walk inside then ascend a short set of stairs to the small second

LITTLE CATALOOCHEE CHURCH ON ITS HILLTOP PERCH

PULPIT'S EYE VIEW OF LITTLE CATALOOCHEE CHURCH

floor. Across Coggins Branch, look for the stone foundation of the Cook's apple barn. Apple growing was an agricultural mainstay in Little Cataloochee and the red fruits were stored here. Sometimes it's hard to imagine agriculture in places like this, given that forest has covered what once were fields.

When the park came to be, the plan was to return even the settled areas of Cataloochee to forest primeval. Many structures were burned, but later the policy was rethought and some buildings were saved for posterity, including this one. And now, continue down the Coggins Branch valley toward the finest structure of them all—Little Cataloochee Church. Along the way you'll see more relics of the past, from fence posts to former fields to metal washtubs. Leave any treasures for other hikers to discover.

At 4.1 miles, come to Little Cataloochee Church, set on a knoll above the trail. The white wooden structure is known for its 400-pound bell situated in the belfry. And you can ring it today, just as they did in the old days,

for church on Sunday and when someone passed away, ringing it one time for every year the deceased person lived. Step inside. White benches face the pulpit. A wood-burning stove centers the structure. Outside a well-kept cemetery inters those who resided in the gorgeous slice of the Carolina mountains.

Originally known as Ola Baptist Church when it was constructed in 1889 (the Little Cataloochee community was named Ola), the bell-holding belfry was added in 1914. During the community's heyday, the church was served by a circuit-riding pastor who served monthly, rotating with other country churches. Gatherings were still held weekly, with Scripture reading and music led by members. Weddings and funerals were also held at hilltop Little Cataloochee Church. Even to this day, services are conducted annually as descendants of former residents gather to worship and hold a reunion. After respectfully touring the locale, give yourself enough time to make the 4.1-mile backtrack.

25

Mount Sterling

TOTAL DISTANCE: 5.4-mile there-and-back

HIKING TIME: 2:45

VERTICAL RISE: 1,940 feet

RATING: Moderate, does have extended climb

MAPS: National Geographic #229 Great Smoky Mountains National Park, USGS 7.5' Waterville NC–TN

TRAILHEAD GPS COORDINATES: N35°42'00.8", W83°05'51.0"

CONTACT INFORMATION: Great Smoky Mountains National Park, 107 Park Headquarters Road, Gatlinburg, TN 37738, (865) 436-1200, nps.gov/grsm

Mount Sterling is a Smoky Mountains icon, a must-visit destination, featuring a fire tower with 360-degree views from the park's eastern end, as well as a backcountry campsite ensconced in the spruce-fir evergreen forests that cloak the highest mantles of the Southern Appalachians. Make your climb to the tower from historic Mount Sterling Gap, winding up the east slope of Mount Sterling Ridge. Enter the high country and climb the Mount Sterling tower, perched at a 5,842-foot elevation.

GETTING THERE

From Exit #451 on I-40, in Tennessee just west of the North Carolina state line, exit under the interstate to bridge the Pigeon River on Waterville Road. After the bridge, turn left to follow the Pigeon River upstream. Come to an intersection with Mount Sterling Road 2.3 miles after crossing the Pigeon River. Turn left on Mount Sterling Road and follow it for 6.1 miles to the trailhead on your right. Parking is limited, so please be considerate.

THE HIKE

If you are coming to hike Mount Sterling, try to do so on a clear day. Also be apprised that in winter the access road, Mount Sterling Road, can be hazardous or even closed. A well-timed hike here will be rewarded with views that are more than worth the climb, for the metal fire tower atop Mount Sterling delivers extraordinary 360-degree views not only of the Smokies but of the mountains to the east and south as well as northeast into East Tennessee and the state line ridge dividing North Carolina from the Volunteer State.

The tower was constructed in

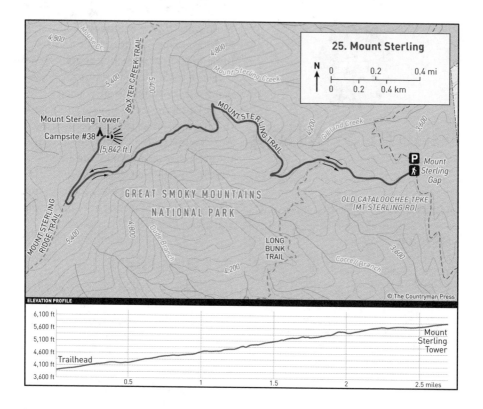

1935 as part of Civilian Conservation Corps efforts to develop and protect what became Great Smoky Mountains National Park on June 15, 1934. The metal tower rises 60 feet above the landscape, above the trees, purportedly the highest elevation metal fire tower standing east of the Mississippi River.

Interestingly Mount Sterling was named for a streak of shiny metal locals found on the lower end of the mountain, thinking it was silver. Alas, the metal turned out to be lead. Nevertheless the name stuck. The winding Mount Sterling Road used to access the trailhead was once the main route between this part of North Carolina and Tennessee, and obviously much more primitive than today, passing through Mount Sterling Gap. During the Civil War the road and gap were scenes of depredations Union

and Confederate irregulars exercised on one another as well as local citizenry. During that time was hard to figure out who was on your side and who wasn't, here in the backwoods of Carolina.

The trail we use was built when the fire tower was constructed, and has been maintained for jeeps to access radio towers after fire towers were no longer staffed by fire spotters living on site. Transmission towers are still in use to this day on Mount Sterling, though the lines between them and lands below have since been removed. Formerly the trail up to Mount Sterling passed under one of these lines. The line cut in the woods is growing over season by season.

We leave Mount Sterling Gap, passing around a pole gate to ascend a wide track wasting no time in gaining elevation. Despite the moderate rating of the hike—and it is relatively short—the trail is also going steadily up, therefore some hikers may take issue with the moderate rating. Pines, buckeye, maple, and Carolina silverbell shade the track. Look for a big oak tree on the right side of the trail at 0.2 mile.

At 0.5 mile, the trail levels off in a gap. Here, the Long Bunk Trail leaves left for Little Cataloochee while we stay straight with the Mount Sterling Trail. At 0.8 mile, the trail makes a big switchback to the right, continuing its measured ascent. Even though we are over 4,000 high at this point, the southern exposure of the trail harbors typically lower elevation species such as mountain laurel, galax, and chestnut oaks, as well as young chestnut trees that haven't succumbed to the chestnut blight that decimated chestnut trees last century. Even today, chestnuts rise from the roots of the old trees only to once again succumb to chestnut blight when they get older.

At 1.1 miles, keep rising. You'll notice the first red spruce trees finding their way into the forest. Continuing uphill, the evergreens become common and are joined by the Fraser fir a little higher in elevation. Typical hardwoods found in this area can't compete with these cold weather–thriving evergreens that have to withstand not only the chill but also harsh winds and heavy snows—and a long winter.

At 2.4 miles, top out on Mount Sterling Ridge. Here, the Mount Sterling Ridge Trail leaves left, but we turn right, gently heading northeast toward

LOOKING DOWN ONTO THE CAMPSITE SITUATED ATOP MOUNT STERLING

THE VIEW FROM MOUNT STERLING'S TOWER EXTENDS AS FAR AS THE SKY'S CLARITY ALLOWS

the apex of Mount Sterling. Pass a horse hitching post, then at 2.7 miles reach Mount Sterling, campsite 38, situated below the tower. Other camping nodes are located among the mountaintop thickets.

Now it is time to climb the tower. The tower steps take you above the tree line and to the views. Immediately below, the cleared spots of the camping area stand out. Looking toward the horizon, tall evergreens rise above the hardwoods but not enough to obstruct your view. The state line ridge rises to fashion a formidable wall of wild national park land. To the east you can scan across the Pigeon River valley toward the Newfound Mountains. Look for the low squat tower at Mount Cammerer to the north. All in all, it's an American national park–level experience, panoramas included.

Mouse Creek Falls and the Midnight Hole

TOTAL DISTANCE: 4.0-mile there-and-back	

HIKING TIME: 2:00

VERTICAL RISE: 548 feet

RATING: Easy

MAPS: National Geographic #229 Great Smoky Mountains National Park, USGS 7.5' Luftee Knob

TRAILHEAD GPS COORDINATES: N35°45'05.9", W83°06'34.9"

CONTACT INFORMATION: Great Smoky Mountains National Park, 107 Park Headquarters Road, Gatlinburg, TN 37738, (865) 436-1200, nps.gov/grsm

This hike explores one of the loveliest streams in the Carolina Smokies, and that is saying a lot. Big Creek is a mountain-bred crashing waterway, slowing in deep pools astride huge boulders, complemented by an everywhere-you-look beauty expected within the bounds of Great Smoky Mountains National Park. The hike is easy, tracing a wide old track on a gentle uptick. You will first come to the Midnight Hole, a deep indigo pool framed in huge grey stones, a popular summertime swimming spot. The final destination is 45-foot Mouse Creek Falls, a tributary stream spilling white into Big Creek.

GETTING THERE

From Exit #451 on I-40, in Tennessee just west of the North Carolina state line, exit under the interstate to bridge the Pigeon River on Waterville Road. After the bridge, turn left to follow the Pigeon River upstream, reentering North Carolina. Come to an intersection with Mount Sterling Road 2.3 miles after crossing the Pigeon River. Proceed straight through the intersection and enter the park soon thereafter. Follow the road along Big Creek, passing a ranger station and parking on your right and the Big Creek Horse Camp on your left before reaching the large Big Creek parking area on your left, 0.9 mile beyond the intersection with Mount Sterling Road.

THE HIKE

The recuperative powers of nature are truly remarkable. The Big Creek watershed of the Smokies demonstrates that. This remote and rugged area, logged mercilessly in the early 1900s, was once barren but has now reforested to

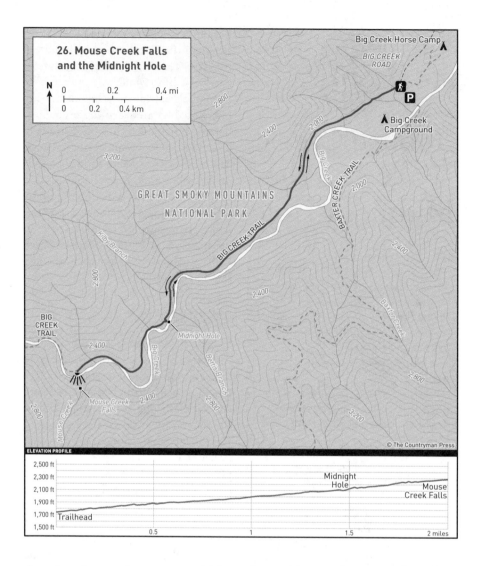

26. Mouse Creek Falls
and the Midnight Hole

the point where, unless you are a biologist specializing in the Southern Appalachians, you would never suspect its history.

Lower Big Creek was lightly populated before Crestmont Logging Company established a timber operation in the flats below the point where this hike starts. A logging railroad was constructed up Big Creek (and is the basic route we follow on this trek). The valley was cut over as World War I spurred the demand for wood. For anywhere from 65 cents to a dollar a day, loggers risked their lives from dusk until dawn, living in shacks that could be moved by rail or even sleeping in rail cars themselves. A company store was located nearby, perhaps in a rail car, where employees could get goods on credit. Dances were organized on Saturday nights. Sunday, the day of rest, was centered on Christian worship, often in the same building that had been the dance hall the night before.

Later, these logged lands became part of the Smokies park. In the 1930s, the Civilian Conservation Corps transformed the logging operation to a national park—constructing trails, roads, and campsites as well as the Big Creek ranger station. For a period, the Big Creek Trail was a road used by visitors driving to Walnut Bottoms, 5 miles upstream, as a hiking, picnicking, and camping base.

Nowadays, the old road is a trail for hikers and equestrians, including us. From the Big Creek parking area, walk back up the road you came a short distance to reach the signed Big Creek Trail. Join the double-track path, shaded by beech, sugar maple, and tulip trees, on the right-hand side of the Big Creek. At 0.2 mile, a narrow spur trail drops sharply left to Big Creek Campground. We stay straight on the wide old railroad grade, passing blasted bluffs that made way for the logging locomotives of yesteryear. The grade is gentle and you are well above the waterway. Large boulders are strewn in the woods above and below as well as in the creek. At 1.3 miles, the Big Creek Trail comes directly alongside its namesake, allowing good looks at the translucent waterway using gravity to find downstream routes among the boulders as only water can do.

The Midnight Hole is not far ahead and you reach it at 1.5 miles. Here, a short track drops down a hill to the sizeable pool spreading forth below a bastion of stone. The chilly pool's depth are an inky blue, giving the pool its name—Midnight Hole—and lightening

MOUSE CREEK FALLS AND BIG CREEK FLOW THROUGH A RICH FOREST

FACE ON VIEW OF MOUSE CREEK FALLS AS IT EMPTIES INTO BIG CREEK

BOULDER BORDERED MIDNIGHT HOLE IS A COOL, CLEAR SWIMMING DESTINATION

as the waters become shallow, exposing gray gravel and lesser tan stones. It is a popular swimming spot when the July heat and humidity roll into the Smokies. In other seasons, the pool is plied only by trout, rising to the surface to feed on insects.

Up the trail, you'll cross small streams flowing from Cammerer Ridge rising high to your right. Doghobble and rhododendron crowd the forest floor. At 1.9 miles, the trail squeezes between a rock bluff to your right and Big Creek to your left.

At 2.0 miles, spot a horse-hitching rack to your left. Walk this way and find Mouse Creek Falls making its reckless plunge across Big Creek. Mouse Creek pops out from the mountainside vegetation as an angled cascade and then gets squeezed in by stone channels before widening to slow in a pool. Here, the creek gathers energy then makes its second stage drop, cascading directly into Big Creek, itself a rushing froth through a boulder garden. These boulders make for ideal contemplation spots. As you look around, it is hard to imagine this watershed was once logged; it has recovered to be a shining jewel of the Smokies and the Carolina mountains.

III.

NORTHEAST NORTH CAROLINA MOUNTAINS

27

Max Patch

TOTAL DISTANCE: 1.5-mile loop	

HIKING TIME: 1:00

VERTICAL RISE: 420 feet

RATING: Easy

MAPS: National Geographic #782 French Broad & Nolichucky Rivers, Cherokee and Pisgah National Forests, USGS 7.5' Lemon Gap TN NC

TRAILHEAD GPS COORDINATES: N35°47'47.6", W82°57'45.1"

CONTACT INFORMATION: Pisgah National Forest, Appalachian Ranger District, 632 Manor Road, Mars Hill, NC 28754, (828) 689-9694, www.fs.usda.gov/nfsnc

Max Patch is one of those places in the Carolina mountains that enthralls me on each and every visit. Each season presents its own portrait of this mountaintop meadow, perched at 4,629 feet on the North Carolina–Tennessee state line. A short loop trail—using portions of the famed Appalachian Trail—leads you around and atop Max Patch and its incredible vistas, often called "the Grandstand of the Smokies" for its views into that special national park. This is a great place to take first-time mountain enthusiasts or less agile trail trekkers, for if the day is clear, your hiking guests are guaranteed to be impressed with Max Patch.

GETTING THERE

From exit 7, Harmon Den, on I-40 west of Asheville, take Cold Springs Creek Road, Forest Road 148, right for 6.3 miles to reach a "T" intersection. Turn left here on NC 1182, Max Patch Road. Follow it for 2.0 miles to the parking area on your right.

THE HIKE

The special characteristics of Max Patch continue to be recognized and appreciated as time goes on. The forest service is continuing to keep this bald open by mowing it and also limiting hiker access to preserve the fields that make it so special. To that end, they have closed the erosive trail that formerly went directly up the bald.

Today, the 300-plus acres of mountain meadow are a reservoir of beauty the Appalachian Trail travels through. Most of us stop for a short visit to Max Patch and just move on, unaware of the past history of this locale. Back in the early 1800s, Max Patch was used to

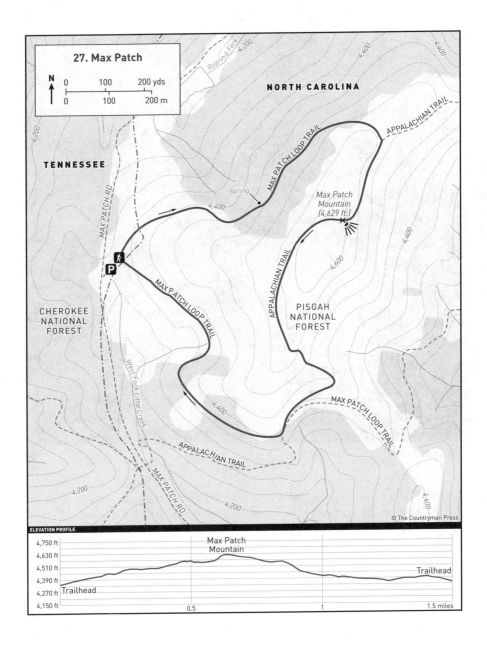

27. Max Patch

N
0   100   200 yds
0   100   200 m

NORTH CAROLINA

APPALACHIAN TRAIL

MAX PATCH LOOP TRAIL

TENNESSEE

MAX PATCH RD.

spring

Max Patch
Mountain
(4,629 ft.)

4,400

4,400

P

APPALACHIAN TRAIL

CHEROKEE
NATIONAL
FOREST

MAX PATCH LOOP TRAIL

PISGAH
NATIONAL
FOREST

West Fork Little Creek

4,400

MAX PATCH LOOP TRAIL

APPALACHIAN TRAIL

MAX PATCH RD.

4,200

4,200

© The Countryman Press

ELEVATION PROFILE

4,750 ft		Max Patch		
4,630 ft		Mountain		
4,510 ft				
4,390 ft				Trailhead
4,270 ft	Trailhead			
4,150 ft		0.5	1	1.5 miles

graze cattle and sheep, all land owned by farmers in the nearby lowlands. No one knows how long Max Patch was open field, for the origin of the Southern Appalachian balds is one of the unsolved mysteries of our time. But we do know that Max Patch's name was changed from its original name of Mac's Patch, the peak being named for a herder by the name of Mac, apparently one of the first to graze stock here, keeping the mountain open.

Later, those flying daredevils of the early days of the airplane decided to use Max Patch as an airstrip in order to claim they were landing at the highest

LOOKING INTO THE CAROLINA MOUNTAINS FROM MAX PATCH

"runway" in the East. Max Patch became such a success as an airfield that air shows were held here in the 1920s and '30s. Instead of being the grandstand of the Smokies, Max Patch was a grandstand of the flying aces.

Max Patch continued to draw visitors escaping city life, or fleeing the summer heat, or simply wishing to view autumn colors. Cabins were built to accommodate these travelers. In the early 1980s, a ski resort was almost built here. However, the Forest Service bought the land to preserve the mountain meadow as well as route the Appalachian Trail through this part of Highland Dixie, and Max Patch entered Carolina mountain hiker lore.

Interpretive signage stands in front of a fence blocking the old trail going directly up the bald, although thoughtless hikers still work around it. Our hike joins the signed Max Patch Loop Trail, following an old grassy roadbed on the side slope of the mountain. You won't have even gotten your legs warmed up before enjoying distant vistas into the state of Tennessee. The meadow is not entirely grass, however. Blackberry and blueberry bushes, along with scattered trees, populate the terrain. A quaint wooden fence borders the trail. At 0.2 mile, the Max Patch Loop Trail leaves the meadow and runs under a canopy of maple trees. If the day is bright, the forest will seem dark and dim compared with the open exposure of Max Patch.

The main field of Max Patch rises above. Ahead on your left, you will pass a spring, used by visitors and livestock as long as both have been coming to Max Patch. At 0.5 mile, the Max Patch Loop Trail leaves the trees and enters open fields again. Just ahead you will intersect the Appalachian Trail, that long-distance path stretching from Georgia to Maine, going directly over Max Patch in between. At this signed intersection, you are in wide open fields, and views explode in all directions. Our loop heads right on the AT, to the crest of Max Patch, marked by a USGS survey marker.

But looking for a metal stake in the ground won't compare with the views that extend in four cardinal directions. In the fore, meadows fall away, yielding to brush and trees below. To the east lies the Blue Ridge, waves of mountains as far as the eye can see. So much to explore! To the southwest stands the rampart that is Great Smoky Mountain National Park, shared by North Carolina and Tennessee. The two most visible peaks are Mount Cammerer with its low stone tower and Mount Sterling with its taller metal fire tower. Field glasses will help you spot them, along the eastern edge of the Smokies. Farther to the west roll the hills of East Tennessee.

From the top of Max Patch, continue the Appalachian Trail, southbound, descending through grasses and brush,

THE FIELDS OF MAX PATCH RISE AWASH WITH WILDFLOWERS IN SUMMER

CLOUDS, SKY AND CAROLINA MOUNTAINS FASHION A SIGHTLY SCENE

a carpet of green by summer and bent grasses of brown in winter. Here you descend the well-marked trail and can see the parking area down to your right. Come to a trail intersection at 1.1 miles. Here, pick up the Max Patch Loop Trail leaving right, as the AT continues descending and the other end of the Max Patch Loop Trail leaves left on an old roadbed. Cruise along the southwest slope of the mountain through berry bushes and young trees as well as grassy areas, returning to the trailhead at 1.5 miles, completing the view-laden adventure.

28

Lovers Leap

TOTAL DISTANCE: 4.1-mile loop

HIKING TIME: 2:00

VERTICAL RISE: 1,440 feet

RATING: Moderate

MAPS: National Geographic #782 French Broad & Nolichucky Rivers, Cherokee and Pisgah National Forests, USGS 7.5' Hots Springs NC TN

TRAILHEAD GPS COORDINATES: N35°53'22.2", W82°48'43.7"

CONTACT INFORMATION: Pisgah National Forest, Appalachian Ranger District, 632 Manor Road, Mars Hill, NC 28754, (828) 689-9694, www.fs.usda.gov/nfsnc

This fun hike next to the cool mountain town of Hot Springs combines the fabled Appalachian Trail with trails emanating from Silver Mine Creek. Your rewards include fantastic views from outcrops protruding above the French Broad River as it cuts through the Appalachians. The trek begins with a trip up narrow and wooded Silver Mine Creek hollow. Make your way up to Pump Gap, meeting the world's most famous path— the Appalachian Trail. Take the AT southbound, rolling along Lovers Leap Ridge to reach outcrops and views, one of which is *the* Lovers Leap. Here, gaze down on the French Broad River, Hot Springs, and the valley beyond before looping back to the trailhead.

GETTING THERE

From Asheville, take I-26 West to exit 19A, Marshall. Join US 25/US 70 21 miles to Hot Springs. Just before crossing the bridge over the French Broad River, just east of Hot Springs, turn right on River Road. Drive a very short distance to the river and turn left on a paved road, Silver Mine Creek Road, following it under the US 25/US 70 bridge. Stay left again as it curves up Silver Mine Creek past houses. Reach the signed Silver Mine parking area on your left, 0.3 mile from US 25/US 70.

THE HIKE

Because the trailhead is literally within walking distance of the town of Hot Springs, make sure to add a trip to this official Appalachian Trail trail town to your hike. Explore the shops, grab a bite to eat and ease those aching hiker muscles with a visit to the thermal springs that gave this Carolina town a name. Before white settlers ever set foot in

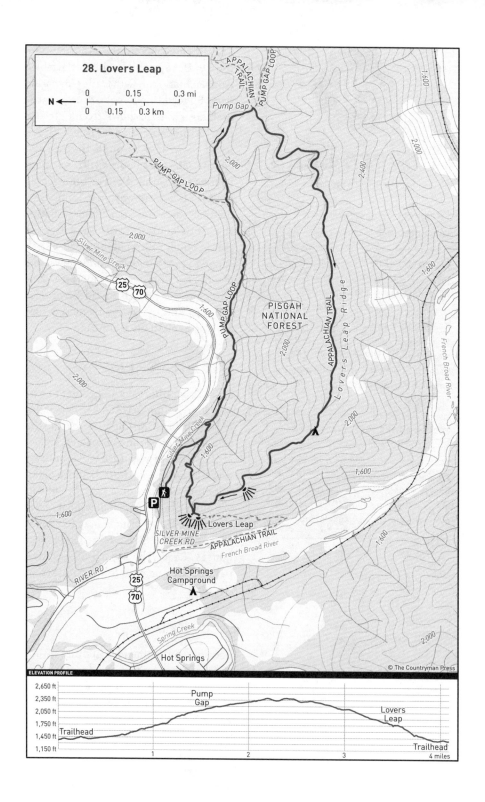

28. Lovers Leap

N ←

| 0 | | 0.15 | | 0.3 mi |
| 0 | 0.15 | | 0.3 km | |

Appalachian Trail

Pump Gap Loop

Pump Gap

2,000

1,600

Silver Mine Creek

25
70

PUMP GAP LOOP

1,600

PISGAH
NATIONAL
FOREST

2,000

2,400

2,000

Lovers Leap Ridge

APPALACHIAN TRAIL

French Broad River

1,600

Silver Mine Creek

1,600

2,000

P

1,600

Lovers Leap

SILVER MINE
CREEK RD

APPALACHIAN TRAIL

French Broad River

1,600

RIVER RD

25
70

Hot Springs
Campground

Spring Creek

Hot Springs

2,000

© The Countryman Press

ELEVATION PROFILE

2,650 ft		
2,350 ft	Pump Gap	
2,050 ft		Lovers
1,750 ft		Leap
1,450 ft	Trailhead	
1,150 ft		Trailhead

1   2   3   4 miles

these parts, the Cherokee soaked in the toasty waters on the banks of the French Broad River. Whether or not the Cherokee believed the 100 degree springs could heal more than aching muscles, the whites who came after them sure did. It started when a man named William Nelson established a "resort" at the springs, the first of a nearly continuous string of operations servicing visitors. In the 1820s, the Buncombe Turnpike crossed the French Broad River here, bringing more visitors, and in 1831 James Patten established a large hotel, luring in visitors, many of whom believed springs such as this, located throughout the South, had healing properties. The popularity of "healing springs" declined after modern medicine evolved, and by 1918, the springs hotel at that time housed German prisoners of war instead of tourists. That hotel burned.

These days, Carolina mountain towns are enjoying a boom for visitors engaging in recreation in the mountains and escaping summer's heat. The Appalachian Trail going through the town has only enhanced the town of Hot Springs' popularity. So has the French Broad River; paddling and rafting has added another outdoor possibility.

We love to hike, but we also don't mind floating rivers, camping, and hanging out in outdoor towns to enhance an already fine hike. Additionally, despite being a mountain hike, the trek stays under 2,400 feet, making it a desirable cool-to-cold weather mountain hiking destination.

HIKING ALONG SILVERMINE CREEK

Start your hike at the parking area for the former Silver Mine Group Camp, joining the single-track Pump Gap Loop Trail. The path traverses the right side of Silver Mine Hollow on a steep slope among white pines, black birch, and rhododendron. Moss covers anything that doesn't move in the stony vale. Quickly drop back along Silver Mine Creek to reach a trail intersection at 0.2 mile. Stay left with the Pump Gap Loop, beginning the loop portion of the trek. Surprisingly, descend to an old road, passing a pair of long-disused concrete dynamite shacks. At 0.4 mile, resume the single-track trail, squeezing past creekside boulders. Strangely, the path climbs over an old roadbed as Silver Mine Creek flows through a culvert. Return to the water upstream and step over the creek and climb among ultra-thick vegetation. At times the trail and stream are one. Continue up the hollow, with Silver Mine Creek singing you along. At 1.1 miles, an arm of the Pump Gap Loop Trail leaves left. That spur circles back to Pump Gap, and you can use it to lengthen your hike if desired. Our hike keeps straight on a lung-testing ascent under towering hardwoods rising above rhododendron tangles. Step over a tributary of Silver Mine Creek. Come to Pump Gap and the Appalachian Trail at 1.5 miles. Notice the treated hemlocks still thriving here.

Turn right on the AT, southbound, now on Lovers Leap Ridge. Roll along the ridge. The hiking is easy. At 2.2 miles, gain the crest of Lovers Leap Ridge under mountain laurel, black gum, pine and chestnut oak. River noise from the French Broad River rises to the ridge. You will also hear town

LOOKING DOWN ON HOT SPRINGS AND THE FRENCH BROAD RIVER

LOVERS LEAP RIDGE RISES LEFT FROM THE STORM-MUDDIED FRENCH BROAD RIVER

sounds from nearby Hot Springs, visible through gaps in the woods. At 2.4 miles, dip to a gap, then edge over to the rocky and piney river side of the ridge. At 2.8 miles, reach a large campsite on your left, descending. At 3.2 miles, a well-worn trail leaves left to a slender spine-like outcrop. Those who dare will walk the narrow stone out to view the river, mountains and town beyond.

After your daring view, resume the AT, still descending. At 3.5 miles, come to a signed trail junction. Your return route, the Lovers Leap Trail, leaves right. Before closing the loop, follow the AT to two overlooks, the first very near the intersection—it delivers a solid river view, while the second, a little ways on the AT, leads to Lovers Leap, an open outcrop. Legend has it the daughter of the leader of an American Indian tribe dove from the rock, perishing after she found out her true love was killed by a rival suitor. Thus, neither lover could have the woman.

Now join the gravel-strewn Lovers Leap Trail, making a sharp switchback to the left at 3.9 miles. Work your way down the declivitous slope of Silver Mine Hollow. Return to the junction with the Pump Gap Loop. Drop left, backtracking to the trailhead at 4.1 miles, completing the hike. Now it is time to visit Hot Springs!

Big Firescald Knob

TOTAL DISTANCE: 10.8-mile loop	

HIKING TIME: 5:30

VERTICAL RISE: 2,380 feet

RATING: Difficult due to distance and elevation gain

MAPS: National Geographic #782 French Broad & Nolichucky Rivers, Cherokee and Pisgah National Forests, USGS 7.5' Greystone NC TN

TRAILHEAD GPS COORDINATES: N36°01'24.1", W82°39'09.0"

CONTACT INFORMATION: Pisgah National Forest, Appalachian Ranger District, 632 Manor Road, Mars Hill, NC 28754, (828) 689-9694, www.fs.usda.gov/nfsnc

This unsung hike is a rolling highlight reel. Set in a remote area of the Pisgah National Forest, the trip first takes you through a wildflower-laden hollow then up Whiteoak Flats Branch, passing a 100-foot cascade. Open onto an old homesite before climbing a well-graded track to meet the Appalachian Trail. From there, walk a stony, knife-edge ridgeline where distant panoramas open in all directions. Stop at an Appalachian Trail shelter before resuming the adventure, descending a very steep side trail to close the loop. The hike, great for backpacking, does gain over 3,000 feet, but the trails are in good shape.

GETTING THERE

From Asheville, take I-26 West to exit 19A, Marshall. Then follow US 25/70 for 21 miles to turn right on NC 208 West and follow it for 3.4 to NC 212. Turn right on NC 212 East and follow it for 10.9 miles to turn left on Big Creek Road, at the Carmen Church of God. Follow Big Creek Road for 1.2 miles. The road seems to end near a barn. Here, angle left onto Forest Road 111, taking the gravel road over a small creek via auto ford. Enter the national forest. At 0.4 mile beyond the barn, veer left onto a short spur road to dead end at Jerry Miller trailhead. You will see a plaque honoring Jerry Miller at the trailhead, as well as a signboard.

THE HIKE

This hike not only has highlights of its own, but you can add a couple more with side trips to Baxter Cliff and White Cliffs. The loop also contains campsites and an Appalachian Trail shelter, making overnight adventures a breeze. However, if you are going to do it as a day

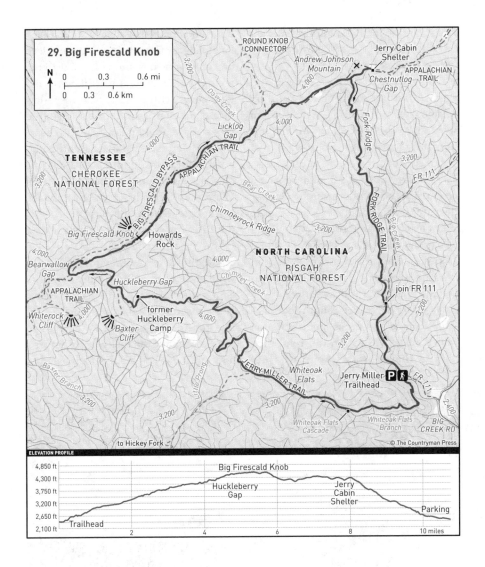

29. Big Firescald Knob

ELEVATION PROFILE

hike, give yourself all day to be able to execute the loop and enjoy the experience along the way.

Leave the Jerry Miller trailhead, immediately crossing Big Creek on a trail bridge, beside which is a memorial to Jerry Miller, a lawyer who fought for more law enforcement in our national forests. His kinfolk, the Sheltons, have property abutting this path. The Jerry Miller Trail cruises through a flat and over a hill where white trilliums bloom

by the thousands in spring. It is an astonishing sight!

Turn upstream into the Whiteoak Flats Branch watershed, a steep richly wooded hollow the raucous mountain stream crashes through. At 0.9 mile, as Whiteoak Flats Branch and the trail finally come together, you'll hear then see Whiteoak Flats Cascade, a 100-foot tongue of whitewater sliding down a stone slab, flanked by heavy vegetation. Despite its length and opulence, no beaten trail to it exists, but the cataract isn't difficult to photograph if you are willing to work for it.

Continue ascending a narrowing hollow, bridging a now gently gurgling Whiteoak Flats Branch at 1.2 miles. Soon open onto Whiteoak Flats, where a former wide clearing is now growing over in pines, locust trees, and tulip trees. Reenter the woods at 1.6 miles, passing a campsite, then work through an upper clearing, also closing. Here, trail blazes follow an old logging road right (the old road going left leads to Hickey Fork and its trails). Gently but steadily, ascend from the Whiteoak Flats Valley, making switchbacks at 2.2 and 2.5 miles.

At 3.0 miles, travel under rhododendron tunnels and cross small streams ahead. At 3.7 miles, an old road dips right to Huckleberry Camp, a former hunting camp. Rise a bit more to reach Huckleberry Gap at 4.1 miles, a modern day campsite and jump off point to the winding spur to Baxter Cliff, with limited views. Climb still, now in yellow birch and evergreen thickets, rising to meet the Appalachian Trail in Bearwallow Gap at 4.6 miles. Head right, northbound, straddling the NC–TN line (If you want to get a good view from Whiterock Cliffs, head south on the AT to a spur leading to the lookout). Ahead, the Big Firescald Bypass heads left, to follow an easier, less scenic track. We stay right with the official AT and soon wind onto the exposed, upturned, knife-edge ridge bordered with growth of low heath that opens views into North Carolina and Tennessee as far as the eye can see. Steps make the rocky, irregular trail less arduous. The ridge was burned to

AUTHOR TREKS THE AT OVER ROCKY BIG FIRESCALD KNOB

bedrock at one time, exposing the stone. Limited post-fire vegetation has left this segment rocky to the extreme but with superlatively scenic vistas.

At 5.4 miles, signed Howards Rock delivers open panoramas that rival anywhere on the entire Appalachian Trail. At 5.6 miles, a newer spur leads left to the Big Firescald Bypass, for those who have had enough of the slow, stony, but scenic track. More views open before you descend into full woods and meet the bypass at 6.2 miles. Continue on the AT, which seems a piece of cake after the rugged trail over Big Firescald Knob. Drop to Licklog Gap and a campsite at 6.6 miles. Water is well down the ridge, though.

The walking is easy as you pass the Round Knob Connector, leading into Tennessee, at 6.9 miles. Roll on the state line ridge under hardwoods, staying above 4,000 feet in elevation. At 7.7 miles, meet the Fork Ridge Trail. This will be your route later, but for now keep northbound on the AT, still dropping to reach Jerry Cabin trail shelter at 7.8 miles. These havens are stretched along the entire Appalachian Trail from Georgia to Maine. A small clearing stands in front of the shelter, in North Carolina, and a spring is easily accessed on the Tennessee side of the ridge. Level campsites are located about 50 yards distant in Chestnutlog Gap. Even if you aren't backpacking the shelter site is worth checking out and taking a break.

After backtracking 0.2 mile from Jerry Cabin shelter, head left, south, on the Fork Ridge Trail. The path is notorious for its steep sections. Luckily our hike takes it downhill. Woe to the hiker climbing Fork Ridge . . . the first mile

LOOKING TOWARD BIG BUTT FROM BIG FIRESCALD KNOB

drops 1,000 feet! You'll find the trail in good shape as it descends through evergreen arbors and among hardwoods. At 9.0 miles, the path hits a gap and even goes up, just to throw you off guard. The descent from here is more gradual, and eventually you'll hear Chimney Creek resounding through the valley.

The Fork Ridge Trail pops out on a parking area along Forest Road 111 at 10.0 miles. Ramble down the valley to ford Wildcat Hollow Creek, then the road fords Chimney Creek at 10.4 miles. Meet the Jerry Miller Trailhead access road at 10.8 miles, walk a few feet to the parking area, then complete your adventurous hike.

30

Mount Mitchell Hike

TOTAL DISTANCE: 5.6-mile loop

HIKING TIME: 2:20

VERTICAL RISE: 912 feet

RATING: Moderate

MAPS: Mount Mitchell State Park, USGS 7.5' Mount Mitchell NC

TRAILHEAD GPS COORDINATES: N35°45'08.0", W82°16'26.0"

CONTACT INFORMATION: Mount Mitchell State Park, 2388 N.C. 128, Burnsville, NC 28714, 828-675-4611, www.ncparks.gov/mount-mitchell-state-park

This hike explores North Carolina's highest state park, heading to the highest point east of the Mississippi. Start at 6,200 feet at Stepps Gap, then trek the crest of the Black Mountains under uncommon spruce-fir forests. Make your way to 6,684-foot Mount Mitchell, gaining big views before looping off the east slope. Return to the trailhead in highland splendor, enjoying more views amid cool breezes. Be apprised this trailhead is often inaccessible in winter. Call ahead before attempting to come here during that season.

GETTING THERE

From Asheville, take the Blue Ridge Parkway north 34 miles to milepost 355. Turn left on NC 128 into Mount Mitchell State Park. Follow the scenic highway 3.0 miles to the large state park restaurant parking on your right.

THE HIKE

Hikes of superlatives are just that—treks to the biggest, the longest, or in this case the highest point not only in the Carolina mountains but in the entire United States east of the Mississippi River. You start at one of the highest trailheads in the East—Stepps Gap. Strangely enough though, Stepps Gap is also home to the state park restaurant, where you could grab a meal before or after your hike during the warm season. Start your hike on the Old Mitchell Trail, northbound on a single-track path. You'll find it near a small building north of the park restaurant. Head uphill among low balsam trees. The Old Mitchell Trail—parts of which have been in use since the 1830s—surmounts a knob, coming near a small water tank. The Mount Mitchell access road comes into view, used by those who

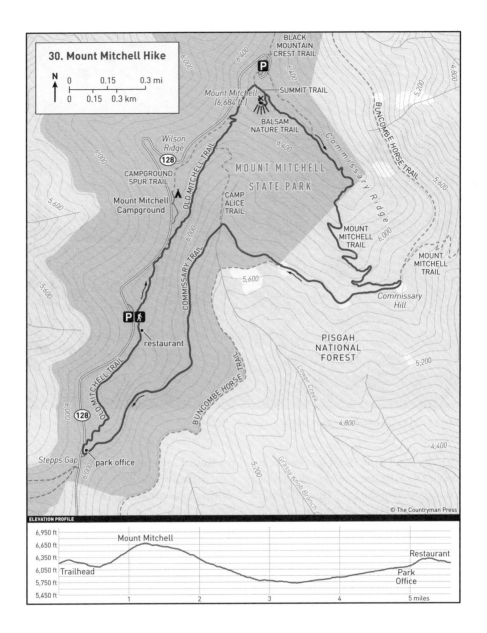

30. Mount Mitchell Hike

N

| 0 | 0.15 | 0.3 mi |
| 0 | 0.15 | 0.3 km |

BLACK MOUNTAIN CREST TRAIL

SUMMIT TRAIL

Mount Mitchell (6,684 ft.)

BALSAM NATURE TRAIL

Wilson Ridge

128

Commissary Ridge

MOUNT MITCHELL STATE PARK

CAMPGROUND SPUR TRAIL

Mount Mitchell Campground

OLD MITCHELL TRAIL

CAMP ALICE TRAIL

MOUNT MITCHELL TRAIL

MOUNT MITCHELL TRAIL

COMMISSARY TRAIL

Commissary Hill

restaurant

PISGAH NATIONAL FOREST

BUNCOMBE HORSE TRAIL

BUNCOMBE HORSE TRAIL

Lower Creek

128

OLD MITCHELL TRAIL

Grassy Knob Branch

Stepps Gap   park office

© The Countryman Press

ELEVATION PROFILE

6,950 ft		Mount Mitchell			
6,650 ft					
6,350 ft					Restaurant
6,050 ft	Trailhead				Park
5,750 ft					Office
5,450 ft		1	2	3	4	5 miles

want but a quarter-mile hike to the peak. At 0.4 mile, we turn away from the road. The trail becomes much more difficult as it curves into a hodge-podge of irregular rocks, bluff, seeping rock slabs, and muddy spots. Luckily the state park has built steps and land bridges to ease you over the most challenging terrain, though travel is slow in places.

At 0.6 mile, hike beneath a transmission line. The trail remains rugged as you start the main climb to Mount Mitchell. Overhead, thick evergreens shade a needle-carpeted forest floor, jeweled with mossy rocks and slowly deteriorating logs. At 0.8 mile, the Camp Alice Trail leaves right, down to Lower Creek, and shortcuts the loop. At 1.0 mile, the

HIKERS GATHER AT THE OBSERVATION PLATFORM ATOP MOUNT MITCHELL

Campground Spur Trail leaves left for the small park campground—the highest campground in the East. Here, stay right with the Old Mitchell Trail, continuing the uptick. At 1.2 miles, head right on the Summit Trail. Enjoy the smooth, wide concrete path, joining casual hikers making the short trek from the upper parking area. Hike beyond the park environmental education building and the Balsam Nature Trail, a signed interpretive walk informing hikers about the boreal forest atop Mount Mitchell.

Come to Mount Mitchell at 1.4 miles. Walk up the observation platform. Note signage delineating the four cardinal directions identifying point on the horizon. On a clear day you will be amply rewarded, but the peak is shrouded in clouds, rain, fog, or snow more than half

the time. Enjoy this perch then take the paved trail back down to turn right, joining the other end of the Balsam Nature Trail. Walk the natural surface trail, past old ranger quarters and rock outcrops while enjoying interpretive information. At 1.7 miles, stay straight, joining the Mount Mitchell Trail. Any potential crowds are left behind. Keep your downgrade, leaving the state park at 2.1 miles, denoted by a sign. Enter the Pisgah National Forest, still in spruce-fir woods. Descend by switchbacks, passing large outcrops, covered in moss. Grab a partial view amid outcrops at 2.6 miles. Note where steps have been cut into the rock upon which you hike.

At 2.9 miles, come to another intersection. Here, head right on the Buncombe Horse Trail/Commissary Trail.

SUMMER WILDFLOWERS GRACE THE COMMISSARY TRAIL

LOOKING ALONG THE CREST OF THE BLACK MOUNTAINS FROM MOUNT MITCHELL

To your left, in a mix of meadow and forest stands the Commissary Hill backcountry campsite. Follow a wide gravelly track on a nearly level trail. The hiking is easy. Blueberry and blackberries rise in scads during summer. At 3.2 miles, on a curve, a stellar view opens. Here, find the Blue Ridge Parkway, the state park above, the state park office, and the restaurant, with ridges and valleys extending into the distance.

At 3.5 miles, the Buncombe Horse Trail leaves left, while we stay right on the Commissary Trail, enjoying more mountain views, following an old railroad line that once took visitors to Mount Mitchell. Reenter the state park, coming to Lower Creek and another trail intersection at 3.8 miles. Just after crossing Lower Creek, the Camp Alice Trail enters on your right. Camp Alice, established in 1914, was an early tourist destination, complete with dining hall and platform tents. Continue an easy, slightly uphill cruise, reaching the state park office in Stepps Gap at 4.9 miles. Here, go around to the front of the office and pick up the Old Mitchell Trail. Head north among low-slung evergreens, climbing a bit before slipping over to the west side of Mount Hallback. Top out before slipping downhill a bit to emerge on the south side of the park restaurant at 5.6 miles. You've burned the calories, therefore you can walk directly into the park restaurant and eat a big ol' meal, guilt-free.

Crabtree Falls

TOTAL DISTANCE: 2.8-mile balloon loop

HIKING TIME: 1:10

VERTICAL RISE: 520 feet

RATING: Easy-moderate

MAPS: Crabtree Falls Hiking Trail, USGS 7.5' Celo NC TN

TRAILHEAD GPS COORDINATES: N35°48'54.1", W82°08'43.2"

CONTACT INFORMATION: Blue Ridge Parkway, 199 Hemphill Knob Road, Asheville, NC 28803, (828) 348-3400, www.nps.gov/blri

Crabtree Falls is one of the most photogenic cataracts in the Carolina mountains. Situated along the Blue Ridge Parkway north of Asheville, Crabtree Falls is part of a greater recreation area that also includes a fine campground. The hike is not difficult, with a mere 500-foot elevation change. Leave the crest of the Blue Ridge, cutting through Crabtree Meadows and the adjacent campground. Descend by switchbacks to Crabtree Creek. A bridge crosses the stream just below the 70-foot falls, presenting a first-rate viewing platform. The climb traces Crabtree Creek before returning to the trailhead.

GETTING THERE

From Asheville, take the Blue Ridge Parkway north to milepost 338.9. Here, turn left into the Crabtree Falls Area. Immediately turn left and reach the upper trailhead parking.

THE HIKE

Interestingly, on official USGS quadrangle maps, 70-foot Crabtree Falls is known as Upper Falls (the government maps also show a Crabtree Falls well downstream). Name aside, this is one attractive spiller that is superlatively scenic and an easy shot for outdoor photographers to bag. For starters, a footbridge with a handrail crosses Crabtree Creek just below the falls, forming an ideal photography spot—no tripod needed, the handrail will do it for you! Crabtree Falls itself makes a classic white spill, widening upon descent, with enough protrusions in the rock to keep the water cascading all 70 feet to a pool. Stately tree growth frames the pourover and the stony stream into which it pours.

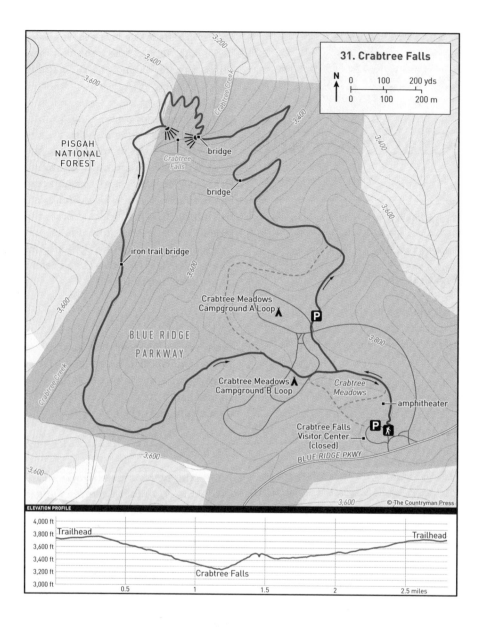

PISGAH
NATIONAL
FOREST

Crabtree Creek

bridge

Crabtree
Falls

bridge

iron trail bridge

Crabtree Meadows
Campground A Loop

BLUE RIDGE
PARKWAY

Crabtree Creek

Crabtree Meadows
Campground B Loop

Crabtree
Meadows

amphitheater

Crabtree Falls
Visitor Center
(closed)

BLUE RIDGE PKWY

© The Countryman Press

ELEVATION PROFILE

4,000 ft
3,800 ft — Trailhead
3,600 ft
3,400 ft
3,200 ft
3,000 ft

Crabtree Falls

Trailhead

0.5   1   1.5   2   2.5 miles

The adventure has still other highlights—the view-rich fields that are left of Crabtree Meadows, a view of Three Knobs Overlook on the Blue Ridge Parkway, and an iron trail bridge as well as a few looks at Crabtree Meadows Campground. The hike starts at the parking area off milepost 339, where a gas station and visitor center were once manned.

Luckily for us, the trail is still in fine shape.

Leave from the upper part of the parking area of the old visitor center on an asphalt path in woods. Quickly pass by the campground amphitheater to enter what is left of Crabtree Meadows. Mountain vistas open and in summer the fields are rife with wildflowers. A few crabtrees still remain, but the area is steadily becoming reforested.

At 0.2 mile, reach an intersection. Here, your return route comes in from Loop B. Our loop stays right toward Crabtree Falls. You soon cross the campground road at the head of Loop A. You can see some of the sites and perhaps look over some empty ones in person. The campground is open from mid-May through October. No reservations are taken. Sitting on a shoulder of the Blue Ridge at 3,600 feet, each of the 71 tent campsites offers a picnic table, fire ring, lantern post, and level tent pad. There are also 22 designated RV sites.

Here, you will also walk through a parking area that was once open to, but now is permanently closed to, day hikers. The trail descends in earnest now under heavy rhododendron topped with black birch, maple and northern red oak. At 0.5 mile, come to another intersection. The trail going left shortcuts the loop and does not go to Crabtree Falls. Stay right here, turning into a hollow created by a tributary of Crabtree Creek. Northern red oaks are well represented. At 0.7 mile, a hiker bridge and exquisite curving stone steps aid your passage. You are finally hearing water sounds. Make a major switchback to the left at 1.0 mile.

Reach Crabtree Falls at 1.2 miles. The bridge over Crabtree Creek—complete with a resting bench—presents an ideal view of the white spiller. The Blue Ridge Parkway is known for its developed overlooks, so it should come as no surprise that they built this trail and bridge with a first-class view in mind. Look upstream. Rock rapids flow under your feet and all the way up to the base of the watery wonder. What I declare "the most photographed tree in the world" stands on an island between you and the falls

CRABTREE FALLS MAKES ITS 70-FOOT DIVE

around which Crabtree Creek flows. Mist drifts onto anything near the falls, including admiring Carolina mountain hikers if the winds are blowing (this mist can be troublesome for waterfall photography, by the way). This is a place to linger, if possible. Summer weekends can be crowded, but if you visit during the off-season, solitude is yours. Speaking of that, because Crabtree Falls faces northeast and is at 3,200 feet elevation, it can turn into a solid sheet of ice during cold spells, and that is another sight altogether. If you are here then, watching ice climbers execute their art may be still another highlight.

The loop switchbacks uphill from

CRABTREE FALLS FRAMED IN SUMMER GREENERY

Crabtree Creek and comes alongside a stone bluff at 1.4 miles. Just ahead, look left for a user-created trail that heads out to an outcrop. When the leaves are off the trees, you can look down on Crabtree Falls. Regardless, you can soak in year-round views of the Blue Ridge Parkway and Three Knobs Overlook. Returning to the official trail, at 1.6 miles, a now-closed trail splits right. From here, begin walking upstream along a much calmer Crabtree Creek, broken with a few modest cascades in a perched valley.

Bridge Crabtree Creek on an iron hiker bridge at 1.8 miles. Admire a little slide cascade and pool just upstream, good for water play for younger hikers.

At 2.1 miles, the loop turns north up a tributary and you cross it on a wooden bridge ahead. Follow this hollow as the stream runs out of water.

Leave the watercourse behind to reach another intersection at 2.5 miles. Here, the loop shortcut leaves acutely left, but you stay straight, coming to Loop B of the campground. Cut straight across the camping area, passing a restroom building along the way. Angle left at the restroom and come to another intersection on the far side of Loop B, near campsite #85. Head left here and soon complete the loop portion of your hike. From here, make a 0.2-mile backtrack to the trailhead.

Tower of Babel Loop

TOTAL DISTANCE: 5.7-mile loop

HIKING TIME: 3:45

VERTICAL RISE: 1.015 feet

RATING: Difficult due to rugged trail first 2.7 miles of hike

MAPS: National Geographic #779 Pisgah National Forest–Linville Gorge Mount Mitchell, USGS 7.5′ Linville Falls

TRAILHEAD GPS COORDINATES: N35°56.419′, W81°55.812′

CONTACT INFORMATION: Pisgah National Forest, Grandfather Ranger District, 109 Lawing Drive, Nebo, NC 28761, (828) 652-2144, www.fs.usda.gov/nfsnc

This hike takes you into Linville Gorge Wilderness, to the Tower of Babel, where you scramble to this peak within a valley and gaze down an untamed canyon, a truly inspiring panorama. From there, climb the nose of a rib ridge, gaining more views before making the rim of Linville Gorge and following a forest road to return to the trailhead. Be apprised the first 2.7 miles of the hike are very slow and challenging, over some of the roughest terrain in the Carolina mountains. Be prepared to work your way over a narrow, stony path, replete with fallen logs and short but continuous ups and downs. The trail rarely gives any quarter. From the Tower of Babel, you will take the Babel Tower Trail up to the west rim of the gorge, then use Kistler Memorial Highway—a simple quiet gravel road—as a much easier conduit back to the trailhead, despite its 700-foot climb, rather than backtracking that very rough 2.7-mile stretch of trail on which you started the hike.

GETTING THERE

From the intersection of US 221 and NC 183, in the town of Linville Falls, turn right on NC 183 East and follow it for 0.7 mile to the gravel Kistler Memorial Highway. You will see a sign indicating Linville Falls and Linville Gorge Wilderness. Veer right here and follow the gravel road for 0.9 mile to the Pine Gap trailhead on your left. Note: along Kistler Memorial Highway, a gravel road, you will pass the Pisgah National Forest access for the trails of Linville Falls and the Linville Gorge Wilderness information cabin before reaching the Pine Gap Trail trailhead.

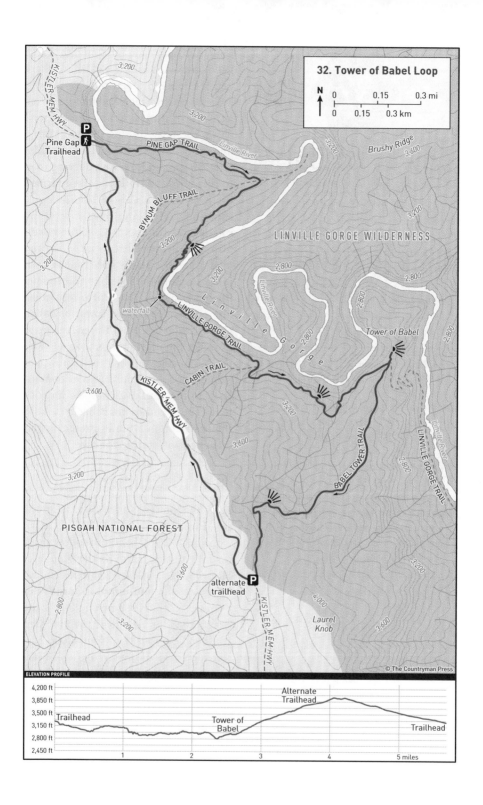

32. Tower of Babel Loop

N

0		0.15		0.3 mi
0	0.15		0.3 km	

Pine Gap Trailhead

KISTLER MEM HWY

PINE GAP TRAIL

Linville River

Brushy Ridge

3,200

3,200

3,600

LINVILLE GORGE WILDERNESS

BYNUM BLUFF TRAIL

3,200

2,800

2,800

L i n v i l l e

Linville River

waterfall

LINVILLE GORGE TRAIL

G o r g e

2,800

2,800

Tower of Babel

CABIN TRAIL

KISTLER MEM HWY

3,200

3,600

BABEL TOWER TRAIL

LINVILLE GORGE TRAIL

3,200

3,200

3,600

3,200

PISGAH NATIONAL FOREST

2,800

3,200

alternate trailhead

KISTLER MEM HWY

4,000

Laurel Knob

3,600

© The Countryman Press

ELEVATION PROFILE

4,200 ft				Alternate			
3,850 ft				Trailhead			
3,500 ft	Trailhead						
3,150 ft				Tower of			Trailhead
2,800 ft				Babel			
2,450 ft		1	2	3	4	5 miles	

THE HIKE

Make no mistake about it, Linville Gorge Wilderness—where this challenging yet rewarding hike take place—is one rugged place, truly deserving of its wilderness designation. Covering nearly 11,000 acres inside the jagged walls of the canyon of the Linville River as it flows off the Blue Ridge, Linville Gorge is a land of extremes: declivitous terrain, expansive rock outcrops, hurtling whitewater, and irregular footing on lightly maintained trails. It is also a place of beauty, including the Tower of Babel and the first-rate views you can gain there, as well as waterfalls and big pools of the Linville River. If you want to camp in the wilderness, backpackers must obtain permits on summer and holiday weekends from the information station on your right,

0.4 mile before reaching the Pine Gap trailhead.

Leave the Pine Gap trailhead on the Pine Gap Trail, bordered in pine, sourwood, and galax. At 0.1 mile, a spur leaves left to a partial overlook into the gorge. From there, follow rough stone steps coming alongside a mean bluff. It is already apparent the path is tough, because the going is slow, even on the downhills. Continue to work along the ragged bluff. The path is just a rock jumble in some places. By 0.4 mile, a series of switchbacks leads you closer to the Linville River. At 0.6 mile, user-created spurs drop left to the water. Stay on the main track, working beneath a craggy cliffline.

Come to a four-way trail intersection at 0.8 mile. Here, the Bynum Bluff Trail goes left a quarter-mile to the Linville River and right up to Kistler Memorial Highway.

THE VIEW INTO LINVILLE GORGE FROM THE TOWER OF BABEL

THE FIRST PART OF THE LOOP TRAVERSES RUGGED TERRAIN

We continue forward, joining the Linville Gorge Trail. You are still paralleling the river, but you and the river have taken a drastic turn to the southwest. Trail conditions are still irregular. Pass an overlook at 1.2 miles. Here, you can peer into the gorge below where the Linville River is fighting downstream as hard as you are.

Descend past a seeping bluff on carved stone steps, then open onto a stone promontory beside the river at 1.3 miles. This is a good place to take a break.

Keep downriver in heavy brush crowding the path, stepping over a tributary. At 1.4 miles, the river bends southeast at a cataract noisily pouring

the Linville Gorge Trail, curving around a drainage pocked with big boulders.

Oaks and sassafras become more common as you lose elevation. At 2.4 miles, come to another overlook into the gorge. Look northeast for the Tower of Babel, a prominence within the gorge but 0.3 mile distant. At 2.5 miles, cross a stream. The trail remains irregular with vegetation cut back to primitive wilderness standards. Descend, passing a spur left down to a waterfall on the river. Stay right and climb to an official trail intersection with the Babel Tower Trail at 2.6 miles. Immediately to your left is a dry rockhouse. Go straight past that and work left, north, around the west side of the tower on a primitive trail, then ascend steeply to the crest, using all fours in places. It isn't easy but once atop, you open onto a panorama of the gorge all around you, a stupendous view. Table Rock, among other crags, stands proudly in the distance.

Backtrack from the tower back to the trail intersection and make your way south, climbing the nose of a ridge on the Babel Tower Trail. The path is a breeze compared with what you've been hiking, despite the continual uphill. Pines, mountain laurel, and chestnut oaks border the single-track path.

At 3.5 miles, pass an open view from an outcrop. Gaze north across the wilderness below. Keep climbing along a perched spring seep and pass a couple of campsites before emerging onto a parking area and Kistler Memorial Highway at 3.9 miles. You will see it is but a remote forest road with a fancy name. Turn right and climb further on the gravel track. Soon you will peak out. It's all downhill from here as you pass the other ends of the Cabin Trail and the Bynum Bluff Trail. Reach the trailhead at 5.7 miles, completing the loop.

15 feet over open rock. At 1.6 miles, pass beside a smaller rockhouse that would help in a storm. By the way, try to hike here when conditions are dry—the trail is challenging enough! At 1.9 miles a user-created trail leads left to a brushy partial view, while just ahead the Cabin Trail climbs right almost 1,000 feet to Kistler Memorial Highway. Continue on

33

Linville Falls

TOTAL DISTANCE: 4.2-miles total on interconnected nature trails

HIKING TIME: 2:15

VERTICAL RISE: 300 feet

RATING: Moderate, can be very easy if hike is shortened

MAPS: Linville Falls Hiking Trails, USGS 7.5' Linville Falls

TRAILHEAD GPS COORDINATES: N35°57.268', W81°55.676'

CONTACT INFORMATION: Blue Ridge Parkway, 199 Hemphill Knob Road, Asheville, NC 28803, (828) 348-3400, www .nps.gov/blri

One of the most rewarding hikes in all the Carolina mountains, the nature trails of 150-foot Linville Falls done in their entirety will deliver multiple looks at multiple waterfalls in uppermost Linville Gorge against the backdrop of the rising Blue Ridge. The hike leaves the visitor center next to the Linville River, crosses the waterway, making an easy trek to cascading Upper Falls. From there, walk your way to three distinct panoramas of 150-foot Linville Falls plummeting through rock and woods in rugged splendor. Return to the trailhead and leave the crowds behind, making your way to the close-up Plunge Basin Overlook of Linville Falls, then take a rugged track to the base of Linville Falls, experiencing an in-your-face view of Linville Falls. On your return, detour to delicate Duggers Creek Falls, a slender spiller pouring through an equally narrow mini-gorge, a study in contrast with Linville Falls. Be apprised that the crowds can be heavy on the first part of the hike, so choose your times wisely.

GETTING THERE

From exit 72, Old Fort on I-40 east of Asheville, join US 70 east for 11 miles to turn left on US 221 North near Marion and follow it 22 miles to meet the Blue Ridge Parkway. Turn northbound on the BRP and follow it for 1.1 miles to turn right onto the access road for Linville Falls visitor center and follow it for 1.5 miles to dead end at the trailhead.

THE HIKE

Sometimes we hikers get an attitude and think we are too cool for little nature trails. However, the nature trails of Linville Falls collectively form a superlative Carolina mountain hiking experience

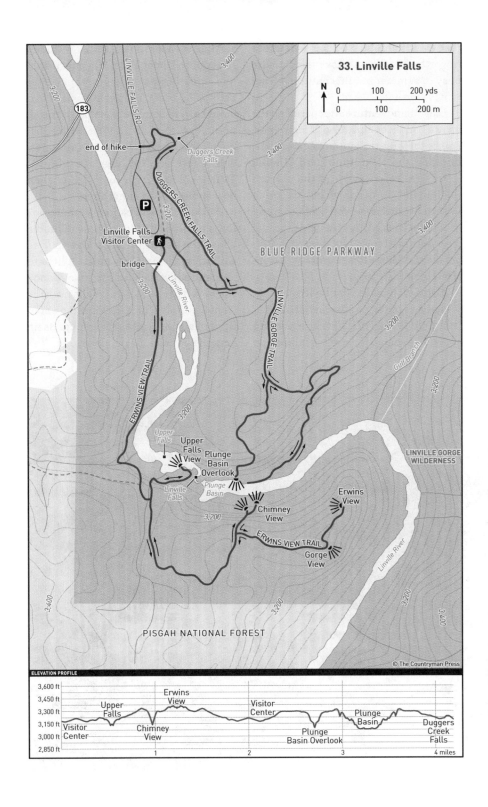

33. Linville Falls

N

| 0 | 100 | 200 yds |
| 0 | 100 | 200 m |

183

LINVILLE FALLS RD

3,400

3,400

Duggers Creek Falls

end of hike

P

DUGGERS CREEK FALLS TRAIL

3,200

Linville Falls Visitor Center

bridge

BLUE RIDGE PARKWAY

3,400

Linville River

LINVILLE GORGE TRAIL

3,200

Gull Branch

3,200

ERWINS VIEW TRAIL

3,200

Upper Falls

Upper Falls View

Plunge Basin Overlook

Plunge Basin

LINVILLE GORGE WILDERNESS

Linville Falls

Chimney View

Erwins View

3,200

ERWINS VIEW TRAIL

Gorge View

Linville River

3,200

3,200

3,400

PISGAH NATIONAL FOREST

3,400

© The Countryman Press

ELEVATION PROFILE

3,600 ft				
3,450 ft		Erwins View		
3,300 ft	Upper Falls		Visitor Center	
3,150 ft				Plunge Basin
3,000 ft	Visitor Center	Chimney View	Plunge Basin Overlook	Duggers Creek Falls
2,850 ft		1	2	3	4 miles

that even the hippest hiker will admit is worthwhile. Yes, parts of the path are busy in summer but this natural attraction is worth it.

Start the adventure after perusing the visitor center, complete with restrooms. Follow the wide trail toward Upper Falls, bridging the clear, tan-tinted Linville River. The waterway forms the heart of the Linville Gorge, of which you are at the head. Pine, preserved hemlocks, and rhododendron border the wide, gravel path designed for significant foot traffic, mostly Blue Ridge Parkway drivers stretching their legs.

Come alongside Linville River. Next bridge a tributary to reach a departing trail right to the Forest Service parking area on Wiseman Road at 0.4 mile. Keep straight then just ahead turn left, taking the spur to Upper Falls. Slip past a bluff and open onto a wide outcrop. Upper Falls spills in two channels about 12 feet amid hard rock into a sizeable churning pool. The roar of Linville Falls—just downstream—echoes up to the waterside overlook. You can see Linville Falls fashion a frightful swirl of white descending into a stony abyss.

Backtrack then rejoin the main track for the trio of vistas to come. Climb a wide rooty trail to reach the spur to Chimney View at 0.9 mile. Split left, descending stone steps to an overlook where you can see Linville Falls from the front. Look also for hikers milling about Upper Falls, as well as the Plunge Basin and the Plunge Basin Overlook. You

HIKERS GATHER AT UPPER FALLS

LINVILLE FALLS AND THE BLUE RIDGE BEYOND FROM ERWINS VIEW

will be both places later. That is one of the finest aspects of this hike—you can see where you were and where you are going while soaking in views of Linville Falls from various settings. Backtrack and head toward Erwins View, passing the Gorge View along the way. The Gorge View opens onto a limited look down fabled Linville Gorge into Linville Gorge Wilderness, one rugged place. Erwins View presents the most wide-open expanses from two separate but adjacent points. Below, the whitewater downspout of Linville Falls creates a focal point from which extend the dark stone walls of the gorge, rising lush woodlands cloaking the mountainsides, and still outward the standing ramparts of the rising Blue Ridge.

You have hiked 1.2 miles. Backtrack to the visitor center. If you forgot something in your vehicle, now is the time to get it. Otherwise, at 2.1 miles, leave the visitor center on the single-track, much, much less used trail to the Plunge Basin. Pass the Duggers Creek Falls Trail then a connector trail to Duggers Creek Falls. You will take this connector trail later. For now, keep rising above the river, well out of sight of the water. At 2.4 miles, head right toward the Plunge Basin Overlook, descending through thickets of mountain laurel and pine. Reach the overlook at 2.6 miles. Peer down into the big pool of the Plunge Basin. It's almost straight down! Linville Falls is making its final two-stage white dive, emerging from a relatively narrow gap the entirety of the Linville River is forced through. Watch how the push of the falls keeps the pool below the

LINVILLE FALLS FROM THE PLUNGE BASIN OVERLOOK

falls in endless movement, a continual churn of highland aqua.

Now it is time to head down there, to the base of the falls, the Plunge Basin itself. Backtrack then pick up new trail as it rolls along the upper gorge woods. Then you drop via steps alongside a rock wall. The going is as tough as the first part of the hike was easy. Twist between boulders, down steep steps, beside fallen hemlocks, all complete with an irregular footbed that forces progress to a crawl. Be careful! Make your way alongside the Linville River and a beach, then you reach the Plunge Basin itself at 3.2 miles. Depending on water levels, you can scramble closer to the falls, the water rumbling and echoing in the stone chamber of the gorge, enhancing the already primeval setting.

It's incredible all the different ways you get to experience Linville Falls— above, below, behind and from varied vantages. Now, make your way back, splitting right on the Connector Trail toward Duggers Creek Falls. Enter an intimate gorge of stone where a bridge crosses Duggers Creek. Scan upstream through a mini-slot canyon framed in evergreens as little ol' Duggers Creek makes a faucet-like drop from a dark ledge. What a contrast to brawling Linville Falls! From here, the trail climbs through a boulder garden then opens onto the access road at the head of the parking area. After seeing all this, you will agree this is one remarkable set of nature trails, for which no one is too cool to hike.

Raider Camp Creek Circuit

TOTAL DISTANCE: 9.5-mile balloon loop

HIKING TIME: 5:15

VERTICAL RISE: 870 feet

RATING: Difficult due to distance and one rugged trail segment

MAPS: National Geographic #779 Pisgah National Forest–Linville Gorge Mount Mitchell, USGS 7.5' Grandfather Mountain NC

TRAILHEAD GPS COORDINATES: N35°58.651', W81°45.974'

CONTACT INFORMATION: Pisgah National Forest, Grandfather Ranger District, 109 Lawing Drive, Nebo, NC 28761, (828) 652-2144, www.fs.usda.gov/nfsnc

One of my favorite hikes in all the Carolina mountains, this loop explores Harper Creek Backcountry, where you will find two spectacular waterfalls standing out among everywhere-you-look beauty along Harper Creek and its tributary Raider Camp Creek. From the trailhead, climb a gap and come alongside Harper Creek to find Harper Creek Falls making its 50-foot double drop with enticing stone swimming pools between. From there, gain solitude, making your way up Harper Creek and its fords. Ahead, work through often-overgrown trail sections passing pools rimmed in beaches, small slides, and scenic lesser cascades to find incredible South Harper Falls, a 200-foot two-tier spiller sating the most avid waterfaller. From there, ascend to an overlook where you can gaze on Grandfather Mountain in one direction and down on the entirety of eye-popping South Harper Falls. Hike upland woods, then close the loop with a trek through the Raider Camp Creek valley, where more waterfalls spill. Note: this hike requires numerous stream fords, making it a warm-weather proposition.

GETTING THERE

From exit 103 on I-40, take the Morganton exit and US 64 East for 0.7 mile, then turn left on US 64 Truck East, also signed as US 64 Bypass. Follow US 64 Truck East for 2.2 miles, then turn left on NC 181 North. Follow NC 181 North for 11.3 miles to Brown Mountain Beach Road. Turn right on Brown Mountain Beach Road and follow it 5.0 miles to turn left as Brown Mountain Beach Road goes left, and the road going straight becomes Adako Road. Look for a national forest sign indicating Mortimer Campground. Follow Brown Mountain Beach Road for

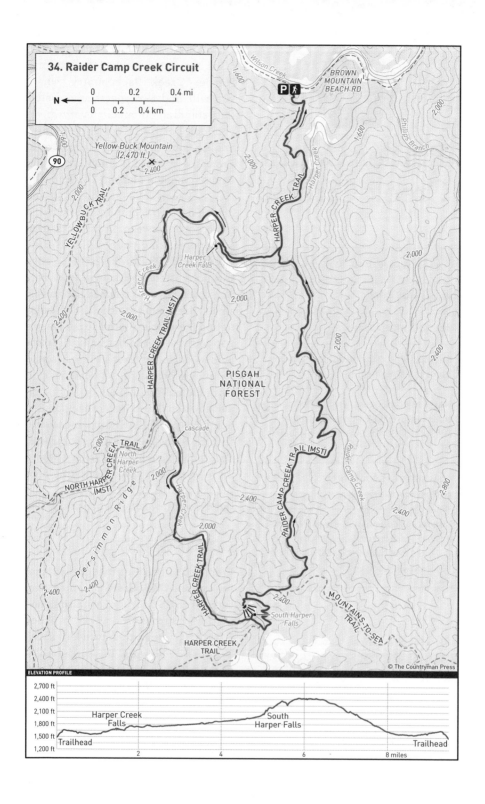

34. Raider Camp Creek Circuit

N ←

| 0 | 0.2 | 0.4 mi |
| 0 | 0.2 | 0.4 km |

Wilson Creek

BROWN MOUNTAIN BEACH RD

P

1,600

90

Yellow Buck Mountain (2,470 ft.)
× 2,400

2,000

1,600

1,400

2,000

HARPER CREEK TRAIL

Harper Creek

Phillips Branch

2,000

Harper Creek Falls

HARPER CREEK TRAIL (MST)

Harper Creek

2,000

PISGAH NATIONAL FOREST

2,000

2,400

RAIDER CAMP CREEK TRAIL (MST)

Raider Camp Creek

cascade

NORTH HARPER CREEK TRAIL

North Harper Creek

NORTH HARPER CREEK [MST]

Persimmon Ridge

2,000

2,400

Harper Creek

2,000

2,400

2,400

2,800

HARPER CREEK TRAIL

2,400

South Harper Falls

MOUNTAINS-TO-SEA TRAIL

HARPER CREEK TRAIL

© The Countryman Press

ELEVATION PROFILE

2,700 ft						
2,400 ft						
2,100 ft	Harper Creek Falls			South Harper Falls		
1,800 ft						
1,500 ft						
1,200 ft	Trailhead					Trailhead

2   4   6   8 miles

7.1 more miles, and the parking area will be on your left.

THE HIKE

Harper Creek is an ideal aquatic summertime destination, and a stream with the name Raider Camp Creek just has to be cool. Hike, fish, swim, and camp your heart away here. I've spend many a night myself along these attractive highland waters, where trout secret themselves in bucolic pools and rich woods avail themselves a respite from summer's heat. Start your trek at Brown Mountain Beach Road, on the Harper Creek Trail, climbing by switchbacks to a gap and a trail intersection at 0.2 mile. Here the Yellow Buck Trail splits right but we stay straight, following a wide and nearly level track. Sounds of Harper Creek waft into your ears. Pass a large camping flat on your left at 0.8 mile.

Soon come alongside the clear creek, walking by a large outcrop. At 1.1 miles, reach another flat and intersection. Here, your return route—the Raider Camp Creek Trail—comes in from across the stream. We stay straight with the Harper Creek Trail, rising from the stream again, going on and off an old logging grade. At 1.3 miles, the route splits again. Here, go left to reach Harper Creek Falls at 1.5 miles. Two user-created trails split left to the falls. The uppermost access lands you in the middle of the stone slab spiller, by way of a rope. Be very careful. The other downstream access is easier and takes you to the base of the lower fall, with its huge swimming pool. Harper Creek Falls makes its two-tiered descent among ragged granite and crystalline water.

Backtrack to the main trail, continuing up Harper Creek, with most day

THE UPPER DROP OF HARPER CREEK FALLS

hikers left behind beyond Harper Creek Falls. White pines tower overhead. The streamside hiking is often easy, especially when you are on the old logging railroad grade. The trail occasionally crosses tributaries flowing into Harper Creek, flowing in pools and rapids, with occasional beaches. At 2.4 miles, hike through a sandy area, deposited on the path from periodic floods. At 2.7 miles, make your first ford of Harper Creek, followed by a second at 2.9 miles. You are on the right bank. Sneak past a pair of rock outcrops directly alongside the water, squeezing the trail between the outcrops and the scenic stream.

THE TWO TIERS OF HARPER CREEK FALLS, DIVIDED BY DEEP PLUNGE POOLS

At 3.7 miles, come to a trail intersection very near the water. It may or may not be signed. Here, the blue blazed North Harper Creek Trail stays on the right bank, while our route, Harper Creek Trail, heads left, fording Harper Creek at the lower end of a big pool where Harper Creek and North Harper Creek converge. You can see this aquatic convergence while making the ford. Once on land, head upstream on the left bank of Harper Creek through thick rhododendron. The next 1.6 miles can be rough and challenging. The path is primitive and often overgrown. Ford Harper Creek at 3.8, 4.0, 4.1, and 4.4 miles. The next crossing, at 4.6 miles, can be confusing; the trail leads across several stream braids before making the right bank. Then you quickly ford again, passing by an open rock slab over which Harper Creek slides. This is a good stopping spot and an area open to the sun, contrasting with the junglesque forest you've been hiking through.

You are at 4.7 miles. The nearly level walking soon ends with another crossing at 5.0 miles. Now ascend the right bank sharply on a steep slope as the rock gorge of now audible South Harper Falls opens to your left. After zigzagging uphill, take a spur leaving left to reach the cataract in the middle of its 200-foot double drop. Above you the spiller flows about 60 feet over slick stone, while below the watercourse pours off an edge, seemingly into oblivion.

Reach the top of the falls and open rock at 5.3 miles. Just ahead, at a signed intersection, head left with the Raider Camp Trail to cross Harper Creek at a bend near private property. Beyond the crossing, turn left, switchbacking uphill. At 5.6 miles, the trail joins an old road-bed, soon reaching the downhill spur to a head-on view of South Harper Falls. You can see both gigantic slides of the lengthy cataract. Turn around. Grandfather Mountain and the crest of the Blue Ridge rise in the yon.

The Raider Camp Trail leaves the overlook southeasterly under oaks and pines, away from moving water, joining wide track, passing an intersection with the Mountains-to-Sea Trail at 6.0 miles. Walk an easy double-track as occasional views open across the Harper Creek Valley. At 6.6 miles, bisect a gap and keep straight, descending toward Raider Camp Creek, which you meet at 7.5 miles. The stream begins its own set of easy-to-hear but near-impossible-to-reach cascades. The valley widens and before you know it, the fast-falling trail makes Harper Creek at 8.3 miles. Turn

SOUTH HARPER FALLS PLUMMETS OVER 200 FEET

upstream, then make the final ford, crossing an island, as well as user created trails and campsites before coming to the signed intersection where you were earlier at 1.1 miles. From this point it is a simple backtrack to the trailhead.

Balds of Roan Mountain

TOTAL DISTANCE: 4.8-mile there-and-back	

HIKING TIME: 2:30

VERTICAL RISE: 950 feet

RATING: Moderate

MAPS: National Geographic #783 Cherokee and Pisgah National Forests—South Holston and Watauga Lakes, USGS 7.5' Carvers Gap TN NC

TRAILHEAD GPS COORDINATES: N36°6.385', W82°6.621'

CONTACT INFORMATION: Pisgah National Forest, P.O. Box 128, Burnsville, NC 28714, (828) 682-6146, www.fs.usda.gov/nfsnc

This hike takes you through open meadows atop the crest of the Appalachians dividing Tennessee from North Carolina. Start your hike over a mile high at Carvers Gap. The fabled Appalachian Trail leads over "balds," or grassy mountaintop locales, as well as through spruce-fir forest, native to only the highest mantles of the Carolina mountains. Roll over Round Bald and Jane Bald, taking in vistas step after step along the way. Leave the AT for Grassy Ridge and more highland hiking to end at an open meadow outcrop and a plaque deservingly lauding these majestic highlands.

GETTING THERE

From Bakersville, take NC 261 North for 12.9 miles to Carvers Gap and the Tennessee–North Carolina state line. Parking will be on your left. Pick up the Appalachian Trail on the east side of Carvers Gap.

THE HIKE

The balds of Roan Mountain deserve legendary status among hikers. When Appalachian Trail thru hikers making their way from Georgia to Maine recall memorable sights, most replies include these open meadows with miles of 360-degree views going on for miles, with meadows, mountain ridges, and forest valleys stretching into the distance as far as the clarity of the sky allows. I live less than an hour's drive from the balds of Roan, and each visit I am stunned by the sheer magnificence and splendor found here.

But what is a bald? Unique to the Southern Appalachians, balds are open, grassy mountain meadows located where no tree line exists that should be forest. Almost all balds are located above 4,000

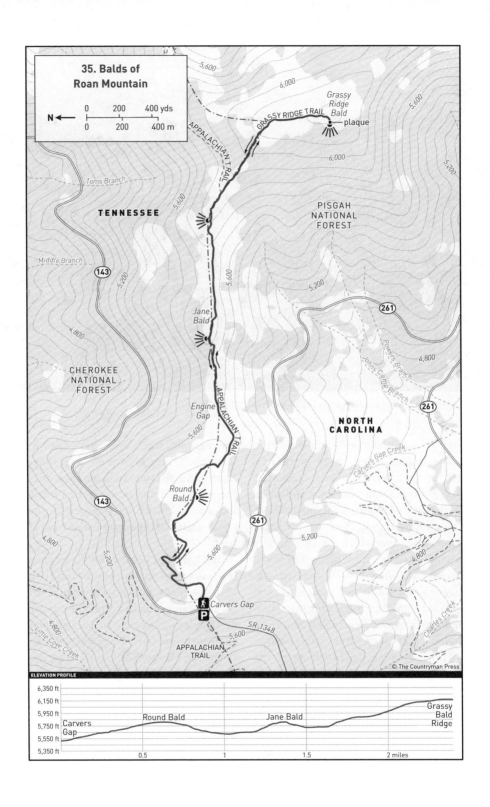

35. Balds of Roan Mountain

N ←

| 0 | 200 | 400 yds |
| 0 | 200 | 400 m |

Grassy Ridge Bald

plaque

GRASSY RIDGE TRAIL

5,600

6,000

6,000

5,600

5,200

APPALACHIAN TRAIL

Toms Branch

TENNESSEE

PISGAH NATIONAL FOREST

5,600

143

Middle Branch

5,200

5,200

261

Jane Bald

4,800

5,600

CHEROKEE NATIONAL FOREST

Powers Branch

4,800

261

Engine Gap

APPALACHIAN TRAIL

NORTH CAROLINA

Johns Camp Branch

143

Round Bald

Carvers Gap Creek

4,800

261

5,600

5,200

4,800

Charles Creek

Little Cove Creek

Carvers Gap

4,800

5,200

P

SR 1348

APPALACHIAN TRAIL

5,600

© The Countryman Press

ELEVATION PROFILE

6,350 ft				
6,150 ft				Grassy
5,950 ft	Round Bald	Jane Bald		Bald
5,750 ft	Carvers			Ridge
5,550 ft	Gap			
5,350 ft	0.5	1	1.5	2 miles

HIKING THE BALDS OF ROAN MOUNTAIN CAN BE A GLORIOUS EXPERIENCE

feet. Yet many balds existed when Americans first climbed these highlands. More than 100 have been documented. Today's balds you visit have almost all been restored or are maintained to keep their grassy crown. Most historic balds have grown over with trees, leaving only a name on topographic maps. The origin of these fields has never been satisfactorily explained, although prior to our era, grazing animals, natural fires from lightning strikes, and clearing by American Indians probably kept the balds clear.

In days gone by, residents of the nearby valleys would drive their cattle to the balds to graze during the summer season while growing winter hay in lowland fields. Grazing sheep and cattle helped keep the balds open then, for when grazing ceased, trees began reclaiming the meadows. The balds of Roan are primarily being kept open by mowing. Other efforts to keep these Southern Appalachian balds open have included goat and cow grazing, burning, and old-fashioned hand cutting. A combination of the above seems to work best.

It's hard not to love the views from the balds, the cooling winds and their very openness. Today, we recognize the balds as being home to rare flowers such as Gray's lily, as well as bird species such as the golden winged warbler. Furthermore, blueberries and blackberries feed wildlife. Many hikers might want to see these balds preserved. However, restoring balds to their "natural" state raises complicated questions. Are the plentiful panoramas reason to save them or should they be kept open for their value to wildlife? Or should they be left alone and allowed to grow over, especially given that we don't understand their origin?

For now, the balds of Roan are being kept open and attract hikers aplenty. Start your adventure at Carvers Gap. Leave Carvers Gap and pick up the Appalachian Trail, northbound, angling up the hillside of Round Bald amid grass and brush to enter contrasting darkness of the rare red spruce and Fraser fir forests that cloak only the highest mantles of the Southern Appalachians. Leave the rocky woods, opening onto Round Bald, dotted with a few spruce and rhododendron islands amid the sea of grass. Views open. Reach the top of Round Bald after walking and gawking at the distant panoramas of North Carolina and Tennessee mountainlands extending in every direction. Be apprised that fog, rain, and clouds are more likely up here, so try to pick a sunny, clear day for your hike.

Drop to grassy Engine Gap at 1.1 miles, to enter brushy country of stunted beech and alder, along with blueberry and blackberry bushes. At 1.3 miles, come to a prominent rock outcrop where hikers gather to sit a spell in wonderment. Others will find a favorable grassy spot to picnic. A little more climbing leads you to the top of brushy Jane Bald.

Descend again on a stony, well-beaten-down track, reaching a top-notch vista at 1.7 miles. Look back at the balds just passed, over which stands the dark wooded mantle of Roan High Knob. Reach a trail intersection and more sitting rocks at 1.8 miles.

ROAN MOUNTAIN RISES BEHIND THIS POPULAR PHOTOGRAPHY SPOT

HIKING TOWARD GRASSY RIDGE FROM ROUND BALD

Here, the Appalachian Trail heads left while the signed Grassy Ridge Trail climbs into thick brush and wind-pruned trees. Ascend southeasterly on Grassy Ridge, still on the Tennessee–North Carolina state line. Rise above 6,000 feet.

At 2.1 miles, the trail bursts back into open grass dotted with dark evergreen copses. The views will stun even the most jaded hiker. At 2.4 miles, the path splits. Head right for a standing outcrop, a natural destination point. Standing atop the stone knob, look back at your route and the balance of the high country. Here, a metal plaque erected by the US Forest Service says it all in a nod to a local Carolina highlander named Cornelius Rex Peake: "A special man who loved God, his country, his fellow men, and this land; a legacy from his forefather. Born in the valley below, April 3, 1887, buried near his birthplace March 23, 1964. Because of his love of nature, his long and close association with this mountain, no one was better versed on the Roan and its people." What an honor to spend a lifetime within sight of "the Roan" as it is locally known. On your return you will be tempted to explore other areas of the balds or even plan a star-watching party or camp out here in the special swath of the Carolina mountains.

36

Calloway Peak via the Profile Trail

TOTAL DISTANCE: 8.2-mile there-and-back

HIKING TIME: 5:00

VERTICAL RISE: 2,096 feet

RATING: Difficult due to elevation gain and terrain

MAPS: Grandfather Mountain State Park, USGS 7.5' Grandfather Mountain NC

TRAILHEAD GPS COORDINATES: N36°07.147', W81°49.965'

CONTACT INFORMATION: Grandfather Mountain State Park, 9872 N.C. 105 South, Suite #6 Banner Elk, NC 28604, 828-963-9522, www.ncparks.gov/grandfather-mountain-state-park

This walking adventure takes place at one of North Carolina's most beloved and respected highland destinations—Grandfather Mountain. Now a state park, this revered mountain offers backcountry hiking at its finest. Our hike uses the Profile Trail to reach the high country and Calloway Peak. Starting at over 4,000 feet, our adventure first goes downhill along the headwaters of the Watauga River before turning up Green Ridge where a view whets your appetite. Continue ascending in gorgeous northern hardwoods with scattered boulders. Eventually rise to spruce-fir forests and very challenging boulder fields. These rocky sections will slow your pace—and the grade is steepening! Reach the ridgecrest and open onto the outcrops of Calloway Peak, where you can soak in highland panoramas extending to the distant horizon.

GETTING THERE

From the intersection of US 221 and NC 105 in Linville, take NC 105 North for 4.6 miles to the signed right turn into the Grandfather Mountain State Park Profile trailhead on your right. Follow the entrance road a short distance to end at a large parking area with water and restrooms.

THE HIKE

Heralded as a special place for centuries, more recently Grandfather Mountain was (and is) known as a private attraction. However, the state of North Carolina acquired undeveloped portions of Grandfather Mountain outside the private attraction boundaries, in addition to obtaining conservation easements to cobble together an important and scenic portion of Grandfather Mountain. Thus

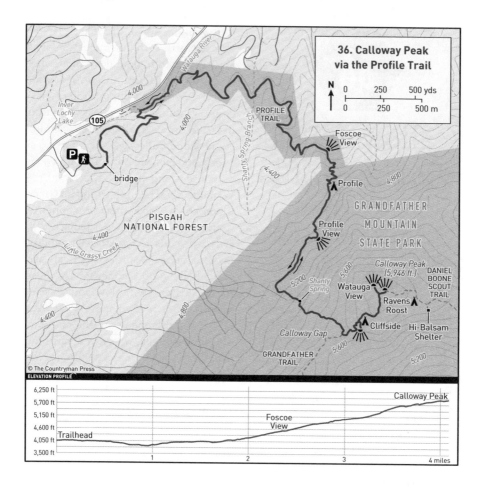

Grandfather Mountain State Park was opened in 2009, bordered by the historic private attraction of Grandfather Mountain, the Blue Ridge Parkway, and the Pisgah National Forest.

Despite the state park's relatively short existence, the Profile Trail has become revered among hiking circles. I don't know if it is the challenging climb, the rugged rocks, the impressive views, or simply so a person can say, "I have climbed Grandfather Mountain."

Make sure and register at the trailhead, even if you are just dayhiking. The Profile Trail inconspicuously leaves the large parking area near the restrooms.

Here a wide, well-graded gravel path enters coves rising above the headwaters of the Watauga River. Trailside hemlocks are being preserved. At 0.1 mile, cross a streamlet on an elaborate steel bridge. The trail is constricted by park boundaries; therefore, it ends up going where you think it won't or shouldn't go. Nevertheless, continue along the river corridor, still descending, crossing more stream branches. Descend by switchbacks to come alongside the creek-like Watauga River at 0.8 mile, under yellow birch, hemlock, and rhododendron.

At 0.9 mile, turn away from the Watauga River and begin the real climb, with 2,096 feet of elevation between you and Calloway Peak. Rise into northern hardwoods of buckeye, beech, and cherry. At 1.6 miles, hop a stream using placed stepping stones, then enter a cool boulder garden. From here, the trail narrows and becomes more primitive. Work into hollows and along rib ridges as you climb, often using switchbacks. At 2.4 miles, reach a cleared panorama, Foscoe View. Look north toward Boone and Elk Knob and beyond that to the mountains of Virginia.

Continue uphill in steep coves where gnarled trunks of yellow birch stand as mute witnesses to the notorious harsh weather found on Grandfather Mountain. In summertime, scads of stinging nettle rises astride the path, but park personnel strive to keep it cut back. Otherwise it would be a very itchy hike. Look for elaborate rock work. At 2.7 miles, pass the Profile Campsite. These backcountry camps must be reserved in advance, should you choose to overnight it. Some camps allow fires, but others don't.

Just beyond here, in bouldery woods, encounter your first spruce trees, the high country indicator. Round leaved viburnum, moss, and ferns grow where rock is absent. At 2.9 miles, come along a massive rock face. At 3.0 miles, reach the disappointing Profile View, where you can look east at the crest of Grandfather Mountain. The trail gets rockier and steeper. Fraser fir joins the red spruce as evergreens continue to become more

POINTING TOWARD THE CREST OF GRANDFATHER MOUNTAIN FROM CLIFFSIDE VIEW

prevalent. At 3.4 miles, come to Shanty Spring, backed against a rock cliff. Shanty Spring is the last sure water source if you are heading to Grandfather's Crest. Here, the Profile Trail turns right and begins an uphill course in irregular rock jumbles. The footing is less than ideal. Use care here; if you get hurt, rescue will be a long ordeal. Avoid accidents before they happen. Assume every rock is slippery.

Reach a high point, then drop just a bit to reach a trail intersection at 3.7 miles. You are in a spruce-fir wonderland, with pockets of mountain ash and yellow birch. Head left on the Daniel Boone Scout Trail, climbing toward Calloway Peak. At 3.8 miles, come to Cliffside Campsite. Take the spur here leading right and pass through the camp to shortly open onto an exposed cliff where views spread wide. Look south at the ridgeline of Grandfather Mountain and scan for hikers trekking along the Grandfather Trail. The Blue Ridge Parkway runs below. Scan for prominent Table Rock in the distance. And beyond, lands roll away to the east, seemingly all the way to Piedmont and on to the Carolina coast.

At 4.1 miles, head left to reach the spur to Watauga View. Commanding vistas open of Linville, the stateline crest, and Elk Knob. Outcrops make for convenient relaxing spots. Now, head back to the main trail and follow

LOOKING OUT FROM WATAUGA VIEW

THIS OUTCROP AT WATAUGA VIEW DELIVERS FIRST RATE PANORAMAS OF THE CAROLINA MOUNTAINS

it, soon finding a short ladder to scale, allowing access to the top of Calloway Peak, which you reach at 4.2 miles. The outcrop here is smaller, but the views are worthy of a 2,096-foot climb. Windswept evergreens encircle the rocky knob, and over them you can look west and north. Look down; you came up that way. On your return, take your time and exercise caution on slippery rocks. After all, you have much more hiking to do among the fantastic Carolina mountains.

37

Boone Fork Circuit

TOTAL DISTANCE: 5.4-mile loop

HIKING TIME: 3:00

VERTICAL RISE: 1013 feet

RATING: Moderate

MAPS: Julian Price Park Hiking Trails, USGS 7.5′ Boone NC

TRAILHEAD GPS COORDINATES: N36°08′22.9″, W81°43′39.1″

CONTACT INFORMATION: Blue Ridge Parkway, 199 Hemphill Knob Road, Asheville, NC 28803, (828) 348-3400, www.nps.gov/blri

This watery hike off the Blue Ridge Parkway starts high at the Price Park picnic area and then follows Boone Fork down a craggy and scenic valley past cascades, culminating in a visit to impressive Hebron Colony Falls, where Boone Fork tumbles over 100 feet in stages through a massive boulder jumble you can scramble through yourself. After that, reach a low point, then ascend along Bee Tree Creek, crisscrossing the small stream time after time (they're very doable at normal flows). Return to the Blue Ridge, following the trail through Price Park Campground to finish the circuit. Be prepared for slow travel in places where the trail is quite rocky. Still other locales are smooth and easy. Add a picnic or a campout to your hike using the Price Park facilities.

GETTING THERE

From the intersection of US 221 and US 321 in Blowing Rock, take US 221 South for 2.3 miles to turn right onto NC 1552 (there will be a sign for Flannery Fork Road and Shulls Mill Road), then quickly turn right again on NC 1571, then again turn quickly, this time left on the Blue Ridge Parkway, and follow it for 1.9 miles to the right turn into Price Park Picnic Area. Follow the main road into the picnic area to park on the left just after the restroom building, also on the left.

THE HIKE

Allow plenty of time for this hike, despite its being less than 6 miles. The going is slow on rocky portions of the trail, especially along lower Boone Fork. Additionally, the side trip to Hebron Colony Falls will take a while if you plan to boulder-scramble along the cataract. The scenery astride the waterways

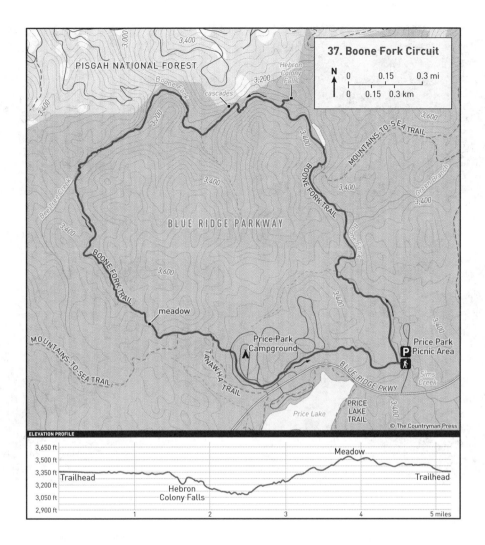

37. Boone Fork Circuit

PISGAH NATIONAL FOREST

BLUE RIDGE PARKWAY

cascades

Hebron Colony Falls

meadow

Price-Park Campground

Price Park Picnic Area

Price Lake

PRICE LAKE TRAIL

Sims Creek

BLUE RIDGE PKWY

MOUNTAINS-TO-SEA TRAIL

BOONE FORK TRAIL

TANAWHA TRAIL

BeeTree Creek

Green Branch

© The Countryman Press

N   0   0.15   0.3 mi
     0   0.15   0.3 km

ELEVATION PROFILE

3,650 ft
3,500 ft
3,350 ft — Trailhead
3,200 ft
3,050 ft
2,900 ft

Hebron Colony Falls

Meadow

Trailhead

1   2   3   4   5 miles

pleases the eye, with dashing rapids and crystalline pools inviting a summer dip.

Leave west from the picnic area, immediately bridging Boone Fork to reach a trail intersection and the loop portion of the hike. Head right on your counterclockwise circuit on the Boone Fork Trail. Boone Fork is gently flowing to your right through mixed woods and meadow, with a healthy dose of rhododendron, mountain laurel and haw. Cherry, buckeye, ferns and blackberry round out the varied vegetation.

Pigpen Knob and other ridges rise from the stream valley. Scattered picnic sites are around you. Kids will be playing in the placid currents amid the picnic area. Look for beaver evidence, including old channels once dammed by the engineering rodents. Julian Price picked this pretty spot as part of a 4,000-acre retreat for his insurance company employees. After Mr. Price died in 1946, his heirs willed the land to the National Park Service, whereupon the getaway became part of the Blue Ridge Parkway.

THIS MULTI-TIERED CASCADE IS BUT ONE OF MANY UNNAMED CATARACTS ON BOONE FORK

Bridge a tributary of Boone Fork at 0.6 mile, still tracing the curves of the stream, sometimes in small glades, sometimes in evergreen thickets. Ahead, walk beneath an overhanging bluff, exiting the greater meadow. Work along the rocky bank of Boone Fork, as the stream and its pools are gaining in size and intensity. Your first cascades come after a mile, with pools and open rocks popular stopping spots. At 1.2 miles, come to an intersection. Here, the Mountains-to-Sea Trail leaves right, bridging Boone Fork. Ahead, pass some noisy cascades, along with a beach and riverside play area. Boone Fork exhibits many faces. The trail turns away from Boone Fork then comes to the signed spur to Hebron Colony Falls at 1.7 miles. Here, you split right, descending back to Boone Fork, to arrive at the base of a massive boulder garden Boone Fork crashes and dashes through. Waterfall height is difficult to calculate here, because no singular drop exists, but the falls displays an amalgamation of chutes and slides, though the highest drop of 20 or so feet is at the top, followed by the cataracts that tumble another 80 feet. Bouldering amid the flow is fun, but exercise caution.

Continue down the Boone Fork valley, now heading west. You are well above the creek, working among rocks. At 2.0 miles, use a short ladder to get through one bouldery locale. At 2.1 miles, come along some unnamed scenic cascades that drop some 40 feet in two stages, with a pool in between, framed in evergreens and yellow birch. At 2.4 miles, a series of steps leads you back down to the water, then negotiate more steps before reaching a low point and turning up Bee Tree Creek at 2.6 miles.

Waste no time making your first crossing of the stream. Navigate up the narrow vale, densely cloaked in doghobble and rhododendron, amid the mosses and rocks, roofed over by a wealth of trees. Heading upstream, most crossings are rock hops, though bridges are present at some crossings. Picturesque mini-cascades enhance the national-park-level scenery.

At 3.8 miles, after a dozen creek crossings, leave the stream then climb a bit more, opening onto a meadow at 4.0 miles. The well-trod trail leads through berry patches, grasses, and young trees trying to reclaim the meadow. Views open onto wooded knobs to the west. The Boone Fork Trail reenters woods and reaches an intersection at 4.2 miles. Here, the Mountains-to-Sea Trail leaves right. Ahead, at 4.3 miles, the Tanawha Trail leaves right to end on the Parkway. At 4.4 miles, come to Price Park Campground near a restroom. Cross the road and begin tracing the now-asphalt path among campsites.

HIKER TREKS PAST BLOOMING RHODODENDRON

BOONE FORK IS A RUGGED, BOULDER STREWN STREAM

However, the way is clear, despite asphalt spurs in the campground. You may smell the aroma of campfires and food cooking, whetting your appetite. Consider an overnighting experience here. The campground offers a variety of sites. I recommend viewing the sites in person; some camps are real dogs, while others may be just what you're looking for.

A spur trail goes right toward Price Lake just before you near the campground registration kiosk at 4.7 miles. The trail becomes dirt again. Walk near another loop of the campground, then descend toward Boone Fork, returning to the picnic area, where you complete the rewarding hike at 5.4 miles.

38

Flat Top Tower

TOTAL DISTANCE: 5.8-mile there-and-back	
HIKING TIME: 2:15	
VERTICAL RISE: 670 feet	
RATING: Moderate	
MAPS: Moses Cone Park Trails, USGS 7.5' Boone NC	
TRAILHEAD GPS COORDINATES: N36°08.940', W81°41.571'	
CONTACT INFORMATION: Blue Ridge Parkway, 199 Hemphill Knob Road, Asheville, NC 28803, (828) 348-3400, www.nps.gov/blri	

Enjoy a foot-friendly hike to an observation tower high atop the Blue Ridge, where you can survey the Carolina mountains in all directions. Your destination is Flat Top Mountain, a peak reached via the series of gravel carriage roads that are part of the former Moses Cone estate, now part of the greater Blue Ridge Parkway. Start the adventure at the home of Moses Cone, complete with a visitor center, craft shop, and gift shop, then make your way along the ridge of Flat Top Mountain, where fields open onto views of Grandfather Mountain. Resume woods walking before reaching the pinnacle of Flat Top, where a tower allows 360-degree vistas from the 4,558 foot summit. The grades are gentle throughout, and the wide gravel track makes for easy hiking.

GETTING THERE

From the intersection of US 221 and US 321 in Blowing Rock, take US 321 North for 1 mile to the Blue Ridge Parkway exit, then turn left on the Blue Ridge Parkway and follow it for 2.2 miles to the entrance to the Cone Manor House. Park and walk to the manor house, then start your hike from the base of the front steps of the house.

THE HIKE

Just to be clear, the carriage roads of Moses Cone Park are closed to vehicular traffic, though they are open to infrequent equestrians. Interestingly, the carriage roads of Moses Cone Park are used by cross-country skiers in winter.

Moses Cone started out as a dry goods salesman for his father, then focused on fabrics, eventually purchasing textile mills. Ultimately, it was through a business relationship with

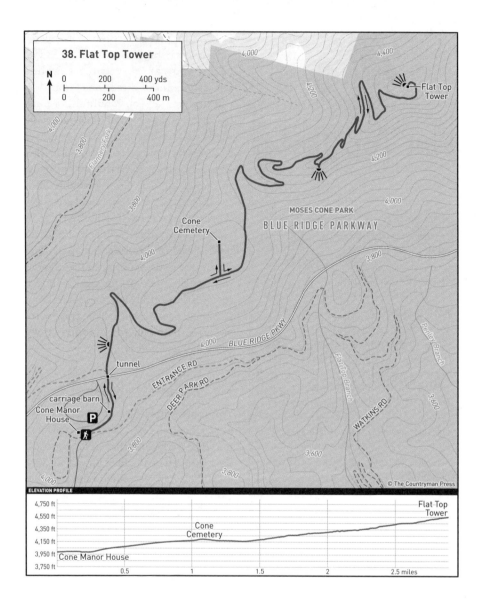

38. Flat Top Tower

ELEVATION PROFILE

the famed jeans maker Levi Strauss and Company—to whom he supplied fabric—that Mr. Cone became known as the "Denim King" (these same companies still provide material for Levi Strauss to this day).

Unfortunately, Mr. Cone suffered from poor health and thus purchased and built his mountain estate Flat Top Manor to revitalize himself in the Carolina highland air. Alas, the Denim King died in 1908. His wife lived another 39 years, then willed Flat Top Manor to the National Park Service. Now the white manse serves as a gathering spot for those touring the home or visiting the craft shop, visitor center, and gift shop.

Our hike to Flat Top Tower starts here as well. As you look out and enjoy

IN FLORIDA THEY SWIM WITH THE DOLPHINS; IN CAROLINA WE HIKE WITH THE COWS

the view from the front porch of Flat Top Manor, nearly 4,000 feet in elevation, walk down the steps to join the carriage road leading left to shortly pass the two-story carriage barn. You are heading northeast. Quickly reach and pass the carriage house on a wide gravel track. If some of the trees and bushes along the way look planted, your hunch is right. Much of the estate was landscaped for scenic value.

At 0.2 mile, walk through the short tunnel under the Blue Ridge Parkway. Immediately following this point, the track splits. The road left leads to Trout Lake but we go right along Flat Top Road. Wander through a meadow, whereupon a view of Grandfather Mountain opens to your left. Locust, oak, and maple border the field of grazing cattle separated from you by a fence. At 0.5 mile, the trail makes a switchback to the right, gaining the nose of the Flat Top Mountain. You are now in full-blown woodland, making a gentle ascent. The 25 miles of carriage roads are characterized by moderate grades throughout, making the entire trail system fun for hikers of all ages.

In fact, the trek to Flat Top Tower is a time-honored family hike along the Blue Ridge Parkway.

Continue rambling in oak-dominated hardwoods. At 0.9 mile, the trail opens onto another meadow. Ahead, you will find the mown spur trail leading to the graves of Moses and Bertha Cone. Follow the spur left to view the memorials, cordoned off by a decorative iron fence. Note the planted spruce adjacent to the east-facing graves. Backtrack to Flat Top

LOOKING NORTH TOWARD BOONE FROM FLAT TOP TOWER

THE CARRIAGE ROADS LEADING TO FLAT TOP MAKE FOR EASY HIKING

Road and continue trekking through the dips and swales of the meadow. Panoramas open toward still-higher terrain, including the balance of Flat Top Mountain and south toward Blowing Rock. Close at hand, wildflowers such as Turk's cap lily brighten the aspect on a summer day.

At 1.6 miles, the road makes a sharp switchback to the right. Avoid shortcutting the switchbacks, because that causes erosion. Continue the quest for the peak, winding higher yet in the gentlest of fashions. At 2.1 miles, look for a short spur leading right to a rock outcrop. Here, you can gaze south, down on the mountain town of Blowing Rock and east toward the Piedmont. The Blue Ridge Parkway forms a black ribbon through the forest below. Pass another second south and east view at 2.2 miles, where the road makes another switchback.

Begin the final climb to the tower.

Angle uphill in woods. Look for yellow birch thriving at this high elevation, as well as some preserved hemlocks. Come to the metal tower and mountaintop clearing at 2.9 miles. Here, the 40-foot metal tower rises in front of you. It replaced a wooden one built in 1900, which quickly deteriorated in the mountain winters of these regal yet unforgiving highlands.

Take the 54 steps and you are at the top of the tower, an open lookout. Look for the town of Boone in the Watauga Valley to the northeast, with Elk Knob rising to the left of Boone. Grandfather Mountain forms a bulk to the west. A host of mountains stretches to the horizon in all directions, offering a first-rate panorama accessed via a moderate trail suitable for hikers of all abilities. Come on up and give it a try. However, note that summertime will offer the most activities in and around the Cone Manor House in addition to the hike.

Elk Knob

TOTAL DISTANCE: 3.8-mile there-and-back
HIKING TIME: 1:50
VERTICAL RISE: 1,040 feet
RATING: Moderate
MAPS: Elk Knob State Park, USGS 7.5' Zionville TN-NC
TRAILHEAD GPS COORDINATES: N36°19'53.7", W81°41'20.8"
CONTACT INFORMATION: Elk Knob State Park, 5564 Meat Camp Road, Todd, NC 28684, (828) 297-7261, www.ncparks.gov/elk-knob-state-park

Take a walk on the high side at one of North Carolina's newer state parks. This adventure in Watauga County starts high and stays high as you begin at the preserve's developed area then begin a steady but moderate uptick to crest out over a mile high. At the peak, you can enjoy extensive panoramas of the nearby Southern Appalachians extending well into Virginia. The air is nearly always cool up here but save your trip for a clear day to enjoy the extensive panoramas earned by those who make their way to this out-of-the-way destination.

GETTING THERE

From the intersection of US 421 and NC 194 in Boone, take NC 194 North for 4.3 miles to turn left on Meat Camp Road and follow it for 5.4 miles to turn left into Elk Knob State Park. Enter the park and drive a short distance to the Elk Knob Trail parking area.

THE HIKE

Established in 2003, Elk Knob State Park harbors and protects the headwaters of North Fork New River. The conical peak rises to a 5,520-foot elevation, standing out on the horizon. It took a while for the park to open to the public, and trails are being developed to this day. However, the path to Elk Knob is already laid out and has become a favorite trek for residents of nearby Boone. You will find a hike here a satisfying experience. Elk Knob wasn't even a candidate to become a state park until the peak was slated for a housing development. Local residents wanted Elk Knob to remain in its natural state. The mountain was then purchased and turned over to the state of North Carolina, at which time it became a state park. In addition to the Elk Knob

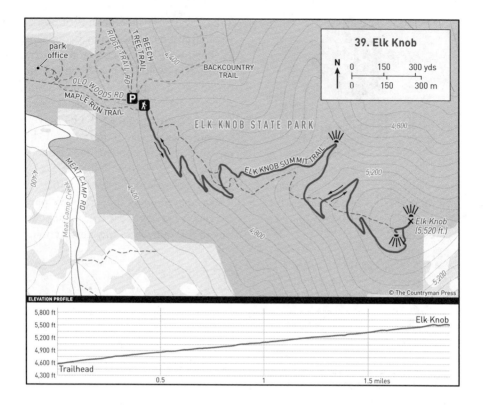

ELEVATION PROFILE

Trail, the preserve also has other pathways that lead to primitive backcountry campsites. The park also presents a wooded picnic area for use before or after the hike.

The hike starts in a saddle on the west slope of Elk Knob. You are already over 4,500 feet in elevation. Walk around a pole gate, joining the Elk Knob Summit Trail in rich northern hardwoods dominated by yellow birch, complemented by buckeye, beech, red maple, and northern red oak.

Yellow birch trees shade mossy rocks and ferns. To identify a yellow birch, look for the yellowish-gold, peeling bark with horizontal stripes. Larger yellow birches will not have bark peeling on their lower trunks, but will still have peeling bark on their upper limbs. The twigs and leaves, when crushed, have a slight wintergreen aroma. Primarily a tree of the north, ranging from Minnesota to Maine, yellow birch stretches south down the spine of the Appalachians all the way to the South Carolina and Georgia mountain regions. It can be found in moist, cool environments throughout the mountain regions of North Carolina. It will often sprout on nutrient-rich rotting logs. Later, the yellow birch grows and the log rots completely away, leaving the yellow birch to look as if it grew up on its root "legs."

The path is in impeccable shape, expertly graded. Grasses sway under the trees, and in later summer, stinging nettle will find its place among the hardwoods. Make your first switchback at 0.2 mile. More switchbacks come in quick succession. At 0.7 mile, you are on the shoulder of Elk Knob, then you curve

A DEER AND ITS FAWN ATOP ELK KNOB

around to its northern side. Note how the hardwoods are stunted and sculpted by the wrath of winter winds. At 1.0 mile, you are rewarded with a fine view to the north. Here, a pattern of mountains and meadows stretches toward the Virginia state line.

More switchbacks ease the climb, and you crisscross an old jeep track up the mountain, now used by rangers for maintenance and rescue. The old track is closed to public use. At 1.4 miles, you are once again on the north slope and its squat trees. The gradient of the trail remains steady. The final part of the hike takes you around the south side of Elk Knob, then rises into a brushy heath community of tightly-woven, head-high bushes.

At the summit at 1.9 miles, the trail splits into two short prongs, one with a south view and another with a north view. On a clear day you will be well rewarded. From the stony south view, you can peer toward Grandfather

FIND TURK'S CAP LILY ALONG THE TRAIL IN SUMMERTIME

THE OVERLOOK AT ELK KNOB EXTENDS CLEAR INTO VIRGINIA

Mountain, with Mount Mitchell in the far distance as well as closer peaks such as Humpback Mountain, Beech Mountain and Snake Mountain.

The north view is my favorite. You are on the actual peak, at 5,520 feet, in a small grassy area, bordered in brush with rock outcrops. Here, a cleared area proffers panoramas of a mosaic of mountains and meadows, rolling valleys, and tall wooded crests, clear into Virginia, including the high points of Mount Rogers, Whitetop Mountain, and North Carolina's Mount Jefferson, a state natural area with trails to explore. The drop-off from the overlook is quite steep—don't look down!

Caudill Cabin

TOTAL DISTANCE: 9.8-mile there-and-back

HIKING TIME: 5:10

VERTICAL RISE: 1,650 feet

RATING: Moderate–difficult due to length of hike

MAPS: Doughton Park Hiking Trails, USGS 7.5' Whitehead NC

TRAILHEAD GPS COORDINATES: N36°22'30.9", W81°08'41.2"

CONTACT INFORMATION: Blue Ridge Parkway, 199 Hemphill Knob Road, Asheville, NC 28803, (828) 348-3400, www.nps.gov/blri

This Blue Ridge Parkway hike takes you deep into Basin Cove, where stands the Caudill Cabin. Along the way, you will enjoy walking along a scenic tumbling trout stream, finding evidence of other mountain people who dwelled in this gorgeous highland country at the foot of the Blue Ridge. The hike leads up along Basin Creek, where you first run into an attractive backcountry campsite. Ahead, range deeper into the mountains where you view a pair of wild waterfalls and other cataracts before arriving at the clearing of the Caudill Cabin. Although the hike is nearly 10 miles round trip, the grades are gentle. However, be apprised that multiple bridgeless creek crossings are necessary, and you will likely get your feet wet, making this trek a more likely warm-weather proposition.

GETTING THERE

From Wilkesboro, take NC 18 North for 16 miles toward Sparta; turn right onto Longbottom Road and follow it for 6.4 miles to a parking area on your right, just after crossing the bridge over Basin Creek. The parking area is on the right of Longbottom Road, whereas the trail is on the left side of the road.

THE HIKE

The Caudill Cabin is the only remaining structure of what was once a thriving community in Basin Cove. Built in 1890 by Martin Caudill, the wood structure is set on a hillside in the shadow of Wildcat Rock. Back then, however, Basin Cove looked very different from the forested wildland it is today. Twenty or more families lived in the valley, and much of the bottomland was cleared and farmed, with products locally consumed and also sent to the nearby Wilkesboro market.

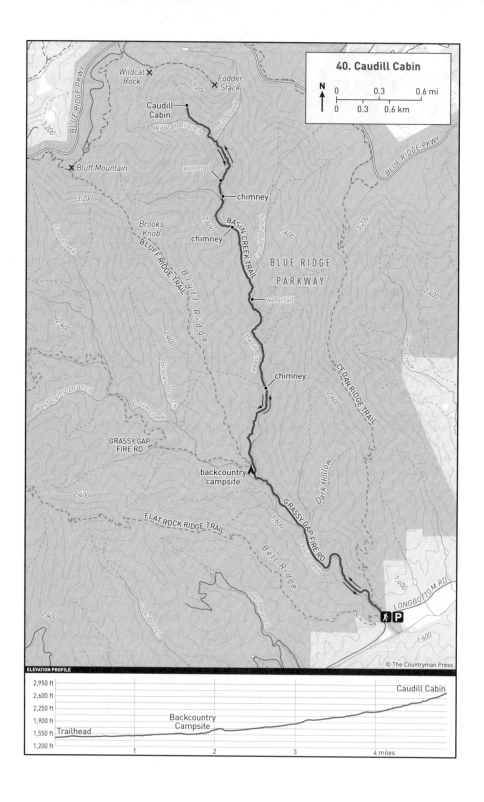

40. Caudill Cabin

N

| 0 | | 0.3 | | 0.6 mi |
| 0 | 0.3 | | 0.6 km | |

Wildcat Rock ✕

Fodder Stack ✕

3,200

Caudill Cabin ■

Wildcat Branch

Basin Creek

BLUE RIDGE PKWY

3,200

waterfall

3,200

✕ Bluff Mountain

■ chimney

BLUE RIDGE PARKWAY

Brooks Knob

2,400

BASIN CREEK TRAIL

BLUFF RIDGE TRAIL

■ chimney

Caudill Branch

2,400

2,400

Bluff Ridge

Cove Creek

■ waterfall

Basin Creek

2,400

■ chimney

Camp Creek

2,400

West Camp Branch

Brooks Branch

Cove Creek

CEDAR RIDGE TRAIL

2,400

GRASSY GAP FIRE RD

Dark Hollow

backcountry campsite ⚠

2,400

FLAT ROCK RIDGE TRAIL

GRASSY GAP FIRE RD

1,600

Bell Ridge

Basin Creek

1,600

2,400

Cook Branch

Bell Branch

LONGBOTTOM RD

1,600

🚶 🅿

© The Countryman Press

ELEVATION PROFILE

				Caudill Cabin
2,950 ft				
2,600 ft				
2,250 ft				
1,900 ft		Backcountry		
1,550 ft Trailhead		Campsite		
1,200 ft				
	1	2	3	4 miles

Basin Creek Union Baptist Church was the social heart of the community, along with its school, open 4 months a year. Life in Basin Cove consisted of farming with the seasons, raising corn and wheat, potatoes, and vegetables. In addition, the men often hunted wild game and the women spun fabric. What they couldn't make on the farm they traded for in nearby Absher.

Life was pretty good until that fateful day in July 1916. The rain fell, and fell more, and fell still more until Basin Creek and its tributaries were raging brown torrents. Before the waters receded, nearly every home in the valley had been uprooted and most of its residents killed. Remaining residents of Basin Creek left en masse. The Caudill Cabin withstood the flood but was abandoned in 1918. In 1938, the Caudill Cabin was bought up by the National Park Service, and the whole area became part of the greater Doughton Park, a Blue Ridge Parkway tract of over 5,000 acres with hiking trails.

Start your hike by leaving Longbottom Road and heading up gated Grassy Gap Fire Road, with Basin Creek to your left. The Flat Rock Ridge Trail begins on the other side of Basin Creek. Walk just a short distance, then the Cedar Ridge Trail leaves right. Stay with the double-track as Basin Creek dances and sings to your left. Pass a small dam. The walking is easy—you only gain 900 feet in the first 4 miles, walking among mixed evergreens and hardwoods while the mountainsides rise steeply.

At 1.1 miles, step over a side creek coming out of Dark Hollow. Beyond here, rise above a big flat separating you from Basin Creek before descending to cross the stream on a wide bridge and enter the Basin Cove backcountry campsite at 1.7 miles. White pines and preserved

hemlocks shade the level scenic area with several designated camping areas, complete with fire rings, lantern posts, and food storage boxes.

Reach a major trail intersection at the upper end of the campsite. Here, Grassy Gap Fire Road and Bluff Ridge Trail leave left, while we stay right, joining the Basin Creek Trail, now heading up the narrowing valley, rich with wildflowers and ferns, national-park-level scenery all around. Big pools are found between rapids, bordered by sizeable mossy boulders.

At 2.4 miles, come to your first trailside chimney. These cabins so close to Basin Creek were probably wiped out during the violent flood of 1916. Make your first crossing at 2.5 miles. There are many more to come, and if you can't make it across this one dry-footed you will likely be fording the rest of the way. By 3.0 miles, the crossings become more frequent, as craggy bluffs force the trail to one side or another of Basin Creek. At 3.2 miles, you are on the left-hand bank and can look down the stream at a 30-foot slide waterfall that is very difficult to access. Ahead, look for more

THE REFURBISHED CAUDILL CABIN STANDS IN THE SHADOW OF THE BLUE RIDGE

FIND THIS 25-FOOT CATARACT ON UPPER BASIN CREEK

evidence of homesites—retaining walls, level spots, and rock piles. It is hard to imagine these regal woods were once open fields.

At 3.3 miles, hop over Caudill Branch, almost as big as Basin Creek, entering on your right. The valley narrows yet again. At 3.7 miles, pass the remains of another chimney. Here, the trail takes you directly through where the cabin would've stood. At 4.1 miles, pass another crumbled chimney. Two streams border this flat. During the 1916 flood, these residents never stood a chance.

At 4.2 miles, you are on the right-hand bank heading upstream, walking a rock slab, and you suddenly come upon an exquisite sight. Below and to your left, Basin Creek spills in a 25-foot cataract, first pouring down over a rock slab, then slowing, then making a second shorter drop into an alluring plunge pool all framed in stone and greenery.

The creek crossings continue in the narrow gorge, replete with big boulders, cliffs and lesser cascades. The ascent sharpens. A clearing opens ahead, and at 4.9 miles you reach the Caudill Cabin. The square log structure has two doors, a fireplace, and no windows. Look around inside. The cabin usually has interpretive information inside. Outside, imagine 15–20 acres cleared instead of what you see now. The homestead was only occupied for 28 years, and yet it is a reminder of life in the Carolina mountains before our day. Allow yourself ample time to return to the trailhead after exploring the cabin.

IV.

SOUTH CAROLINA MOUNTAINS

41

Opossum Creek Falls

TOTAL DISTANCE: 4.6-mile there-and-back

HIKING TIME: 2:15

VERTICAL RISE: 770 feet

RATING: Easy-moderate

MAPS: Sumter National Forest—Andrew Pickens Ranger District; USGS 7.5' Rainy Mountain GA-SC

TRAILHEAD GPS COORDINATES: N34°46'23.8", W83°18'14.8"

CONTACT INFORMATION: Sumter National Forest, Andrew Pickens Ranger District Office, 112 Andrew Pickens Circle, Mountain Rest, SC 29664, (864) 638-9568, www.fs.usda.gov/scnfs

This is the most westerly marked and maintained trail in the mountains of South Carolina, located in the tip of Oconee County near the Georgia state line. This hike offers a walk from high to low on a well-maintained and nicely graded trail that leads to the famed Chattooga River. An alluring beach and swimming hole are located on the federally designated wild and scenic river. In the warmer season, you will often see rafters and kayakers paddling the Chattooga. The trail then turns away from the river and up the cool incised valley of Opossum Creek to reach a dramatic 55-foot waterfall descending in a series of drops, saving its biggest splash for last.

GETTING THERE

From Westminster, South Carolina, take US 76 West for 13.5 miles to near Long Creek. Turn left on Damascus Church Road (the Long Creek Volunteer Fire Department is here). Follow Damascus Church Road for 0.9 mile to Battle Creek Road. Turn right and follow Battle Creek Road for 1.9 miles to Turkey Ridge Road, gravel Forest Road 755. Follow Turkey Ridge Road for 2.1 miles and you will see the Opossum Creek Trail on your left. However, continue up the road another 50 yards to a parking area on your left. Backtrack to the trail.

THE HIKE

Enjoy rewarding views along the drive to the trailhead here, especially of Rabun Bald, across the Georgia state line. From the parking area, backtrack just a bit on the forest road to join the trail to Opossum Creek Falls, bordered by boulders. Begin the nearly painless 770-foot descent on the well-contoured pathway, entering dry piney woods.

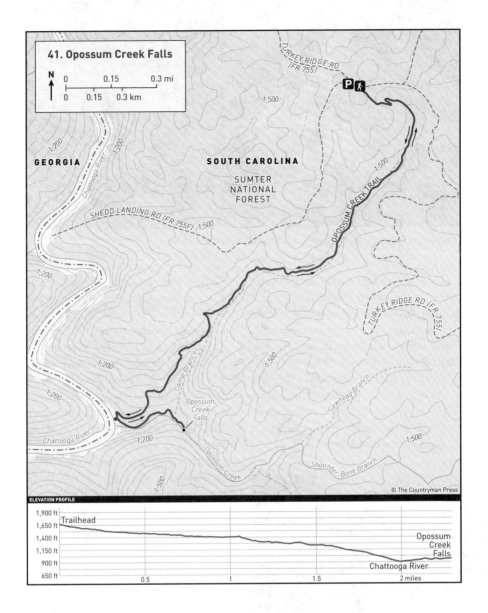

41. Opossum Creek Falls

ELEVATION PROFILE

Circle into the valley of Camp Branch, which feeds Opossum Creek. You will be in this valley for most of the hike. Hickories, oaks and dogwood trees prevail along the upper part of this streambed.

As the trail deepens into the now more moist valley, holly, sycamore and magnolia appear. At 0.5 mile, a spur creek flows in from the left and the valley widens. The going is easy in this perched vale

that transitions into Southern Appalachian streamside forest, with black birch and rhododendron added to the mix.

At 0.6 mile, hop over upper Camp Branch amid doghobble. Ahead, the valley narrows again, slicing through tight hills, forcing the stream to run narrow over rocky chutes under evergreens. At 1.0 mile, leave the old roadbed you've been following and resume the single-track

DESTINATIONS LIKE OPOSSUM CREEK FALLS MAKE HIKING IN THE CAROLINA MOUNTAINS SPECIAL

trail well above the creek. Camp Branch is diving sharply for the Chattooga and making its own noisy waterfalls, in cascading stages, mostly unseen through the rhododendron. The cataracts are very difficult to access due to the sheer slope between the trail and the water. The path now works around the big drop to your left, circling into tiny feeder streamlets, and even going uphill some, continuing its quest for the Chattooga River.

LOOKING OUT ON THE CHATTOOGA RIVER NEAR ITS CONFLUENCE WITH OPOSSUM CREEK

White pines tower overhead and the valley widens further. You sense the breadth of the Chattooga Valley ahead, maybe even feel warmer air on a summer day, and begin to hear the deeper roar of the rapids versus the splashy drops of Camp Branch. Reach the Chattooga River at 2.0 miles. The wooded flat is sandy and paths diverge, as previous hikers have been anxious to view the big waterway. Opossum Creek is coming in at an angle, flowing left to right, while the Chattooga is flowing right to left. Walk out to the river, where the Chattooga is bending to the west. A wonderful sand beach is located here, crafting an ideal swimming spot. If it is a warm day, especially on weekends, you will see rafters plying the series of rapids upstream, and jumping off a big rock well upriver. The immediate series of named upstream rapids are Class IV–V and include Corkscrew Rapid, Crack-in-the-Rock, Jaw Bone, Sock 'em Dog, and Shoulder Bone. These, and the ones just below the bend which you are at, are the lowermost rapids on the Chattooga before the river is dammed as Tugaloo Lake.

River floaters will tell you Chattooga River deserves its wild and scenic designation, and then some. Culled from

OPOSSUM CREEK FALLS PLUMMETS 55 FEET IN ITS ENTIRETY

South Carolina's Sumter National Forest, the Nantahala National Forest of North Carolina and the Chattahoochee National Forest of Georgia, this wild and scenic river corridor protects one of the most significant free-flowing streams in the Southeast. The river itself is 50 miles long, starting in North Carolina, then heads southwest, forming the Georgia-South Carolina border before meeting the Tallulah River and forming the Tugaloo River.

The Chattooga is perhaps best known for being the backdrop of the Burt Reynolds movie *Deliverance*. It was around this time, in 1974, that the Chattooga was designated a wild and scenic river, a place where rafters, canoers, kayakers, and anglers enjoy this valley of massive boulders, clear trout and bass filled waters, and deep forests. Hikers have miles of river corridor hiking that link to adjacent national forest lands.

The Opossum Creek Trail turns left at the river and upstream along Opossum Creek. Bisect a small campsite then slice between carved beech trees, entering a slender vale. At this point, the trail is more heavily used, because the cataract is accessed by boaters. Reach Camp Branch just above its confluence with Opossum Creek at 2.1 miles and step over this small stream. Turn up Opossum Creek. The trail becomes jumbled with boulders just before reaching 55-foot high Opossum Creek Falls at 2.3 miles. Here, the stream makes an initial slide to the left, then comes toward you in a drop. The creek splits and turns, always descending, before gathering one last time for a single sliding dramatic plunge onto a stony bed, where it continues working its way toward the Chattooga. The area just below the falls features alluring observation boulders. Sit awhile before your return trip to the trailhead.

Station Cove Falls via Historic Oconee Station

This hike begins at one of South Carolina's first mountain frontier outposts, Oconee Station, that you can explore before circling around a pond to then enter Sumter National Forest along Station Creek. Here, beavers have dammed the lower reaches of the stream in a large wide cove, and streamlets trickle toward Station Creek beneath lush woodlands, rife with wildflowers in spring. The valley narrows and the trail enters a steep valley harboring Station Cove Falls. On your return trip, circle the other side of the pond. Consider bringing a picnic lunch, because Oconee Station has an excellent picnic ground.

GETTING THERE

From the intersection of SC 28 and SC 11 in Walhalla, South Carolina, head north on SC 11 for 6.3 miles to Oconee Station Road. Turn left on Oconee Station Road and follow it for 2.1 miles to the park entrance, on your right. Follow the park road to dead end at a parking area, adjacent to a picnic ground, restroom, and small park office. From the parking area, follow the trail uphill to Oconee Station.

THE HIKE

Just uphill from the trailhead are Oconee Station and the William Richards house. Take the time to see the buildings. A trail leads from the parking area to the site. Guided tours are held on Saturday and Sunday, 1–5 p.m. Oconee Station was erected in 1792, the first in a series of fortifications to protect settlers from American Indian attacks as they moved into what was then the western frontier. Tensions mounted as settlers moved into the Cherokee Foothills, leading to run-ins with the Cherokee. The government response was to build seven outposts such as Oconee

---

TOTAL DISTANCE: 3.1-mile loop with spurs

HIKING TIME: 1:20

VERTICAL RISE: 280 feet

RATING: Easy

MAPS: Sumter National Forest—Andrew Pickens Ranger District, Oconee Station State Historic Site; USGS 7.5' Walhalla SC

TRAILHEAD GPS COORDINATES: N34°50'45.9", W83°04'11.8"

CONTACT INFORMATION: Oconee Station State Historic Site, 500 Oconee Station Road, Walhalla, SC 29691, (864) 638-0079, www.southcarolinaparks.com; Sumter National Forest, Andrew Pickens Ranger District Office, 112 Andrew Pickens Circle, Mountain Rest, SC 29664, (864) 638-9568, www.fs.usda.gov/scnfs

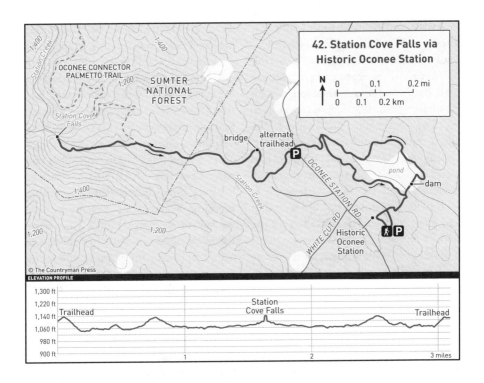

42. Station Cove Falls via Historic Oconee Station

N
0   0.1   0.2 mi
0   0.1   0.2 km

OCONEE CONNECTOR
PALMETTO TRAIL

SUMTER
NATIONAL
FOREST

Station Cove Falls

bridge
alternate trailhead

OCONEE STATION RD.

pond

dam

Station Creek

WHITE CUT RD.

Historic
Oconee
Station

© The Countryman Press

ELEVATION PROFILE

1,300 ft
1,220 ft
1,140 ft — Trailhead
1,060 ft
980 ft
900 ft

Station Cove Falls

Trailhead

1   2   3 miles

Station in the South Carolina upstate. The brick structure housed soldiers over an 8-year period, after which area American Indian tribes were subdued and settlements were well established, making attacks unlikely. During this period, the outpost also became a trading post. Troops were removed for good by 1799.

William Richards was the lead trader at the outpost and built the brick house next to Oconee Station in 1805. At this time, deer skins were in high demand across the Atlantic. Local American Indians hunted deer and brought their skins to the trading post, to exchange for goods ranging from iron pots to guns to whiskey to cotton clothing. Guns were the most highly prized; the Indians could use the guns to gain tactical advantage over their foes as well as to hunt deer. Over time, they brought thousands of deer skins to the station. Imagine all the trading and interactions two centuries

back. However, the American frontier moved westward and Oconee Station became a backwater. Now the 210-acre site, listed on the National Register of Historic Places, is part of the South Carolina state park system.

HISTORIC OCONEE STATION WAS ERECTED IN 1792

At the trailhead, a path leads just a few yards uphill to Oconee Station. Explore the buildings, then take the trail leaving north to cross the park access road. Pass a trail kiosk, then join a natural surface path, descending in woods to reach an intersection at 0.2 mile. To the left, a sign indicates the falls, but keep straight and downhill, reaching the historic site pond. Walk over the pond dam, open to the sun. This lake can be popular with bank fishermen, going for bream and other species. The trail then curves to the right, away from where you think it should go. Give it time, as it curves back to the left then circles the pond in pine, sweetgum, and sourwoods about 30 feet above the lake. Step over a couple of dry streambeds that lead to quiet coves in the pond.

Join an old roadbed along the pond, circling to its head, then reach a trail junction at 0.6 mile. Turn right here, now on the track to Station Cove Falls. Cross Oconee Station Road and reach an alternate trailhead, with parking area and kiosk at 0.8 mile. Dip back into woodland on a wide track through white oak dominated woods and meet the first of several small feeder branches of Station Creek. Span the stream on a wooden footbridge at 1.0 mile. This forested cove displays wildflowers aplenty in spring.

To your left is Station Creek, but you can't hear it flowing. That's because beavers have dammed up the creek, forming a mountain wetland. Beavers were once common all over the Palmetto State, save for the coast, but were trapped to the point where many biologists believed the rodent to have disappeared from South Carolina. In 1940, six beavers from Georgia were reintroduced to the Sandhills National Wildlife Refuge in Chesterfield County. Around that same time, beavers from the Savannah River basin in Georgia came over the border themselves. From these two populations, beavers have spread throughout the state and are now

HIKERS GATHER AT THE BASE OF STATION COVE FALLS

STATION COVE FALLS CAN RUN LOW IN EARLY AUTUMN

in all 46 South Carolina counties. Beavers create shallow ponds such as this, which attract other wildlife, especially waterfowl, and are in general a boon to any ecosystem. Their dams slow watercourses, settling sediment and filtering waters to make them cleaner.

The hollow narrows beyond the beaver pond and Station Creek flows anew. Cross more side streams. Enter Sumter National Forest at 1.2 miles. At 1.4 miles, reach a trail junction and stile. Here, the Oconee Connector of the Palmetto Trail leaves right and uphill, to make Oconee State Park via Station Mountain. The stile here lets only hikers continue to the falls. The hollow narrows and steepens.

Rock hop translucent Station Creek on a wide rock slab to reach the falls at 1.6 miles. Here, Station Cove Falls pours over a rock lip, descends in stages, slows for a brief period, then widens over a final dive, completing a 60-foot fall. The rock cathedral around the cascade is the catch point for many fallen logs.

From here, backtrack along Station Creek, crossing Oconee Station Road to reach the trail junction near the park pond at 2.6 miles. This time, take the right fork, circling around the south side of the lake, crossing intermittent branches to finally climb back to Oconee Station, completing your hike at 3.1 miles.

Pigpen Falls and Lick Log Falls

TOTAL DISTANCE: 2.0 mile there-and-back

HIKING TIME: 1:10

VERTICAL RISE: 260 feet

RATING: Easy, does have scramble at hike's end

MAPS: National Geographic #785 Nantahala National Forest—Nantahala & Cullasaja Gorges, Sumter National Forest—Andrew Pickens Ranger District; USGS 7.5' Tamassee SC

TRAILHEAD GPS COORDINATES: N34°55'30.1", W83°07'21.2"

CONTACT INFORMATION: Sumter National Forest, Andrew Pickens Ranger District Office, 112 Andrew Pickens Circle, Mountain Rest, SC 29664, (864) 638-9568, www.fs.usda.gov/scnfs

This short hike deep in the gorge of the wild and scenic Chattooga River leads to waterfalls sure to please the eye, as well as a good look at the Chattooga River itself. Start on the venerated Foothills Trail at the remote Nicholson Ford trailhead, then wind through rich woods, following Pigpen Branch to its confluence with Licklog Creek and beyond to wide 10-foot Pigpen Falls. Enjoy this spiller then work farther downstream, where Lick Log Falls makes two major drops, the first of which is a 25-foot curtain-type cataract while the second is more of an angled cascade, dropping 65 feet where it meets the Chattooga River. Be apprised that though the hike is easy, the last part to reach the base of Lick Log Falls is steep and irregular.

GETTING THERE

From the intersection of SC 28 and SC 107 near Mountain Rest, South Carolina, take SC 107 north for 3.4 miles to turn left on Village Creek Road and follow it for 1.8 miles to turn right onto Nicholson Ford Road and it becomes gravel. Follow it for 2.1 miles, crossing a couple of small creek fords, then split right onto Pigpen Branch Road (if you stay straight here you enter a private drive) to shortly dead end at the trailhead.

THE HIKE

This hike offers aquatic rewards aplenty for the effort. And you use two of South Carolina's most scenic pathways on one hike—the Foothills Trail and the Chattooga Trail, both of which traverse the federally designated wild and scenic Chattooga River. Also known as the Thrift Lake parking area, the Nicholson Ford trailhead offers access to the

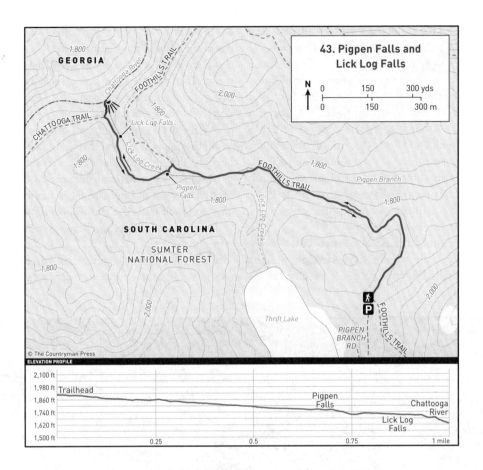

By 0.3 mile, you can hear Pigpen Falls and Lick Log Falls elevation profile. (1,800 ft, 2,000 ft, GEORGIA, SOUTH CAROLINA, SUMTER NATIONAL FOREST, Thrift Lake, Pigpen Falls, Lick Log Falls, Chattooga Trail, Foothills Trail, Pigpen Branch Rd.)

Foothills Trail in two directions. Make sure you join the segment of the Foothills Trail heading toward the Chattooga River and Burrells Ford. The well-marked and maintained single-track path runs under towering white pines, flanked by mountain laurel, maple and holly. Golden needles carpet the trailbed. Ferns add a touch of green to the forest floor.

By 0.3 mile, you can hear Pigpen Branch singing in the hollow below. Rhododendron thickens near Pigpen Branch. At 0.5 mile, the Foothills Trail leads past a streamside campsite partly shaded by tall white pines. Ahead, cross clear rushing Pigpen Branch on

a footbridge. Notice the speckles of pyrite—fool's gold—sparkling in the creek bottom. Ahead, cross Lick Log Creek. Pigpen Branch is a tributary of Licklog Creek. Both of these names are farming-related. The derivation of the name Pigpen is self-explanatory. However, Lick Log is a term used by yesteryear farmers. When running cattle, salt was used to supplement the cow's diet. Farmers would use hollowed-out logs to hold the cow's salt supplement, and the salt would hold in the hollowed out part as well as seep into the log itself, creating a salt lick. And because the salt lick was on a log, you have the name Lick Log for this creek!

Think about that when you cross Lick Log Creek another again, this time by bridge. You are now on the right-hand bank, descending. Come to a trail intersection at 0.8 mile. Here, the Foothills Trail stays straight, aiming for the Chattooga River and onward to Table Rock State Park. Our hike splits left and downhill, now on the Chattooga Trail. Immediately return to Lick Log Creek and reach the base of Pigpen Falls. Here you will find a large but shallow pool at the base of a wide rock ledge. The primary thrust of Pigpen Falls drops dead ahead but at the far right side of the ledge you will see a second, lesser cascade. A sizable sandbar collects at the outer edge of the plunge pool.

From Pigpen Falls, take the Chattooga Trail across Lick Log Creek by bridge, then continue down the Lick Log Creek valley, cutting a deeper gorge now. Ahead, on your right, you will hear a roar then see the upper cataract of Lick Log Falls. Here, the mountain stream pours over a lip, creating a curtain-type drop. This part of Lick Log Falls is not easy to reach from the trail. The valley widens and the Chattooga River comes into view below. Just as the Chattooga Trail curves downstream, look for a user-created path dropping right, very

A FACE ON VIEW OF LICK LOG FALLS

LICK LOG FALLS FLOWS DIRECTLY INTO THE CHATTOOGA RIVER

steeply, down to the confluence of Lick Log Creek and the Chattooga River. Carefully clamber down, using arms and legs for balance. Then you reach the meeting of the creek and the river at 1.0 mile. Here, stand on a sandbar and gaze upstream at Lick Log Falls. This is a gorgeous ledge cascade, widening as it spills 65 feet in stages, alternating rock and water, finally adding its flow to the Chattooga River, which in turn tumbles in rapids and fulfills its role as the boundary between South Carolina and Georgia, just across the river. With care you can work your way up to the upper part of Lick Log Falls.

King Creek Falls and Big Bend Falls

TOTAL DISTANCE: 7.6 mile there-and-back with spur

HIKING TIME: 4:10

VERTICAL RISE: 250 feet

RATING: Moderate, does have scramble to Big Bend Falls

MAPS: National Geographic #785 Nantahala National Forest—Nantahala & Cullasaja Gorges, Sumter National Forest—Andrew Pickens Ranger District; USGS 7.5' Satolah GA–SC–NC

TRAILHEAD GPS COORDINATES: N34°58'17.1", W83°06'52.9"

CONTACT INFORMATION: Sumter National Forest, Andrew Pickens Ranger District Office, 112 Andrew Pickens Circle, Mountain Rest, SC 29664, (864) 638-9568, www.fs.usda.gov/scnfs

This hike travels entirely within the Chattooga Wild and Scenic River corridor, reaching two entirely different yet equally attractive falls. The first, King Creek Falls, is widely considered to be the most scenic falls in the entire Sumter National Forest. It drops 80-plus feet over a rock face, ever widening to end at a catch basin bordered by a large gravel bar. The second, Big Bend Falls, is simply the power of a large river following gravity. Delicate beauty versus raw power. Leave Burrells Ford parking area, with its primitive walk-in camping area nearby, then cruise downstream along the wild and scenic Chattooga River, with its everywhere-you-look beauty, to reach Kings Creek shortly. A spur trail takes you up King Creek to its falls. The hike continues down the inspiring Chattooga River valley, curving past the actual big bend of the Chattooga River, then come to Big Bend Falls. Your return trip will yield more sights and scenes of the river to imprint an album of superlative memories.

GETTING THERE

From the intersection of SC 11 and SC 28 just east of Walhalla, South Carolina, drive west on SC 28 for 9.5 miles to SC 107, then turn right. Follow SC 107 for 8.9 miles to Forest Road 708. Descend on gravel FR 708 for 3 miles. Burrells Ford parking area will be on your left. The hike starts near the signboard on the south side of the parking area.

THE HIKE

Leave the gravel parking area for Burrells Ford Walk-in Campground, on the access trail by the trailhead signboard. Immediately meet the Foothills Trail. Turn right here, heading away from

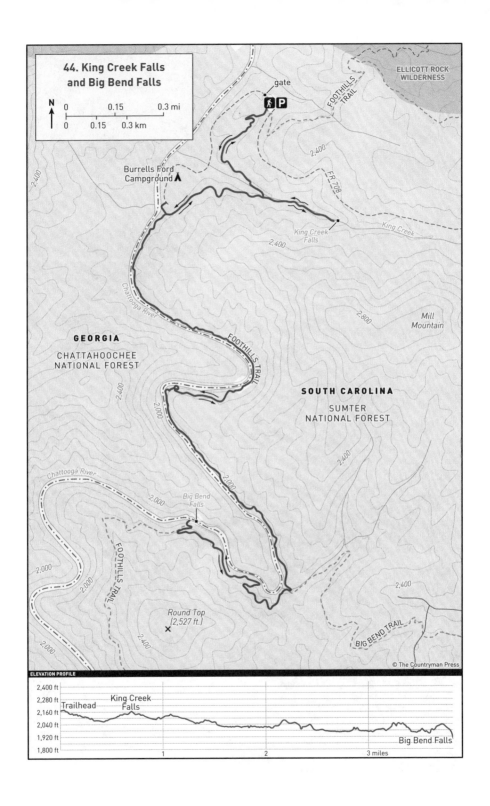

44. King Creek Falls and Big Bend Falls

N

| 0 | 0.15 | 0.3 mi |
| 0 | 0.15 | 0.3 km |

ELLICOTT ROCK
WILDERNESS

gate

FOOTHILLS TRAIL

FR. 708

Burrells Ford
Campground

2,400

King Creek
Falls

2,400

King Creek

Chattooga River

2,800

Mill
Mountain

GEORGIA

CHATTAHOOCHEE
NATIONAL FOREST

2,400

FOOTHILLS TRAIL

2,000

SOUTH CAROLINA

SUMTER
NATIONAL FOREST

2,400

2,000

Chattooga River

2,000

Big Bend
Falls

2,000

2,400

FOOTHILLS TRAIL

2,000

Round Top
(2,527 ft.)
×

2,400

BIG BEND TRAIL

© The Countryman Press

ELEVATION PROFILE

2,400 ft	
2,280 ft	King Creek
2,160 ft	Trailhead Falls
2,040 ft	
1,920 ft	Big Bend Falls
1,800 ft	
	1 2 3 miles

PROFILE VIEW OF 80 FOOT KING CREEK FALLS

Forest Road 708, southbound on the Foothills Trail, which winds through thick woods of white pine and holly with mountain laurel aplenty. Follow the single-track trail as it switchbacks through a hollow on a rooty track.

Descend to reach King Creek at 0.4 mile. A spur trail leads right toward Burrells Ford Campground. Our hike crosses King Creek on a wooden bridge. The trail then turns upstream in dense rhododendron. A campsite lies to your right. Reach a trail junction ahead. To your left, a spur trail leads 0.2 mile to Kings Creek Falls. To your right, the Foothills Trail leads downstream toward Big Bend Falls. Take the spur up toward Kings Creek, which is crashing to your left, gathering in surprisingly large pools. Keep ascending to get well above the stream, appreciating the deep valley King Creek has cut. Falling water noises echo through the valley as you reach King Creek Falls at 0.7 mile. Here, the spectacular aquatic feature makes a white dive over a lip of rock, executes three quick drops, then spreads wide in multiple cascades and flows according to the rule of gravity. The plunge pool is limited in depth, but a large gravel bar lies at the fall's base and makes for a good viewing spot. Fallen logs and boulders offer seats in the amphitheater of beauty created by water and time.

Backtrack from the falls, then continue down the Chattooga River on the Foothills Trail, swinging around the western edge of Mill Mountain, dipping into occasional hollows. At 1.3 miles, an old roadbed comes in on your right. This roadbed-trail leads to the Burrells Ford camping area. Stay south with the Foothills Trail as it nears the Chattooga but stays above the watercourse, passing seeps that feed the river.

Rock boulders and bluffs border the trailbed. Small bridges and waterbars have been installed to make the going easier on the rougher areas. Galax is especially fragrant on this steep slope. From this perch, you can look down on the river, and its attendant gravel bars. The going is rocky, rooty, and slow, as the trail works above bluffs below. The path passes along some rocklines itself. Switchbacks lead you down to the river and a sand beach at 1.9 miles. This could be a good swimming spot for those inclined. Pass more exposed rocks, ledges, and shelves on the river that would make good sunning spots when the water is low.

Leave the riverside and climb, leveling off a good 20–30 feet above the flow, soon to reach the river again at 2.6 miles after a couple of downhill switchbacks. Ahead, the trail and the river are a mere foot or two apart. In these spots, the path is ragged; flood alters the land and the vegetation. Enjoy some looks at the designated wild and scenic waterway.

The trail climbs away from the river and turns into a hollow and stream to meet the Big Bend Trail at 3.2 miles, just above a sliding cascade of an unnamed creek coming in from the left. Cross the wooden bridge and stay right on the Foothills Trail as it crosses an old closed forest road. Ahead, travel well above the river in thick brush, reaching some switchbacks that work along rough rock ledges. Continue downstream along the river as it spills over singing rapids and rocks. The trail lingers on the sloped mountainside, curving in and out of little hollows. Reach a second set of switchbacks since the Big Bend Trail intersection at 3.9 miles. You will hear Big Bend Falls before you see it. These switchbacks descend to reach the unofficial, user-created spur

HIKER ADMIRES KING CREEK FALLS

trail to the falls at 4.0 miles. Work down through rhododendron and laurel thickets. The user-created trail splits. The trail leaving right passes under a large rockhouse with many fallen boulders at its base, and you end up at the top of the 30-foot riverwide fall. Be very careful here, because everything is slippery. The trail to the base of the falls splits left, then finds a break in a ledge to reach an open rock a few feet from the falls. Power is the essence of Big Bend Falls. The cataract charges perhaps 30 feet in its entirety, bounding over layers of rock in a white froth. Exercise caution.

Ellicott Rock Wilderness Hike

TOTAL DISTANCE: 8.4-mile there-and-back	

HIKING TIME: 4:20

VERTICAL RISE: 420 feet

RATING: Moderate–difficult

MAPS: National Geographic #785 Nantahala National Forest—Nantahala & Cullasaja Gorges, Sumter National Forest—Andrew Pickens Ranger District; USGS 7.5' Tamassee SC–GA

TRAILHEAD GPS COORDINATES: N34°59'07.7", W83°04'20.0"

CONTACT INFORMATION: Sumter National Forest, Andrew Pickens Ranger District Office, 112 Andrew Pickens Circle, Mountain Rest, SC 29664, (864) 638-9568, www.fs.usda.gov/scnfs

This historic yet scenic hike start at the Walhalla State Fish Hatchery, constructed by the Civilian Conservation Corps (CCC) in the 1930s, to enter the Ellicott Rock Wilderness, then heads down the rugged East Fork gorge, passing waterfalls and an immense rock bluff before meeting the Chattooga River. Here the trek turns north and travels along the wild and scenic waterway. Circle Bad Creek and return to the Chattooga, gaining up-close looks at the river, where gravel bars and sand beaches form, while hiking a tough track. Rocks, thick vegetation, and uneven terrain make it a challenge to reach Ellicott Rock. This rock, insignificant in its own right, forms the border where the states of South Carolina, North Carolina, and Georgia meet. Here you can clamber down to the streamside where, back in 1812, Andrew Ellicott, while surveying the boundary between the Carolinas, etched the exact boundary in stone. Interestingly, Ellicott helped survey the capital city of Washington, the western boundary of Pennsylvania, and "Ellicott's Line," which divided Alabama from Florida at 31 degrees north. His final act for our country was surveying the border between Canada and the western United States, at 45 degrees north. Part of the border between South Carolina and Georgia follows 35 degrees north. Ol' Ellicott really got around. Also look for Commissioners Rock, etched just a few feet away, which was a resurvey. On your return trip, you will doubtless see more exceptional beauty on display alongside these streams. While you're here, visit the hatchery to see the trout of varying sizes in their rearing ponds. And bring a picnic—the hatchery has a nice picnic area, along with a stone picnic shelter also built by the CCC. The hatchery is open daily from

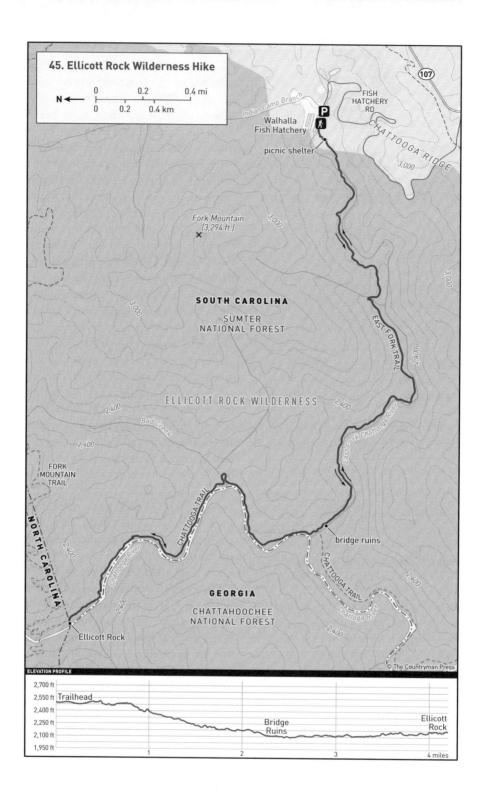

45. Ellicott Rock Wilderness Hike

SANDBARS LIKE THIS ARE DEPOSITED DURING HIGH WATER EVENTS ON THE CHATTOOGA

8 a.m. to 4 p.m., save for Christmas Day and inclement winter weather.

GETTING THERE

From the intersection of SC 11 and SC 28 just east of Walhalla, South Carolina, take SC 28 West for 9.5 miles to SC 107. Turn right onto SC 107 and follow it for 11.7 miles to Fish Hatchery Road. Turn left and follow Fish Hatchery Road for 1.7 miles to the hatchery, veering left to bridge East Fork and reach the parking area.

THE HIKE

From the parking lot, follow a paved path leading past the restrooms. The hike soon follows a wooden boardwalk with a side trail leading right to the hatchery. The main trail stays left. Ahead, a spur leads right to a fishing pier but we stay straight, soon reaching the

stone-and-wood CCC shelter with picnic tables and a large stone fireplace inside.

The East Fork Trail shortly enters Ellicott Rock Wilderness. Wind amid tall trees to soon cross a large wooden bridge spanning the East Fork at 0.3 mile. Officially enter the Ellicott Rock Wilderness, as marked by a sign. The trail joins a wide old roadbed coming in from your right. At this point, both the trail and the river begin their descent into the East Fork Chattooga Gorge. Below you the East Fork is carving its way down, in falls, cascades, and rapids. The trail begins circling in and out of hollows, passing a drip cascade on your right at 0.6 mile. You get a good view of the cascade from an elaborate footbridge with handrails spanning the watercourse.

Enjoy looks down on the East Fork before the path turns into an intriguing side hollow. Here, at 1.0 mile, you cross a slick slide cascade on concrete steps set in the middle of the slide. Note the small

THE CHATTOOGA RIVER FLOWS THROUGH UNTAMED
ELLICOTT ROCK WILDERNESS

falls just upstream of the slide. Ahead, leave the roadbed, aiming for the river in lush woods. Reach an overhanging bluff beside the stream at 1.6 miles. The now narrower trail briefly climbs then makes an uneven descent, as does the East Fork. The river drops and the trail chases it downward, all amid Southern Appalachian woodland beauty. Drift through rhododendron tunnels then come alongside the river near a rock slab at 2.3 miles. In the middle of the slab, you'll see an old bridge foundation. The rest of the former footbridge was washed away by flood. Ahead, meet the Chattooga Trail at 2.4 miles; a high wooden bridge with handrails leads left to a camping flat. Consider going over there and making your way to the confluence of the two streams, where the rocky and fast-moving East Fork meets the slower Chattooga at the lower end of a long pool. A rapid begins downstream just below the confluence.

This hike, however, turns northbound on the Chattooga Trail, away from the bridge, traveling along this silent mountain pool. Doghobble, mountain laurel, and rhododendron crowd the trail, as do rock ledges. Swing into a flat, circling the stream to rock-hop Bad Creek at 3.1 miles. Curve back toward the Chattooga where you find a large, flat rock extending into the Chattooga.

The Chattooga Trail climbs away from Bad Creek and continues up the river, picking up an old roadbed to return soon to the river's edge after passing through a deep, dark rhododendron tunnel. The riverside scenes vary as it divides into islands, shoals, big boulders, gravel bars, and pools in a swirling mosaic of beauty. White pine towers over magnolia, birch, and the ever-present rhododendron, galax, and moss. In places the trail crosses muddy seeps, tiny feeder streams, and slick rocks. The trail, because it's in the wilderness, is managed more lightly; logs left unremoved can become obstacles that may have a cut in them to allow for easier passage.

Come along the river's edge, passing washed-out spots. Cross a small branch on a small wooden bridge. Take note here; Ellicott Rock is not far away. At 4.2 miles, you'll reach the spur trail dropping left just a few feet to the water's edge and Ellicott Rock, which may be marked with surveyor's tape. It is not easy to find. When you get there, you'll wonder where the rock is—there is no significant rock around. Scramble down a mossy, slick slab, bordered with rhododendron, to a rapid. At the water's edge you'll see Ellicott's carved inscription, "NC." Just downstream, above the water, Commissioner's Rock, also carved, states, LAT 35, AD 1813, NC + SC. After finding the rock enjoy the wilderness yet again on your backtrack.

46

Lower Whitewater Falls

TOTAL DISTANCE: 4.4-mile there-and-back	
HIKING TIME: 2:00	
VERTICAL RISE: 730 feet	
RATING: Moderate	
MAPS: Foothills Trail—Bad Creek Trail Access; USGS 7.5' Reid NC-SC	
TRAILHEAD GPS COORDINATES: N35°00'44.8", W82°59'57.2"	
CONTACT INFORMATION: Jocassee Gorges, 1344 Cleo Chapman Highway, Sunset, SC 29685, (864) 868-0281, www.dnr.sc.gov	

This trek leads you to view one of the most spectacular falls in the Southeast, which is saying a lot. I believe it's even more spectacular than its upstream cousin, Whitewater Falls. But there is a difference between the two cataracts— Lower Whitewater Falls sees less than a tenth of the foot traffic of the Whitewater Falls. You'll leave Duke Power's Bad Creek Complex, then descend to the Whitewater River. Bridge the stream and join South Carolina's stellar Foothills Trail, climbing to skim the side slopes of Whitewater Mountain before reaching a head-on vista of Lower Whitewater Falls, a 400-foot-high white froth dashing down over gray stone, acclaimed as one of South Carolina's tallest cataracts.

GETTING THERE

From the junction of SC 11 and SC 130 just north of Salem, South Carolina, head north on SC 130, S. Bruce Rochester Memorial Highway. Keep north for 10.2 miles to the gated entrance to the Bad Creek Project. Drive up to the gate and it will open (from 6 a.m. to 6 p.m.). Pass through the gate and keep downhill for 2.1 miles, turning left at the sign for the Foothills Trail. Continue 0.3 mile to a large parking area. The Bad Creek Access Trail starts in the far left-hand corner of the parking area.

THE HIKE

It is easy to see how the Whitewater River was named, considering it has two 400-foot waterfalls on it, as well as numerous other cascades dropping off the Blue Ridge escarpment. Born in highlands of the Nantahala National Forest in North Carolina, the river pours south, forming the boundary between Transylvania and Jackson Counties

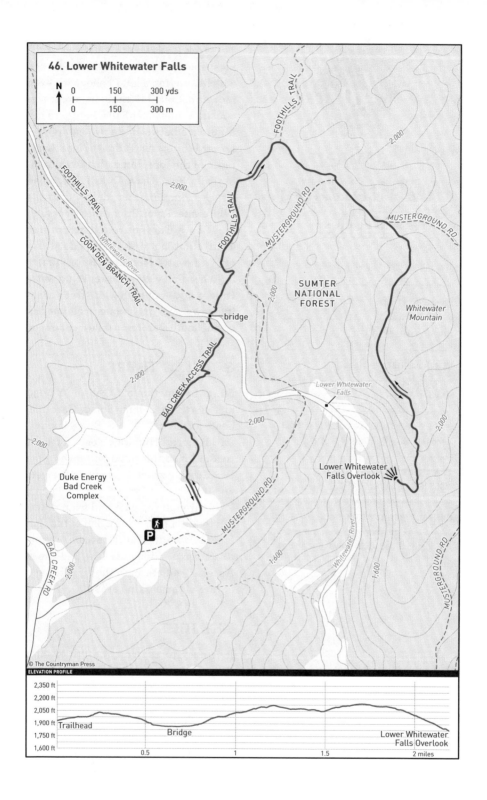

46. Lower Whitewater Falls

N

| 0 | 150 | 300 yds |
| 0 | 150 | 300 m |

FOOTHILLS TRAIL

2,000

FOOTHILLS TRAIL

MUSTERGROUND RD.

2,000

MUSTERGROUND RD.

COON DEN BRANCH TRAIL

Whitewater River

SUMTER
NATIONAL
FOREST

Whitewater
Mountain

bridge

BAD CREEK ACCESS TRAIL

Lower Whitewater
Falls

2,000

2,000

2,000

Duke Energy
Bad Creek
Complex

Lower Whitewater
Falls Overlook

MUSTERGROUND RD.

P

BAD CREEK RD.

2,000

1,600

Whitewater River

1,600

MUSTERGROUND RD.

© The Countryman Press

ELEVATION PROFILE

2,350 ft			
2,200 ft			
2,050 ft			
1,900 ft	Trailhead		
1,750 ft		Bridge	Lower Whitewater
1,600 ft			Falls Overlook

0.5   1   1.5   2 miles

before taking its famous dive as Whitewater Falls then pushing into South Carolina and diving yet again as Lower Whitewater Falls. Beyond the second major cataract, its waters are slowed in Lake Jocassee, where it merges with other streams.

Our hike takes place just a few miles above where the Whitewater River meets Lake Jocassee. Leave the large Bad Creek Access parking area, taking a graveled brushy path bordered by scrubby trees, grass, and regrowth over disturbed land. You can hear the Whitewater River flowing to your right, before it's stilled as part of Lake Jocassee. Keep east, then turn left, walking through a tree-dotted flat. Ignore user-created spur trails in this area. At 0.2 mile, the trail climbs into full-blown woods, heavy with mountain laurel. The Bad Creek Access Trail skirts the west side of a

small knob then gently descends into a flat, where you can hear the Whitewater River again. Drift across the wooded riverside flat to reach a trail junction and the first of two bridges over the Whitewater River at 0.6 mile. To your left, before the bridge, is the 1.0-mile Coon Den Branch Trail. This path shows much less use than any other trails in the area, but it's easily followed, should you want to explore Coon Den Branch Natural Area. To reach Lower Whitewater Falls overlook, cross the two iron bridges over the Whitewater River to meet the Foothills Trail and an inviting bench. Here the Foothills Trail leads left for 2.8 miles to Whitewater Falls Overlook, an additional hiking opportunity.

Our hike stays straight on the Foothills Trail. Head uphill in mixed woods, only to switchback and climb onto a ridgeline. The wide trail is rooty. The ridge

THE VIEW FROM THIS OVERLOOK IS YOUR REWARD ON THIS HIKE

LOWER WHITEWATER FALLS IS ONE BIG AND MAJESTIC WATERFALL

CROSSING THE TRAIL BRIDGE OVER THE WHITEWATER RIVER

steepens and the Foothills Trail slips over to the right-hand side of the wooded ridge, joins an old roadbed, turns right, and makes a trail junction 1.2 miles from the Bad Creek Access. Here, the Lower Whitewater Falls Access Trail keeps straight while the Foothills Trail leaves left. From here to the falls overlook, the trail primarily traces old woods roads.

At 1.4 miles, the trail emerges onto a hunter parking area at Musterground Road, open to public access in fall hunting season. Follow the road southeast. The wide pea-gravel track makes for easy hiking, but you soon leave the road at 1.5 miles. This is a signed right turn away from the gravel road.

Pine, sourwood, and cane border the trail as it gently climbs the west slope of Whitewater Mountain. You can't help but wonder where the trail is going as you climb without hearing any water. The trail reaches a high point then begins a gentle downgrade that steepens. You are on the slope of Whitewater Mountain and curving toward the rim of the gorge created by the Whitewater River, though it only seems as if you are jumping on and off old woods roads. Have no fear, the way is blazed and clear. Water sounds enter your ears. A final right turn and a narrowing to single-track path heralds your arrival at the Lower Whitewater Falls Overlook at 2.2 miles. It is 340 feet down from the high point of Whitewater Mountain to the overlook.

But you probably find that the trip was completely worth it. The overlook brings you face-on with Lower Whitewater Falls, which drops across a chasm lying between you and it. The river makes a few warm-up tumbles, just for kicks, then displays a final practice drop before diving off a sheer ledge in a roaring sheet of white bordered in gray granite, framed in dense forest, with mountain ridges and sky beyond. The general claim is that the falls are 400 feet high, but the single biggest drop is a little over 200 feet. Either way, the cataract is another good reason to hike in the Carolina mountains.

Laurel Fork Falls at Lake Jocassee

TOTAL DISTANCE: 10.6-mile there-and-back	
HIKING TIME: 5:45	
VERTICAL RISE: 1,080 feet	
RATING: Difficult due to distance	
MAPS: Jim Timmerman Natural Resources Area at Jocassee Gorges, Foothills Trail; USGS 7.5' Eastatoe Gap, Reid NC–SC	
TRAILHEAD GPS COORDINATES: N35°02'37.9", W82°50'17.1"	
CONTACT INFORMATION: Jocassee Gorges, 1344 Cleo Chapman Hwy, Sunset, SC 29685, (864) 868-0281, www.dnr.sc.gov	

This hike, an excellent overnight backpacking for those inclined, travels through the Laurel Fork Heritage Preserve, a scenic area and one the finest mountain valleys in South Carolina. You'll leave Laurel Fork Gap to briefly follow a forest road, soon meeting the Foothills Trail. From here the hike winds among thickly wooded steepsided ridges graced with copious doses of mountain laurel. Drop into the Laurel Fork watershed and enjoy Carolina mountain splendor, topped off with a visit to 25-foot Virginia Hawkins Falls. Continuing down the valley, the hike traces numerous bridges spanning Laurel Fork and leads to the lip of the gorge over which 90-foot Laurel Fork Falls drops. The stages of watery descents will blow you away. Beyond the spiller, the Foothills Trail leads to Lake Jocassee, a clear mountain-rimmed impoundment that may just lure you in for a swim. The valley is also a good spring wildflower destination.

GETTING THERE

From Pickens, take US 178 West to SC 11. Hit your odometer at SC 11, and continue on US 178 for 8.1 more miles to Laurel Valley Road, which is shortly past the community of Rocky Bottom. Turn left at Laurel Valley Road, but stay right and uphill on the gravel road; follow this gravel road, Horsepasture Road, for 3.6 miles to Laurel Fork Gap. Here the road splits. Horsepasture Road heads left and Canebrake Road goes right. Park at the limited area where the two roads split. Start walking right up Canebrake Road.

THE HIKE

Leave Laurel Fork Gap, ascending northwest on gravel Canebrake Road,

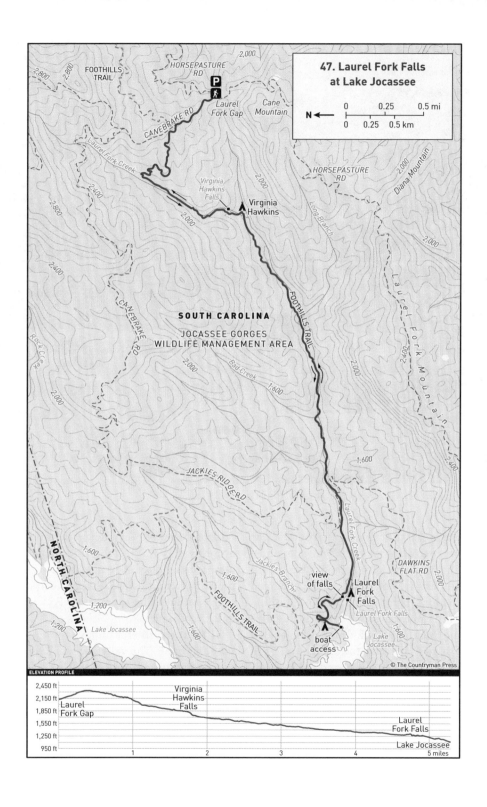

VIRGINIA HAWKINS FALLS SPILLS OVER A WEATHERED LEDGE

reaching the signed, perpendicular crossing of the Foothills Trail at 0.3 mile. Turn left here, joining the Foothills Trail and briefly walking a smaller, canopied roadbed before tracing the Foothills Trail right as a single-track path entering thick forest. Wind along steep-sided hollows, working toward Laurel Fork amid mountain laurel and oak aplenty. Appreciate the trail work, with steps helping you negotiate the declivitous slopes.

As you near Laurel Fork on steep switchbacks, the mountain laurel evolves to rhododendron, and the noisy stream becomes audible. Reach Laurel Fork at 1.2 miles. Turn downstream in a tight valley full of tulip trees, black birch, doghobble, and fern. Mossy bluffs protrude from hillsides. Reach the first of five bridges that span Laurel Fork in quick succession.

After the fifth crossing, you are on the right bank. The valley opens. Keep descending to reach Virginia Hawkins Falls, formerly known as Double Falls, at 1.9 miles. This is a low-flow, multi-tiered 25-foot drop. The initial pourover is over a sheer stone slab, followed by shorter, stair-step-like spills. Beyond Virginia Hawkins Falls, the Laurel Fork Trail descends, reaching the Virginia

Hawkins campsite at 2.0 miles, complete with fire rings, to meet a gated roadbed that has descended from Laurel Gap. You can trace this roadbed back up to the gap on your return if you wish. The very last part of that return is on a foot trail with steps. You cannot see this road from Laurel Fork Gap, but you can see the foot trail heading downhill from the gap. It's about a mile back to the gap from Laurel Fork, but you'll miss all the bridges and Double Falls.

The Foothills Trail keeps descending, immediately crossing a bridge to the right bank from Virginia Hawkins campsite. The trail hops off and on the old road as it works around side streams and passes through wooded flats. Farther downstream, the trail uses old wooden road bridges to span the creek.

At other times it parallels the old road in woods. Smaller footbridges will span feeder branches while you walk the trail, including Long Branch at 2.8 miles, coming in on your left.

The gorge tightens at 3.2 miles, forcing the stream, the Foothills Trail and the roadbed to squeeze through a slot for about 0.25 mile. The valley opens again. At 3.5 miles, Bad Creek comes in on your right. Amid all the hiker and old road bridges, the next bridge, at 3.7 miles, will stand out. This is a suspension bridge that crosses over to the left bank. You will gain good looks up and down the stream. The forest floor is covered in galax, while white pines form a superstory over the balance of the lush forest.

Laurel Fork gains momentum as more

A VIEW FROM THE DIFFICULT TO REACH BASE OF LAUREL FORK FALLS

THE UPPER DROP OF LAUREL FORK FALLS

it downstream, leads to the top of Laurel Fork Falls. Here you can see it slide over the lip of the gorge to reach Lake Jocassee after tumbling downward numerous times and in numerous forms. It is an impressive cataract, yet it is hard to categorize.

To gain a better view, continue along the Foothills Trail, cruising beside a blasted cliff to reach a long vista of the falls through the trees at 4.8 miles. Near here, a dangerous unmaintained trail leads very, very steeply down to the midlevel of the falls. You can look up at the first two drops of Laurel Fork Falls, which end in a plunge pool before gathering momentum and dropping even more.

The highlights aren't over yet. To continue to Lake Jocassee, follow the Foothills Trail, now on a wide roadbed, as it slices through a blasted gap and works around to reach Jackies Branch and a trail intersection at 5.1 miles. Stay left here on a spur, descending past a few cascades of Jackies Branch and a small campsite to reach the lakeshore and boat/hiker access for the Foothills Trail at 5.3 miles. The aquamarine water, normally very clear, will lure you in for a swim on a sunny day. Laurel Fork Falls, roaring away farther up the cove, can be heard but not seen from the access. On nice weekends boaters will motor to the fall's base, reaching the cataract much more easily than you. However, the beauty of the Laurel Fork Gorge will be more than worth the effort we hikers exercise to see this superlative South Carolina mountain magnificence.

feeder branches increase its flow. At 4.0 miles, emerge at Dawkins Flat Road and an auto accessible campsite, when the forest roads here are seasonally open. Bridge the creek here, descending on the right bank, passing near other auto campsites.

At 4.6 miles, a marked spur trail leads left across a hiker suspension bridge spanning Laurel Fork Creek, reaching Laurel Fork Falls campsite at a former homesite. The campsite trail, if you follow

48

Beech Bottom Falls

TOTAL DISTANCE: 1.8-mile there-and-back

HIKING TIME: 1:00

VERTICAL RISE: 320 feet

RATING: Easy

MAPS: Jim Timmerman Natural Resources Area at Jocassee Gorges; USGS 7.5' Eastatoe Gap NC-SC

TRAILHEAD GPS COORDINATES: N35°04'08.7", W82°47'43.2"

CONTACT INFORMATION: Jocassee Gorges, 1344 Cleo Chapman Hwy, Sunset, SC 29685, (864) 868-0281, www.dnr.sc.gov

This hike uses a newer trail in the Jocassee Gorge WMA to view a tall waterfall in a rugged gorge. The hike is a bit on the short side, but you can add to it with the short drive and walk to South Carolina's high point atop Sassafras Mountain, enjoying 360-degree views from an elevated and developed vista point accessible by all.

GETTING THERE

From Pickens, take US 178 North to SC 11. Keep straight on SC 11 for 7.2 miles to Rocky Bottom and F. Van Clayton Memorial Highway, a two lane paved road. Turn right on F. Van Clayton Memorial Highway and follow it for 1.9 miles to the parking area on your left, just after the Chimneytop Gap crossing of the Foothills Trail.

THE HIKE

Jocassee Gorges contains many of South Carolina's special places within its confines and 60-foot Beech Bottom Falls is one such place. The Beech Bottom Trail was opened in 2019 and replaced a dangerous alternate route to what was formerly called Pinnacle Falls but is now called Beech Bottom Falls.

From the parking area, used for both the Foothills Trail and the Beech Bottom Falls Trail, walk F. Van Clayton Memorial Highway north a short distance to a gated road, the beginning of the Beech Bottom Falls Trail. Follow the double-track path west, running along a small branch feeding Abner Creek. The path eases downhill then comes to a strange looking cylindrical structure. It is a bat roost, placed by South Carolina Department of Natural Resources. Bats are the only mammals capable of true flight and are an important part of the ecosystem,

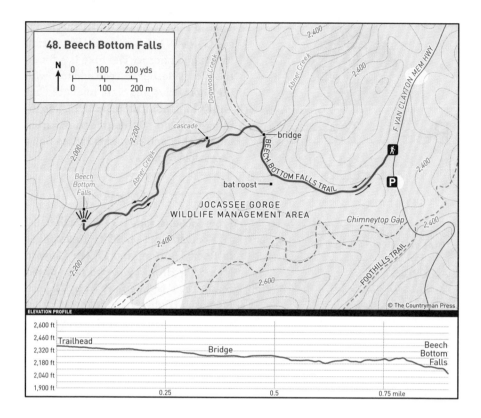

48. Beech Bottom Falls

ELEVATION PROFILE

consuming mosquitoes and other troublesome insects. This bat roost helps prop up declining bat populations, mostly due to white nose syndrome, a fungus-based illness killing these mammals all over the United States.

Continue descending beyond the bat roost, crossing crystalline Abner Creek on a cool trail bridge with decorative railing constructed from local mountain laurel. Just ahead, at 0.4 mile, leave the double-track left on a foot trail. Bridge back over to the left bank of Abner Creek. The single-track path now enters a thickly wooded steepening gorge. At 0.5 mile, you come along Abner Creek at a pool and cascade. This is as close as you are going to get to the stream from here on out, as Abner Creek drops steeply and the narrow trail works along

a very sharp slope, slightly rising or dropping to find the most sane passage. Some trail segments offer handrails to make the trail safer.

At 0.9 mile, the more-level-than-not track makes a quick descent to a horizontal wooden viewing platform with handrails. Here, enjoy a face on view of Beech Bottom Falls. The stream dives 60 feet off a widening rock face in a forbidding and dangerous gorge. Don't even try to walk to the bottom of the falls. Enjoy the perch.

After making the return trek from Beech Bottom Falls, get in your vehicle and continue the drive up scenic F. Van Clayton Memorial Highway for a little less than 3 miles to the Sassafras Mountain parking area and the walkway to South Carolina's highest point at 3,553

BEECH BOTTOM FALLS TUMBLES 60 FEET OVER AN IRREGULAR ROCK FACE

ENJOY A VIEW FROM SOUTH CAROLINA'S HIGHEST POINT, SASSAFRAS MOUNTAIN, LOCATED NEAR THIS HIKE'S TRAILHEAD

feet, plus the added height of the low slung observation tower, opened in 2019. Enjoy views in all directions, including south all the way to Georgia. The North Carolina-South Carolina state line cuts across the tower. The large parking area is not only used for the observation tower, but also for those hiking the Foothills Trail leading to Table Rock State Park as well as the Foothills Spur Trail leading along the North Carolina-South Carolina state line to Jones Gap State Park.

However, by far most people are here to bag South Carolina's high point of Sassafras Mountain. There exists a whole class of adventurers whose goal it is to visit all the highest points in every state. They are known as high pointers. Some high points can be driven to, while others require modest walks like this, or Clingmans Dome in Tennessee, or Missouri's Taum Sauk Mountain, while others require a more substantial hike, like that to Virginia's Mount Rogers or Maine's Mount Katahdin. Still others require mountaineering skills that your average hiker doesn't have—or need, unless you want to climb Washington's Mount Rainier or Alaska's Denali. That being said, there are still other high points that are significant only in context to being inside the boundaries of their given state—such as Britton Hill in Florida, or Ohio's Campbell Hill.

The first high pointers began making such quests in the 1930s. To this day, members of high point clubs or soloists on a personal mission will be found at places like Sassafras Mountain, topping another summit and checking off another state. So after hiking to Beech Bottom Falls and Sassafras Mountain perhaps you can begin your own quest to be a high pointer.

Table Rock State Park Hike

TOTAL DISTANCE: 8.0-mile loop

HIKING TIME: 5:00

VERTICAL RISE: 2,267 feet

RATING: Difficult due challenging, rocky trail

MAPS: Table Rock State Park; USGS 7.5' Table Rock

TRAILHEAD GPS COORDINATES: N35°01'55.2", W82°42'01.4"

CONTACT INFORMATION: Table Rock State Park, 158 Ellison Lane, Pickens, SC 29671, 864-878-9813, www.southcarolinaparks.com

This tough loop offers rewards aplenty, including waterfalls and vistas, as well as the chance to summit Pinnacle Mountain at 3,425 feet. Start on the famed Table Rock Trail, passing cascades and a great view from the Civilian Conservation Corps (CCC) shelter before joining a wooded ridgeline traveling west. The trail trends ever upward, topping out at wooded Pinnacle Mountain. A sharp descent on the Pinnacle Mountain Trail meets the Foothills Trail, then descends past my favorite view at Table Rock State Park, Bald Rock, where the Palmetto State stretches to the horizon. Finally, work your way along a sharp mountain slope to join Carrick Creek, presenting more falls of its own. Allow plenty of time; the trails can be slow and rocky in places.

GETTING THERE

From Pickens, drive north on US 178 West for 9.0 miles. Turn right onto SC 11 and follow it for 4.4 miles to West Gate Road. Turn left onto West Gate Road, continuing to the park entrance. From the park entrance station, follow the main road for 0.7 mile to Carrick Nature Center and trailhead. The hike starts behind the nature center. A parking fee and trailhead registration are mandatory.

THE HIKE

Leave the nature center breezeway, crossing Carrick Creek on the Table Rock Trail. Take the paved path along the stream, reaching 8-foot Carrick Creek Cascade and plunge pool, the first place you'll be whipping out your phone for a photo op. The paved path continues up the valley, crossing Carrick Creek to find a trail junction at 0.2 mile. Split right with now-natural surface Table Rock Trail. The path sides

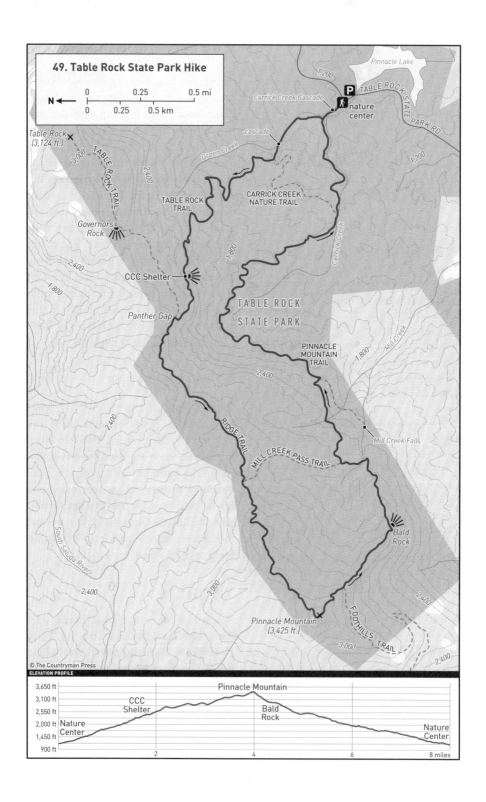

49. Table Rock State Park Hike

N ←

| 0 | 0.25 | | 0.5 mi |
| 0 | 0.25 | 0.5 km | |

Table Rock
(3,124 ft.)

Pinnacle Lake

1,200

TABLE ROCK STATE PARK RD

Carrick Creek Cascade

nature
center

cascade

Green Creek

1,200

3,000

TABLE ROCK TRAIL

2,400

TABLE ROCK
TRAIL

CARRICK CREEK
NATURE TRAIL

Carrick Creek

Governors
Rock

1,800

CCC Shelter

TABLE ROCK
STATE PARK

2,400

1,800

Panther Gap

PINNACLE
MOUNTAIN
TRAIL

1,800

Mill Creek

2,400

2,400

RIDGE TRAIL

MILL CREEK PASS TRAIL

Mill Creek Falls

South Saluda River

Bald
Rock

2,400

2,400

3,000

Pinnacle Mountain
(3,425 ft.)

FOOTHILLS TRAIL

3,000

2,400

© The Countryman Press

ELEVATION PROFILE

		Pinnacle Mountain		
3,650 ft				
3,100 ft	CCC			
2,550 ft	Shelter		Bald	
2,000 ft			Rock	
Nature				Nature
1,450 ft	Center			Center
900 ft				
	2	4	6	8 miles

LOOKING OUT FROM THE HISTORIC SHELTER ON TABLE ROCK MOUNTAIN

along shaded Green Creek, spanning the stream. Watch for a 4-foot ledge drop just above the crossing. Continue up the valley, passing a stair-step cascade of 40 feet. A second ledge cascade lies ahead. Cross Green Creek again to meet the Carrick Creek Nature Trail at 0.5 mile.

Stay with the Table Rock Trail as it ascends stone steps amid boulders and trickling branches under fire-managed woods. Keep working up a wash, weaving through car-sized stones. Pass two cabin-sized boulders, climbing along them, at 1.2 miles. The ascent steepens, and partial views open from the mountainside. Reach the CCC shelter and overlook at 1.8 miles. The roofed wooden structure stands in the woods just above a huge rock face that offers expansive views. Paris Mountain and Greenville are to your left. Below lies the state park's Pinnacle Lake. Beyond, hills give way to South Carolina's Midlands.

More views open beyond the shelter; you'll reach Panther Gap and a trail junction at 2.0 miles. Here the Ridge Trail leaves left for Pinnacle Mountain.

If you're itching for a view, walk east on the Table Rock Trail for 0.6 mile to Governors Rock. Otherwise ascend west from Panther Gap on a narrow ridge nose. The Ridge Trail is shaded by oak, birch, beech, and hickory. Notice how much less this trail is used compared with the Table Rock Trail. Slip over to the south side of the ridge in thick woods draped with vines aplenty.

Reach a gap, then climb again, only to work over to the north side of the ridge. The Ridge Trail enters rhododendron thickets, tunneling down to a gap and a trail junction at 3.0 miles. The Mill Creek Pass Trail leaves left. If you're tired, you can shortcut your loop by taking this trail, but you'll miss two major highlights—Pinnacle Mountain and Bald Rock.

Work your way directly up the ridgeline on the Ridge Trail, then gain your elevation via switchbacks. Top out on the pinnacle of Pinnacle Mountain at 3.9 miles, elevation 3,425 feet. The wooded summit is designated with a survey marker, but no views. A small clearing

LOOKING LEFT TOWARD TABLE ROCK FROM BALD ROCK

stands at the crest. Head left here, now on the Pinnacle Trail, nose-diving down the south face of the Pinnacle Mountain. Keep the brakes on before meeting the Foothills Trail at 4.0 miles.

Stay left as the Foothills and Pinnacle Trails run in conjunction beneath tunnels of mountain laurel. Work down the rocky nose of a ridge, losing elevation fast to open onto Bald Rock and a superlative view, my favorite in the Palmetto State, at 4.4 miles. To the northeast you can clearly see Table Rock; swinging east, as much land as the eye can behold. To the south lies yet more wooded country. Bald Rock has many vista points and exploration areas, so plan to linger here awhile.

To continue your loop, keep heading downhill and east on the open rock to find the blazed trail opening into the woods, dominated by fire-scarred pine and laurel on a rocky root-filled track to meet sparkling Mill Creek amid rhododendron. The trail was rerouted here a few years back. Pay attention. Cross Mill Creek at 5.0 miles, then meet the Mill Creek Pass Trail at 5.1 miles.

Work along the side slope of Pinnacle Mountain, passing bluffs, then come to another trail intersection at 5.8 miles. Here, a spur leads 0.3 mile right to Mill Creek Falls, a 60-foot spiller amidst other cataracts and cascades that make it difficult to distinguish one from the other. Continuing the loop, the Pinnacle Creek Trail crosses intermittent drainages on a bluff-rich slope, bridging uppermost Carrick Creek at 6.2 miles. Look for huge boulders and boulder fields in the adjacent woods. Keep a moderate but steady descent, returning to Carrick Creek and the other end of the Carrick Nature Trail at 7.2 miles. Leave the solitude behind here to come alongside Carrick Creek—and enjoy the ride, as Carrick Creek makes its own fall-, chute-, and cascade-laden descent for the lowlands. Many of the drops here are rock slab slides. White pines rise above the rooty, well-beaten trail. Cross Carrick Creek a total of three times by rock-hop and reach a final junction, meeting the Table Rock Trail at 7.8 miles. From here, backtrack 0.2 mile to the nature center, finishing the challenging but worthy Carolina mountain trek.

50

Raven Cliff Falls

TOTAL DISTANCE: 3.8-mile there-and-back

HIKING TIME: 1:50

VERTICAL RISE: 550 feet

RATING: Easy-moderate

MAPS: Mountain Bridge Wilderness, Foothills Trail; USGS 7.5' Table Rock

TRAILHEAD GPS COORDINATES: N35°06'56.6", W82°38'17.4"

CONTACT INFORMATION: Caesars Head State Park, 8155 Greer Highway, Cleveland, SC 29635, (864)836-6115, www .southcarolinaparks.com/caesarshead

This there-and-back hike takes you to a well-visited overlook of famed Raven Cliff Falls. Start in South Carolina's high country near the North Carolina border at rugged Caesars Head State Park, within the confines of the Mountain Bridge Wilderness, rambling above 3,000 feet, to enjoy a long-range view of the 320-foot cataract. If you are feeling feisty, you can make an arduous loop to see the falls up close, but this requires ample time and stamina. Most hikers are satisfied with the simple hike to the falls overlook, with its more distant view, and back to the trailhead. But you can travel down to the cool mountain valley of Matthews Creek then climb away from the trout-teeming stream to an overlook astride Raven Cliff Falls, passing rockhouses and other stone features, before crossing upper Matthews Creek on a dramatic suspension bridge. Join South Carolina's main mountain track, the Foothills Trail, for some more highland rambling, completing the circuit. This added loop makes for a total hike of a strenuous 7.9 miles, thanks to the drop to Matthews Creek and subsequent climb out.

GETTING THERE

From Pickens, take SC 8 North for 15 miles to SC 11. Veer right onto SC 11/ SC 8 and follow it to the point where SC 8 turns left. Stay with SC 8 for 1.3 more miles, then keep forward on US 276. Follow US 276 as it climbs, passing the Caesars Head State Park Visitor Center at 6.4 miles (a Mountain Bridge Wilderness map can be purchased here). Continue on US 276 for 1 mile past the visitor center to reach the trailhead on your right. A parking fee and trailhead registration are mandatory. The Raven

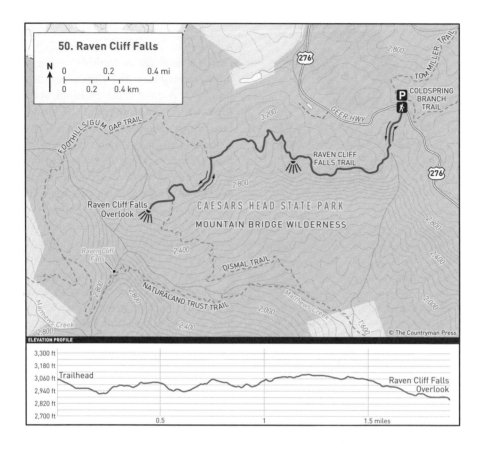

50. Raven Cliff Falls

N

| 0 | 0.2 | 0.4 mi |
| 0 | 0.2 | 0.4 km |

276

2,800

TOM MILLER TRAIL

COLDSPRING
BRANCH
TRAIL

GEER HWY

FOOTHILLS/GUM GAP TRAIL

3,200

RAVEN CLIFF
FALLS TRAIL

276

2,800

Raven Cliff Falls
Overlook

2,800

CAESARS HEAD STATE PARK

MOUNTAIN BRIDGE WILDERNESS

2,400

2,400

Raven Cliff
Falls

2,800

DISMAL TRAIL

2,000

NATURALAND TRUST TRAIL

2,800

Matthews Creek

2,000

Matthews Creek

2,800

2,400

2,000

1,600

© The Countryman Press

ELEVATION PROFILE

| 3,300 ft |
| 3,180 ft |
| 3,060 ft | Trailhead |
| 2,940 ft |
| 2,820 ft |
| 2,700 ft |

Raven Cliff Falls
Overlook

0.5   1   1.5 miles

Cliff Falls Trail starts on the opposite side of US 276 from the parking area.

THE HIKE

Three trails emanate from the parking area on US 276. The Tom Miller Trail and the Coldspring Branch Trail leave directly from the parking area on the east side of US 276, heading into adjacent Jones Gap State Park. Many hikers mistakenly take these trails for Raven Cliff Falls. Don't do it. Instead, leave the trailhead and registration area and cross over to the west side of US 276 to join the Raven Cliff Falls Trail. It starts out as a wide gravel track, descending in mixed hardwoods complemented with ferns and rhododendron. The Foothills

Trail and Palmetto Trail run in conjunction with the Raven Cliff Falls Trail here. Pass under a power-line clearing and outbuilding at 0.2 mile. Here, veer right, crossing a little tributary stream of Matthews Creek, now on a foot trail that follows an old roadbed. The wide natural surface track meanders westerly on the cusp of the deep 1,500-foot dropoff into Matthews Creek and features great winter views to the south. You can hear the stream and falls roaring below. The aquatic roar adds a little pep to your step.

The nearly level track passes over some rock slabs in a pine-oak-laurel forest. Pass side trails leading left to stone slabs with partial views at 0.8 mile. The Raven Cliff Falls Trail descends into

THE MAIN DROP ON RAVEN CLIFF FALLS IS A DOOZY

THE BLUE RIDGE RISES ABOVE RAVEN CLIFF FALLS

confounded by all the names the locals had given their flora.

Beyond the evergreens, the Raven Cliff Trail rises back into dry woods to pick up an old ridgetop roadbed at 1.3 miles. Reach a trail intersection at 1.5 miles. Here the Foothills/Palmetto and Raven Cliff Trails part ways; stay left with the Raven Cliff Falls Trail. Descend, still on the edge of the gorge. Meet the interestingly-named Dismal Trail in a gap at 1.8 miles. This is the beginning of the arduous loop, should you choose to do it. Note that the state park has put signs up warning hikers of the challenge; the rangers have had to rescue a few who bit off more than they could chew.

No matter whether you choose the challenging loop or not, first make the trek to the Raven Cliff Falls overlook. Keep straight here, tracing the Raven Cliff Falls Trail out a wooded ridge. At 1.9 miles, reach a trail shelter and wooden viewing platform. Through a cleared window framed by trees, you can observe the 320-foot falls plunging over a sheer rock face. It's a long-range vista but does deliver a face-on shot of this diving froth of white as it slaloms through a wooded vale then makes its daring dive before splashing at the base of a cliff and flowing out of sight through the trees, deep into the gorge below. The cataract is formed when the perched watershed of Matthews Creek, draining the most northwesterly corner of Greenville County flows east off the Blue Ridge into a canyon dividing Caesars Head from Raven Cliff. Much of the hike travels along this gulf. Matthews Creek goes on to feed the South Saluda River.

tangles of mountain laurel and rhododendron. Rhododendron, with bigger, leathery evergreen leaves, prefers shaded ravines and being near streams but will also grow along moist slopes and on high-elevation well-watered ridges such as here. Mountain laurel, with smaller evergreen leaves, prefers dry, south facing ridges amid pine-oak forests. That being said, the two often overlap habitats, as is the case here. To add to the confusion are their historical names. Many pioneers called mountain laurel ivy. They called rhododendron laurel. Botanists of the last century, while cataloging the vast array of plants in the South, must have been